Settling in Thailand:
An Expat Guide

RICHARD McCULLY & STEPHEN SAAD

ARUN
PRESS

Preface 5
Acknowledgments 7
Introduction. 8
Glossary and Other Keys 15

The Basics of Life in Thailand

Accommodation and Areas 21
Finances and Budgeting 35
Setting Up Your Life in Thailand 56
Getting Sick. 77
Food 84

Interviews with Expats in Thailand 1–6

Interview 1: The Bar Manager 93
Interview 2: The Retiree 101
Interview 3: The (Working) Mum. 108
Interview 4 – The Middle-aged Man Who Married a Bargirl. 115
Interview 5 – The Ajarn 124
Interview 6 – The Entrepreneur. 136

Lifestyle in Thailand

Before we begin 141
Some cultural preliminaries. 142
First Impressions 147
Getting around. 159
Social Life 167
Leisure and Relaxation 181
Nightlife 195
Some Final Random Practicalities. 204

Interviews with Expats in Thailand 7–13

Interview 7: The Hotel Owner 224
Interview 8: The Tech Boss. 235
Interview 9: The Filipino. 245
Interview 10: The Banker 251
Interview 11: The Expat Who Did Not Stay. 260
Interview 12 – The Sportsman. 263
Interview 13: The Filmmaker. 267

Staying in Thailand (Some Final Thoughts) 271

Some Useful Resources. 278
About the Authors. 281

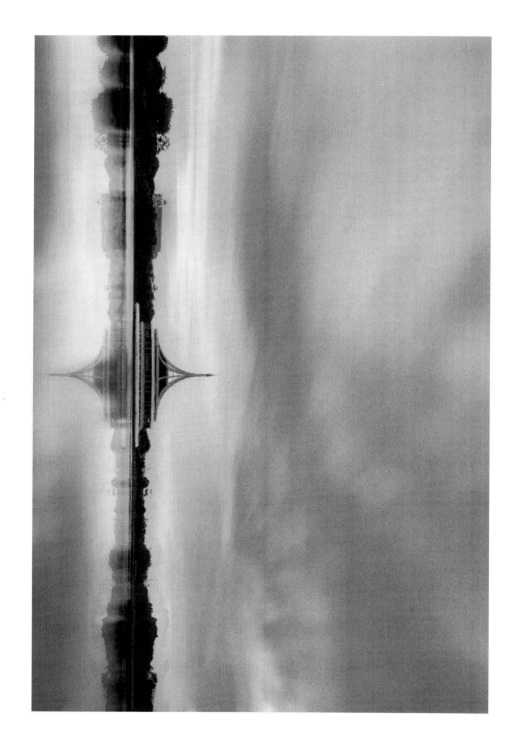

Preface

I wanted to write a book on what it feels like to live in Thailand and provide some insight into how things work over here. Most people coming to Thailand, either as a tourist or as a long-term visitor, will have some idea of the basics, either from research pre-trip on the Internet or picking up a guide to Thailand at the airport...or both. These sources give visitors an excellent overview of the country, the people, the practical basics – the currency, the key areas of Bangkok etc, and so on. This book seeks not to regurgitate all of this well-known material but act as a complement to these by going through the key aspects of day to day life in Thailand for an expat and also describing what life is like in Thailand from the perspective of expats who live here.

I have a 15 year plus association with Thailand, having first come here on a business trip from London back in 2001. After moving here to work in a banking software company, learning the language, getting married to a Thai colleague, moving back to the UK to continue my career, I now find myself back in Thailand all over again. Having spent so much of the last 15 years either working in Thailand, travelling to Thailand once or twice a year to visit in-laws or talking about Thailand with friends and relatives in the UK, I felt it was worth passing on what I have learnt and observed over the years to the benefit of those considering a move here or those already here and wanting to understand this wonderful country better. After writing a couple of books on the Thai language, I chose this to be my third and quite possibly, most ambitious writing project in Thailand.

Over the years I have come across many blogs and websites on Thailand written by expats. While none of these can be said to be 'wrong' (because any description of one's own perspective and experiences cannot be wrong), I felt that some of these were either too narrow in their perspective or based on a limited understanding of how things work in Thailand. Conversely, some commentary on Thailand is close to evangelical, where everything is great and life is great here etc. Indeed, some people think an expat life here is just one long day on a beach in Phuket and partying at night.

Obviously, the truth is somewhere in between – life in Thailand has just the same number and diversity of frustrations, errands and responsibilities, as well as memorable experiences, as anywhere else but they may apply to different things and circumstances than back home. So, something that might be an easy 10-minute job back home might take a couple of hours here but something that would be mundane back home often turns out to be a pleasant experience here and convinces you that you made the right decision to move here.

So, this book aims to provide a balanced and unbiased description of the practicalities of life in Thailand as well as insight into some of the cultural and social aspects that may not be obvious to a newcomer. I have teamed up with Richard McCully, an English teacher and expat here in Thailand for five years, not only because of the fact that he has settled here but mainly because he shares approach of taking a balanced perspective of life in Thailand – neither too cynical nor too naïve, neither too shallow nor too introspective. Most importantly, Richard, through his website, describes life in Thailand in a witty and non-judgemental way that serves to highlight the challenges of life in Thailand (and there will be many) as well as the some of the great things about life here.

I hope this book helps potential and existing expats to settle in Thailand and have a positive experience here during their stay. Thailand is, quite simply, an amazing country and with a little investment in mindset, language and cultural adjustment, expats can live here in a more liberal, peaceful and harmonious way than back home. If, like me, you want to live in Thailand, use this book to better understand your new home and get the best out of your stay in Thailand.

Steve Saad

Acknowledgments

The authors would like to thank the following people for their help, advice and support in the making of this book. Without them this book would not have been possible, simple as that.

- The interviewees who gave their time to this project with nothing offered in return apart from the opportunity to 'tell their story'.
- Bangorn Maneekong, for having the idea to do this book in the first place and supporting it throughout. Steve, as he does with each of his books, would also like to thank Bee for being his wife!
- Tako Edson for his fantastic caricatures of the interviewees' job roles or stereotypes. He did a really good job and helped to bring the book alive.
- Lertnapa Bongbut for his beautiful photography and his enthusiasm in offering his work toward this project.
- Phil Williams for his support of the project as a whole and proofreading.

Introduction

Settling in Thailand takes a broad and deep look at the main aspects of beginning a new life here in Thailand, from the practical aspects of setting up one's life to the subtler aspects of the culture and social norms. The book is split into two main sections – the first section, covering several chapters are more geared toward imparting information on key aspects of expat life e.g. accommodation, health etc. while the second section is more on lifestyle where we discuss some of the cultural, social, communication and other more intangible aspects of life here in Thailand. While both sections contain insight and opinion, in general, the second section will be more so than the first where the aim is to describe the 'lay of the land' first and foremost.

The book is a joint effort between two writers where the first section – 'The basics of life in Thailand' is mainly written by Richard McCully with a couple of sub-sections written by me while the latter section of the book – 'Lifestyle in Thailand' – is the other way around. There is a short third section – 'Staying in Thailand (Some Conclusions)' – where Richard, Phil – our primary editor, interviewee and previous Thailand blogger – and I summarise our thoughts on how to successfully live here in Thailand long term. Interwoven between these three sections are three sections of sets of interviews done with expats with experience of living in Thailand. More on the interviews later in this section.

We have used "I" to refer to ourselves throughout the book without specifying any more granularly which of us is writing that sub-section because it does not really matter. As we said, roughly speaking, Richard has written the stuff on practicalities and I have written most of the rest on social interactions and lifestyle observations.

Themes – Throughout this book we will endeavour to weave in a set of themes that will give some meaning and comparability to the comments we make on life in Thailand. These themes are:

- the difference between a tourist perspective and living in Thailand for real
- frustrations in Thailand
- the underlying reasons behind why things are done the way they are
- pleasantly surprising aspects of life in Thailand

Not every theme will necessarily be relevant for every chapter but taken as a whole, these themes will give some colour and context to the descriptions within this book.

Disclaimers and fundamental principles – A book of this nature will, by definition, contain lots of generalisations and avoiding this would lead to either a research paper on Thailand or a comparatively bland 'Lonely Planet' style guide to Thailand, which, obviously, already exists. Therefore, readers are advised of the following points before proceeding any further:

- The book is not a research paper and therefore, there will be no statistics or data to back up statements or opinions. Attempting to do this would be pointless and as most people know, data can be used to present pretty much any side of an argument or opinion. This book is based on the perspectives and opinions and experiences of the authors and interviewees and makes no attempt to verify whether these are proven to be correct by conducting surveys etc.
- There are no official facts in this book and this book should not be used as an official source of information on which to base important decisions such as applying for visas and suchlike, While the authors have attempted to provide lots of information on life in Thailand, this information is to the best knowledge of the authors and is only intended as a guide and in no way is this book a substitute for official information from the relevant institutions in Thailand or official websites; the authors take no responsibility whatsoever for any readers using this book as a reference source on which to base major decisions in Thailand.
- The authors will neither set out to deliberately criticise aspects of life in Thailand nor will they avoid offering opinions and perspective on social interactions and experiences from an expat's point of view in Thailand. Furthermore, the book will balance commentary on generalisations by highlighting exceptions or underlying reasons (cultural, social) why things seem to be a certain way.
- This book is not a relationship book on how to find a Thai wife or how to understand Thai women and so on. Neither does the book spend most of its time on the Thailand nightlife scene or the so-called Bangkok underbelly or other cheap stereotypes of Thailand. On the other hand, the book does not take a sanctimonious or morally judgemental position on that scene and neither does it try to sanitise it or present it in more politically correct terms. The book simply presents life in Thailand across as large a cross-section of expats as possible.
- The book is written, mainly from a male, Western expat's point of view,

as, a) that is the background of the authors and b) this represents the majority of foreigners who may be interested in this book, given that there is more of a cultural divide with Thai culture than with other Asian expats such as Chinese or Filipino. Having said this, the book contains a couple of interviews with Western females as well as an interview with a Filipino long-term resident so breadth and balance of opinion has been ensured. We did not, however, interview any Chinese or Japanese expats as we did not believe they would add much new insight to the book and we were aware of language issues in doing interviews in English with these nationalities.

It should be noted that throughout this book, when we refer to "Westerner", we generally mean expats who are from developed countries in the West i.e. UK, US, Canada, Europe and so on. In most cases, we actually probably mean Australian, New Zealand, South African, Russian too, as all of these would be seen by Thai people as 'farang' or 'white foreigner'. As I do not want to use 'farang' to refer to us expats, I have chosen to use 'Westerner', which, as I say, in most cases, will apply to pretty much any Caucasian foreigners.

If, like me, you are a non-Caucasian expat from one of the aforementioned countries, again, in most cases, when we refer to 'Westerner', our comments should apply to you too. There are some sentences where it should be obvious from the context that we are referring to 'white'-skinned foreigners and so, again, rather than tie ourselves in knots trying to constantly clarify these points, we have left it to your common sense.

Interviews – As well as the narrative and perspectives of the authors, this book contains a series of interviews with expats in Thailand. Interviews were conducted mainly by the authors one-to-one but some were by email and interviewees were encouraged to give an honest and interesting description of their time in Thailand. Several of the interviewees have chosen to remain anonymous while others have not. Interviewees are mostly either acquaintances or friends or professional contacts of the authors, although one or two people were unknown personally to the authors beforehand. All were chosen based on their value to the book i.e. the possibility that they had something interesting to say about life in Thailand, either because of their length of stay here or because of their lifestyle / line of work.

The authors also tried to ensure diversity within the set of interviewees so that, for example, not too many ended up coming from an English teacher background, even though this is probably the most common background of a Western expat in Thailand.

Finally, although it may appear as if the interviews asked a homogenous set of questions, this was not the case. Many of the actual questions sent or asked in person to interviewees contained several sub-questions to add context and explanation; one question went to over 100 words! Also, questions were not phrased exactly the same way to each interviewee. Finally, many of the interviews contain questions outside of the core set of common questions, where these questions were asked as a follow-up on a specific theme the interviewee seemed to be broaching. Readers can therefore be assured that, despite the fact that the interviews seem to be homogenous, the underlying approach was much less robotic and much more context-rich. Even the very first question on asking about interviewees' background contained several sub-questions to indicate to interviewees that we wanted to know what the circumstances were behind their move to Thailand, whether they had been to Thailand before for holiday, whether they had mostly stayed in cities or outer provinces etc.

Key differentiators to other books in the market – In the construction of this book the authors came across one or two seemingly similar books available for sale in Thailand. It is therefore worth pointing out at this early stage how this book attempts to be different:

- Not written by angry or sleazy Westerners in Thailand – A lot of material on the Internet such as Thai expat forums and discussion sites contain chat that can only be described as angry, critical and contemptuous of life in Thailand, usually based on a particular bad experience. One or two books go down the same route albeit with a toned-down narrative – from angry to sarcastic / "you've been warned – this is Thailand" snobbery. Without knowing for sure, the impression one gets from reading these types of comments is that they are written by the stereotypical 'farang' in Thailand i.e. the foreigner who understands little of Thai culture, cares even less, speaks only the most rudimentary Thai, has no interest in learning more, spends every day amongst expat friends and never interacts with Thai people apart from when a customer.
- While there is no doubt that there is a grain of truth in most of these types of opinions, the authors of this book have a fundamentally different approach, which is to offer a balanced view of life in Thailand that recognises the expat perspective (frustrations, bemusement etc) but also highlights why things work the way they do and what the underlying nuances of social interactions may be. Furthermore, where relevant, the

11

book attempts to suggest what expats need to do to deal with these frustrations. Ultimately, this book does not take the easy option of wallowing in a sea of criticism of how things in Thailand are different to 'back home' because, at the end of the day, nobody has forced expats to move here!

- Similarly, this book does not focus on bargirls or how to pick up Thai women or suchlike. The book is entirely unbiased and non-judgemental so where interviewees have mentioned nightlife and relationships with bargirls, this has been treated no differently to English teaching or any other aspect of life in Thailand.

- Not written by evangelists on Thai culture – At the opposite end of the spectrum are the foreigners who are so in love with Thailand and so interested in Thai culture, they are almost more Thai than Thais! This book will not gloss over frustrations of life in Thailand or ignore things which seem plain wrong to expats who experience them in Thailand. Apart from anything else, whether those feelings were based on misunderstandings or not, they represent the perspective of foreigners in Thailand and therefore, cannot be wrong and it is legitimate and necessary for this book to represent a balanced recognition of these.

- This book will not preach to readers to 'become Thai' or to understand and accept and practise every single aspect of Thai culture. This is not a culture book and the authors do not expect readers to live their lives in Thailand on a mission to become Thai. Expats in Thailand come from all walks of life from all parts of the world and while the onus is more on the expat to fit into Thailand rather than the other way around, it does not mean that this book will present a biased, evangelical account of Thailand where expats are always wrong or do not understand and the Thai way is always right. As much as possible, this book deals with all aspects of expat life in Thailand in a balanced way.

- To summarise the previous points and therefore, the central ethos of this book, in short, as the Thai wise old saying goes – "deuhn taang săai glaang" – "walk in the middle of the road" (neither one extreme nor the other).

- The interviews, as mentioned previously, are a further attempt to ensure the authors represent a balanced and broad perspective of life in Thailand, not just the experiences of the two main authors (which is already one more than other books on Thailand). Where interviewees have given an account of their experiences that is markedly different to the authors', there has been no attempt to downplay these whatsoever; indeed, interviewees were selected based on the fact that they have a different background to the authors and therefore, would likely have something different to say about life in Thailand.

- Finally, it is worth emphasising the breadth and scale of the undertaking the authors have embarked upon in bringing this project to market. Apart from the countless man-hours spent on writing and producing the book, conducting the interviews and so on, the book offers almost 150 years' worth of experience of Thailand across the two authors and interviewees. Above anything else, this should ensure the book is as broad and insightful as possible.

Taken together, the authors hope these differentiating factors make this a landmark project and a more honest, balanced and fair representation of what to expect from a life in Thailand. There have been many books – fiction and non-fiction – published over the years here in Thailand that seek to illustrate an expat's view of Thailand. In general, these have been geared more toward the 'pulp fiction' sector of the market or, in non-fiction, more toward being written by expats who really do not understand Thailand and the little they do, was more based on the nightlife scene and the expat sitting in an expat bar scene.

With modern Thailand opening up its economy, encouraging foreign investment and business setup and entrepreneurship, the type of expats who are settling in Thailand now is also changing. It is no longer the case that the only foreigners in Thailand are retired British or American divorced men or young backpackers. There is a growing middle-class expat scene in Bangkok, with many people coming to Bangkok to work, earning good money, not because they are escaping life back home or have failed but because Bangkok is fast becoming a big Asian city like Singapore and Hong Kong. There is a long way to go but Thailand is attracting working age business people, investors and professionals who see Thailand as a place to succeed. Consequently, literary tastes have also moved on, mainly because there is more to Thailand than the subjects covered in the pulp fiction of the previous generation. The authors hope that readers recognise, appreciate and differentiate this book from other books written on life in Thailand.

On the other hand, the authors have been very careful not to take a puritanical or morally superior view of the kinds of lives expats lead in Thailand. All the contributors to the book have been treated equally, non-judgementally and therefore, this book neither indulges in the nightlife scene nor does it avoid it when interviewees talk about it. So, as mentioned earlier, the driving ambition of this book is to be balanced and broad in its perspective and to represent the lives of the types of expats in professional jobs or other walks of life that do not get represented in most books out there.

It is not easy to adjust to a life in a country on the other side of the world with different customs and social norms but hopefully this book will assist expats to make the transition more smoothly and fit into Thai society enough to make a life in Thailand more fulfilling and enjoyable. Real life is different to a holiday but with a little effort, adjustment and patience, expats may discover that life in Thailand is even better than as a tourist, which is saying something since Thailand is one the most popular tourist destinations in the world and Bangkok the most visited city in the world.

Glossary and Other Keys

Throughout this book we will use several terms which are used by Thais or expats in Thailand.

Farang	Term used to describe a foreigner in Thailand. This is usually reserved for Caucasian foreigners. This word can have negative connotations. Some expats hate this word, as it seems sometimes disrespectful, as Thai people will use it to describe you rather than just calling you a person.
Baht (THB)	The currency used in Thailand. Baht is the main unit and there is a smaller, rarely used, unit called a satang.
7/11	A convenience store with branches throughout the country.
Hi-So	Short for High Society. This term is used to describe upper class people. Usually it is reserved for people with luxury cars, living in high end houses who shop at designer stores. Sometimes it is used jokingly among people, for example if you have Starbucks rather than a local coffee your Thai friends might call you Hi-So. Some people use the phrase "high Thais" which has the same meaning.
Soi	This word is basically a small road off the main street. Most areas in towns and cities have one main road and several sois which makes it easy to navigate around as they are all numbered.
BTS / MRT / Airport Link	The BTS is a skytrain system in Bangkok. The MRT is a subway system in Bangkok. The Airport Link is another skytrain which runs from the city center to the main airport in Bangkok.
Songthaew	A pickup truck which has been transformed to allow passengers to sit in the back. Used throughout Thailand these cheap public transport vehicles allow quick passage around town.

TRANSLITERATION

Throughout this book and significantly in the music section, you will see transliterated Thai i.e. Thai written in English characters. The following is a much cut-down guide to my system, which I use in my other Thai learning books. As this is not a language learning book, I will not explain all the vowel sounds and leave it to you to get as close as you can, based on the English letter combinations but here is the bare minimum you need to be able to read the few transliterated words in this book:

- There are five tones in Thai – medium or monotone, lòw, hígh, rĭsing (like "oh yeeaah??") and fâlling ("oh nooo!!").
- Short sounds are underlined while long sounds are not. The underline, or absence of it, always takes precedence over whether the word is spelt with a single or double vowel. So, hèd is a long sound even though it is spelt with a single e while tóok is a short sound.
- The k in Thai is a bit of a rough k and is almost a kh. Indeed, many books spell it Khun, not Koon, as I spell it.
- A dt consonant is a softer t sound, halfway to a d sound. Similarly, a bp consonant is halfway between a b and a p.

The vowels and vowel combinations are extensive so I have not explained these individually; the eu sound is like "errr" and the eu sound is like a Californian teenager saying "dude" with the mouth stretched wide.

GUIDE TO PRONUNCIATION OF COMMON THAI (AND ENGLISH!) WORDS

This book is not a Thai language book but there are two aspects of language that I (Steve) feel will be useful to expats and potential expats:

- Thai names and other common words of everyday life written in English alphabet.
- English words absorbed into Thai and pronounced as Thai; called táp sàp in Thai.

Pronouncing transliterated Thai words

There are some basic points that will help you pronounce the Thai you see in airports, street signs and in other aspects of everyday life. Here is a non-exhaustive list:

- 'Ph' words are NOT pronounced as an 'f' sound. The reason Thais add the 'h' is because they are differentiating a 'p' sound as in 'Putin' from a 'p' sound in 'suppose'. In Thai, these two sounds are represented by two different consonants i.e. a hard, more breathy 'p' and a softer, more 'lippy' 'p'.
- So, it is NOT 'Fooket' or even, god forbid, 'F**k It', it is 'Poogèt'. Similarly, it is not 'Faya Thai', it is 'Paya Thai'.
- Conversely, it is 'Bprà-dtoo-náam', with a soft 'p' and a soft 't'.
- 'Suvarnabhumi' is a literal transliteration, letter by letter, not a phonetic translation. The 'i' is not pronounced out loud and there is no 'v' sound in Thai, it is a 'w' sound. So, it is 'Sòo-wan-ná-poom'.
- There is no 'th' sound in Thai. Similarly to the point above about 'ph', the reason for adding the 'h' to the 't' is to differentiate the hard 't' e.g. 'tiger' and the soft 't', which is more like a 'dt'; they are two different consonants in Thai.
- So, 'Thailand' is not pronounced with a 'th' sound…obviously.
- 'Singha' – the 'ha' is silent. This is another case of Thais transliterating the word from Thai letter for letter, as opposed to transliterating how it is actually pronounced in Thai, which is 'Sĭng'. If asking for a Singha Beer, ask for 'Beer Sĭng'.
- 'Koh' is nothing like what the word for island sounds like in Thai. It is more like 'Gàw' i.e. a low, short, stunted 'aw' sound preceded by a hard and deep 'g' sound. When speaking to Thais, pronounce it the Thai way, when speaking to fellow Westerners, feel free to say 'Koh'.
- Thais often get confused on how to transliterate a hard 'g' and a 'k' (for good reasons) so, as you have noticed already, many words are mistakenly transliterated with a 'k' when they should be spelt with a 'g'.
- Examples are 'kin' where it should be 'gin' (to eat) and similarly for 'Kanchanaburi'.
- The same point applies for words spelt with a 'ch' when they are pronounced with a 'j' sound in Thai
- Examples are 'Phloen Chit' where it is 'Ploen Jit' and similarly for 'Chatuchak'.

Understanding English words spoken Thai style

Thai has absorbed many English words into the language and these words are used as pseudo-Thai words. This is nothing unique to Thai, many French and other foreign words are absorbed into English and used as English words and pronounced in an English way. Also, it is worth highlighting how Thais pronounce English when it is spoken with a strong Thai accent.

- As mentioned above, there is no 'v' sound in Thai so 7/11 is pronounced with a 'w' sound and a high tone i.e. '<u>se</u>-<u>wén</u>'. The 11 is usually left out for brevity – you will soon realise that Thai speech is all about convenience so if something can be pared down to one syllable, it will be!
- 'Wine' is pronounced as 'wai' because Thai does not have 'ine' sounds.
- 'You' is pronounced, slightly comically, as 'yoo'.
- 'More' is pronounced 'maw' and similarly for other 'ore' or just 'o' sounds.
- 'Jeans' are 'gaang geng yeen' – the 'j' becomes a Dutch 'j'.
- 'Strawberry' is pronounced quite differently. Thais struggle with sounds where two consonants are pronounced simultaneously because it is less common in Thai and there are certainly no 'st' sounds. So it sounds like 'sa-dtaw' and without bothering with the 'r'.
- Because 'st' is a tricky sound for Thais, they refer to me (and you if your name is Steve) as 'Mi-dtar Sa-dteeb'. Also, Thai syllables cannot end in an 'f' sound so you get 'Sa-dteeb'.
- 'Table' is pronounced 'tay-<u>bûn</u>' because Thai does not have words with an 'l' ending sound; 'l' sounds get converted to 'n' sounds in Thai if they are at the end of a syllable. 'Mobile' ends up as 'mow-baai' with a faint 'n' sound at the end.
- 'Free' is pronounced 'fèe' as in '<u>mâi</u> fèe'.
- In Thai, words cannot end in an 's' sound either and this is why Thais have such a hard time with plurals in English. 'Maai fen wan too meet yoo' = 'My friends want to meet you'. Without knowing whether the Thai person is referring a singular or plural, some situations can become confusing! Similarly, Thais will struggle with words such as 'six' and say 'sick'.

If you stay in Thailand for any length of time, you will get used to the Thai accent when they speak in English with you and over time, you will not be stumped by strange pronunciations. In fact, you will probably end up deliberately mispronouncing English words in the local style because it is pointless trying to stress to local people that the word is actually an English word originally. Also, after all, you are in Thailand and you will want to be understood easily and go with the flow.

CURRENCY CONVERSION

Throughout the book prices are listed in Thai Baht (THB). This will help you to get used to thinking in Baht, something you must do if you become an expat. Thailand is a popular destination for expats from around the world so it made no sense to use another currency such as USD or EUR as it wouldn't mean anything to others reading the book.

Below you can see a basic table showing currency conversion rates as of early 2018. Before reading you should use a source such as xe.com to find the latest rates to help you understand pricing.

Approximate currency conversion table based on early 2018:

1 US Dollar	31.6 Thai Baht
1 British Pound	43.8 Thai Baht
1 Australian Dollar	24.7 Thai Baht
1 Canadian Dollar	25.2 Thai Baht
1 Euro	38.9 Thai Baht
1 Japanese Yen	0.3 Thai Baht (100 Yen = 30 Baht)
1 Indian Rupee	0.5 Thai Baht (100 INR = 50 Baht)
1 Chinese Renminbi	5 Thai Baht
1 Swedish Krona	3.9 Thai Baht
1 New Zealand Dollar	23 Thai Baht
1 Singapore Dollar	23.8 Thai Baht
1 Russian Ruble	0.5 Thai Baht (100 RUB = 50 Baht)

The Basics of Life in Thailand

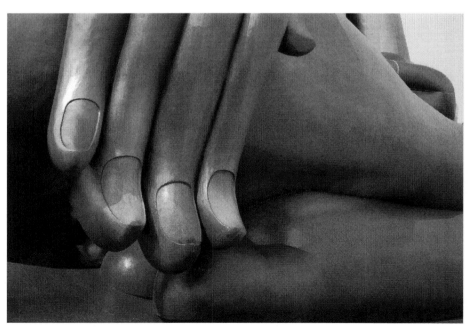

Accommodation and Areas

One of the most important things you have to decide when you move to a new country is where you want to live. It can impact a lot on your enjoyment and quality of life.

Thailand has a lot to offer so don't just go to the first place you like and settle there. Make sure you try a few different locations before making such a big decision. It is also not worth confirming long term accommodation before arriving unless you have been to Thailand before. You should book into a hotel for at least a few days to give yourself a chance to look around.

I would suggest ddproperty.com as the best site in English to look for property in Thailand. DDproperty also has a section to find agents who will take your requirements and find your dream place. Rental agents charge the landlord a fee for finding a tenant so you shouldn't pay an agent to find you a rental property.

You can also just choose an area and walk around to find a building you like. Inside most condos and apartments there will be a front desk and they should be able to show you available units or arrange a time for you to come back and see one.

About Me

I arrived here in Thailand when I was 26. I had been working in the UK in a sales job but wanted to experience life abroad. I'd been to Thailand before and booked a teacher training course.

I planned to stay in Thailand for a couple of years but continued to progress so have stayed. The relaxing lifestyle and ease of life here are my favourite things.

Currently I work for an international language school as an English teacher. I also run the website lifeinanewcountry.com which is all about living in Thailand. On my site I share my cost of living and thoughts on life here.

BANGKOK

The capital city of Thailand is where many working expats choose to locate themselves. By being in Bangkok you benefit from the best transport options, a wide choice of facilities and ease of travel to other places in Thailand and internationally. With just over 12 million people living in Bangkok it is easy to meet new people and, with a lot of tourists, it does feel like a very international place. There are a couple of business centres and a large demand for teachers which makes Bangkok a great place to find high paying work.

The downside to living in Bangkok is that it lacks a lot of the charm that you find in other towns and cities around Thailand.

Thai people are very quick to tell you about the famous "Thai smile", that all Thai people are happy and smile all the time. To be honest I've seen that in the countryside, around the beaches and in Chiang Mai but not so much in Bangkok. The city seems to chip away at people through the pollution and hours of traffic jams, which can make life a bit miserable sometimes.

When it comes to choosing an area in Bangkok to live in there are many factors you must consider. Pricing of accommodation varies and different areas have different vibes. Most expats choose to base themselves next to an MRT (subway) or BTS (sky train) station. Rents do tend to be higher the closer you are to these transport options but it will save you a lot of time and money compared to paying for taxis or using the bus network.

Ari

Ari is located towards the end of the BTS line, a couple of stops before Mo Chit. It is famous for being a mini financial and business district and has quite a lot of Western professionals living there, most in well-paid jobs in IT or finance. It is also well-known for its dining options. Soi Ari has a huge number of great places to eat local and international food. Places such as SALT are famous in Bangkok but bear in mind the prices make these restaurants treats rather than regular dining spots for most.

There are a number of craft beer bars dotted around and a few Thai-style restaurants to give it a bit of a local feel. The large number of condos springing up in the area show that it is now becoming more gentrified than it was five or so years ago. It is also quite expensive to buy or rent a place compared to neighboring areas.

Asok

Asok is a key area in Bangkok as it is one of the main intersections between the BTS and MRT meaning it is quite simple to get to any station from here. It is also a good location for being on lower Sukhumvit which has many bars (of all types), malls and offices.

Condos within walking distance of the train stations can be astronomical and pretty poor value for money compared with being a few stations further down Sukhumvit. Expect to pay at least 15,000 baht for a small room within 10 minutes of the station. 40sq metre rooms go for over 20,000 baht a month.

Thong Lor

Thong Lor is quite a trendy area and is located two stops away from Asok. It is famous for bars and restaurants. A lot of rich Thai people go to this area to eat and socialize.

It is especially popular with Japanese expats, as is neighboring Ekkamai. There are a number of new condo buildings in the area. The prices are a little lower than Asok but rents are getting more expensive.

On Nut

For expats wanting to be on the BTS line but looking to keep costs down, On Nut is a popular area. When we say "keep costs down", we mean for an expat on a reasonable expat salary or with reasonable wealth. Many Thais would call On Nut rental rates expensive.

The neighbourhood has developed over the past five years and there are many good restaurants and bars to be found. Using the BTS you can be in the city center within 20 minutes. 40sq metre condos start from around 13,000 baht a month.

Silom

Silom is another interchange area for the BTS and MRT. As such it is an easy place to travel around Bangkok from. It is also the area where a lot of business-es are based. As an expat you might find yourself working here. Rental prices are high in this area.

At night it is home to a famous gay area and a red-light district. It can get quite lively here.

Ratchada

Ratchada is the area between Ratchadapisek and Param 9 MRT stations. In total there are five stations in this area. The accommodation is cheaper than around the BTS but offers good access to the city center and a wide choice of dining options. Ratchada Road is quite a wide dual carriageway and so the environment is a little less residential and more 'office block-y'.

Also note that Ratchada is the epicentre of the soapy massage parlours of Bangkok. All the action happens discreetly indoors but the, often huge, buildings are typically fronted with massive neon signs. It might not be a desirable location for some people to be in but for others it is a bonus to have all forms of entertainment on their doorstep!

Expect to pay around 15,000 baht for a decent condo within a few minutes' walk of an MRT station.

Mo Chit

Home to a world-famous market and two huge parks, this area is good for those wanting to be on the outskirts of town but still on the transport lines. Both the MRT and BTS have stations in this area. Prices are reasonable but it will take around 30 minutes to get to the centre of the city.

Also, it is useful to be in this area if you plan to fly around the region using the low-cost airlines as almost all of them fly out of Don Mueang which is nearby. Similarly, it is convenient for getting out of Bangkok and upcountry easily by road, especially if you plan to go northwards, as Mo Chit is to the north of Bangkok and is the location of the Northern bus terminal. As such you do not need to negotiate the dreaded traffic trying to get up and out from Sukhumvit and can get to all over Thailand easily from here.

Ladprao

Ladprao has an MRT station and provides access to the outskirts of the city. Rents in this area are reasonable and there are a number of shopping malls in the vicinity. The main road does experience horrible traffic jams throughout rush hour. Many people like this area because it is a bit more like 'real' Thailand; there are expats here and high-rise condos etc. but it still feels a bit more Thai, certainly much more than Sukhumvit. Also, there are lots of great Thai restaurants on the Kaset-Nawamin Road by the tollway just off Ladprao. Again, these are more targeted toward Thai clientele so more authentic flavours, live Thai music in some places and a more chilled out atmosphere (compared to a high-end Thai restaurant in Sathorn, for example).

How Close Should I Live to My Work?

During my time in Bangkok I have had three different jobs and lived in five different condos. I can safely say that I have been happiest when living closer to work, even if the area wasn't as desirable or the apartment not as nice.

Traffic in Bangkok can be horrific and it isn't fun being stuck for over an hour going to work each day. The heat and pollution also make it a miserable experience traveling across the city every day. Take my advice, find out where you're working and then arrange your accommodation within a 30-minute commute.

CHIANG MAI

Chiang Mai is a popular expat location for many reasons. Firstly, there are all the facilities you need to live but in a much quieter environment than Bangkok. You can travel to fantastic places within a few hours by road and be totally "in the wild" within half an hour.

Over recent years Chiang Mai has started to suffer from the traffic problems which bring Bangkok to a halt. The government is planning to build a monorail around the city in the next few years which should help greatly.

Chiang Mai is also marketed as the destination for digital nomads, people working remotely. There are a lot of internet cafes and shared office spaces set up to cater for this market. Chiang Mai has the highest concentration of Buddhist temples in Thailand and generally attracts digital nomads, 'hippies', creative people, spiritually starved people…you get the idea. Also, lots of retirees who have lived in Bangkok for a few years and want a more chilled out, more suburban style life head to Chiang Mai.

Chiang Mai University area (Suthep)

This area is the location many students at the university live in so there is a large supply of cheap accommodation and food. Cheap apartments start from around 4,000 baht a month. A decent 35sq metre condo will cost around 10,000 baht a month.

Nimmanhaemin

Possibly the trendiest area of Chiang Mai with plenty of bars, restaurants, working spaces and malls. You will also find supermarkets with imported goods in this area. This area is the most similar to Thong Lor or Ekkamai in Bangkok.

It is the most expensive area of Chiang Mai to live in but still you can get a good place in the 15-20,000-baht price range. The top condos in this area go for around 30,000 baht a month.

Hang Dong

More suited to families who want to live in a house with a decent garden. Around 15km from central Chiang Mai you need a car to come into the city but it is close to international schools. A lot of western families choose to be in this area because of the space, schools and to be closer to nature. Western style houses will cost between 20-40,000 THB a month depending upon the size and facilities.

Future Public Transport

These days a lot of expats choose to live close to public transport, especially if they don't have a car or motorbike. At the moment the BTS, MRT and Airport Rail Link in Bangkok are the most convenient forms of transport. Unfortunately, they only cover a small area of the city. The good news is that there are big plans in the next five to ten years to improve public transport not just in Bangkok but all over Thailand.

In Bangkok there will be many new BTS, MRT and Monorail lines built within the next 10 years. Some of these have already started construction with projected completion dates between 2020 and 2023. This will make it easier to travel around the city and reduce the need to sit in traffic jams. There is also a plan to link the two main airports in Bangkok via an extension to the Airport Rail Link.

In Chiang Mai there are discussions taking place about building either a monorail or a light-rail transit system in the city. Whilst plans have not been confirmed it is seen as an important project which will go ahead in one form or another.

There are plans to build a light-rail transit system in Phuket. It will cover roughly 60km and have 23 stations. This will make Phuket more accessible for tourists and people who live there. There is also a similar system being planned for Khon Kaen in the north east of Thailand.

Finally, current intercity railway lines will be improved in a bid to cut down travel times between strategic cities in Thailand.

PATTAYA and JOMTIEN

Pattaya has a worldwide reputation for its after dark activities but there is a lot more to this area. The Thai government turn a blind eye to prostitution in the main and many focus on the fact that Pattaya is a popular destination for Thai families and coachloads of Chinese package tourists.

Pattaya is a popular destination for expats so if you decide to locate yourself in Thailand's sin city, you will have lots of opportunities to meet fellow foreigners. The local expat scene in Pattaya and neighbouring Jomtien means that there are many expat societies and groups you can join. There are also many golf courses and this, in itself, is something that draws many people to this part of Thailand.

Jomtien is your best bet if you want to avoid the bars of Pattaya. It is more focused towards retired expats but there are many international families living in the area too.

One thing which is fantastic about this region is the availability of cheaply priced international food. Pattaya and Jomtien have a great range of restaurants which can be up to 50% cheaper than the fancier Bangkok options.

Accommodation is available at all price levels from 3,000-baht apartments to 50,000-baht houses.

HUA HIN

Hua Hin is a quieter version of Pattaya with less nightlife and fewer tourists. The town itself has a lot of positives such as world class golf courses, a great mix of dining options and national parks within a short drive.

The beach at Hua Hin is a slight improvement on Pattaya but you are probably not going to want to spend an awful lot of time there.

The nearby area of Cha-Am is also popular. In all honesty if you are looking at beach life then the only benefit Hua Hin has is that prices are cheaper than Phuket and it is a little quieter than Pattaya.

There is a wide range of accommodation options suiting all budgets. The closer to the beach you are the more expensive it will be.

PHUKET

Phuket is probably your best option if you want to be on the beach but with a range of facilities nearby. The difference between the beach in Phuket, compared to Pattaya or Hua Hin, is that in Phuket there are world class white sand beaches with crystal clear water.

The east side of Phuket is normally cheaper and has fewer tourists than other parts of the island. There is a large selection of long term rental properties in this area and great shopping options, including a mall. The downside to the east of Phuket is that the traffic is worse and you will probably be around 15 minutes' drive from decent beaches.

The western side of Phuket is where most luxury properties and hotels are located. There are many fine dining options and you can live next to world-class beaches. However, this does come with a high financial cost. If budget isn't an issue and you want the idyllic beach lifestyle then this is probably your best choice.

If you want to be in the centre of Phuket nightlife then the area around Patong beach is your best option. Although not quite as notorious as Pattaya's walking street, Patong does have a number of bars aimed at sex tourists.

The downside to Phuket is that it is expensive for many things. A lot of restaurants have three prices, one for local Thais, another for visiting Thais and the most expensive for foreigners.. Another key factor to consider is that public transport can be very expensive. Taxis are a rule to themselves and charge up to 10 times the price of a Bangkok taxi. If you choose to live in Phuket then you really should get a car or motorbike to get around.

Accommodation costs vary widely. It is possible to find cheap apartments but prices for condos start at around 12,000 baht. Luxury beach front houses can cost over 300,000 baht per month.

OTHERS

Islands such as Koh Samui are quite popular with expats. It can be quite expensive to live here and the major drawback is that it requires a boat or plane to get off the island which is quite time consuming. Being a tourist destination, Koh Samui does have a lot of facilities and restaurants. The main consideration is whether you want to live on an island and are happy being there all year round.

Essan (or Isaan) is the area in the North East of Thailand. It is famous for its rice fields and women. The stereotype of a foreigner with a Thai partner is that the partner will be from this region. Many people do settle down in this area to be with their partner's family and report that life is simple and quiet. Essan does lack a lot of facilities but there are regional cities such as Khon Kaen and Ubon Ratchathani where you can find shopping malls and western restaurants.

There are of course many other cities, towns and islands where you can happily live in Thailand, we just don't have enough space to list them all!

Living in the Sticks – Paradise or Hell?

For three months, I lived in an area called Lam Lukka, which is located just north of Bangkok and I hated pretty much every minute of it after the initial buzz of arriving in a new place had faded.

I could look out of my window and see rice fields and there weren't any other foreigners around which was pretty cool to begin with. After a few weeks however, I found myself running out of town as quickly as possible on a Friday night and staying in Bangkok until Sunday evening. I couldn't hack being in such a quiet area.

To make things worse, Lam Lukka actually is quite a major road so I would have beautiful views one way and then a six-lane major highway the other. It was a visual paradise one way and an eyesore the other.

Since then I have lived in areas away from the city center but within a 30-minute journey so I can get in and take advantage of what the city offers without paying high central prices or dealing with tourist traps.

TYPES OF ACCOMMODATION

The three main types of accommodation that expats in Thailand live in are condos, apartments and houses. In all major towns you will find a mixture of these at a range of price points.

A key factor to consider is transport. Usually houses require you to have either a car or motorbike as they are not normally close to public transport. Condos and apartments are normally built in town or city centres which means they are more convenient if you don't have your own set of wheels.

Condos and apartments sound similar but there are a couple of key differences. Condos are owned by individuals whereas an apartment is owned by the building. Condos will use government water and electric rates whereas apartments usually charge higher utility bills paid directly to the building owner. Finally, condos are normally built to a higher standard than apartments, in most cases.

Apartments are usually studio rooms ranging from around 25-75sq meters. They will be basically furnished and at the low end will not have kitchens or western style bathrooms. Apartments are the choice of a lot of Thai people on a budget and it is not uncommon for them to share with friends. The quality of the buildings varies and older apartments suffer from damage and don't provide a luxury feel.

Condos are usually in the same size bracket as apartments but the difference is you will have studio, one, two and three-bedroom options. Condos provide separate living areas and western bathrooms as well as at least a simple kitchen area. You also tend to find more condos have leisure facilities such as swimming pools and fitness rooms.

Houses come in different forms. Town houses are what we would call terraced houses in the UK, houses connected to each other. Detached houses are called single houses in Thailand. Usually you will get at least three bedrooms which makes these ideal for families or perhaps as house share options with friends. Many houses are built in "villages" – a term which describes a housing complex in Thailand.

Unless you have a family or are given housing as part of a job package most expats will focus on condos if they choose to live in Bangkok. Houses in central Bangkok are extremely expensive and many expats don't need so much space. Outside of Bangkok houses are much cheaper to rent and become a good option for many people.

RENT OR BUY

A big question for many expats is whether they should rent or buy a place here. We will take a look at this in the next chapter of the book so skip ahead if you want to read up on that in more detail.

As a quick overview it is not worth buying if you are just here for the short term. There are many hurdles to jump through to buy a place in Thailand the sales process can take a long time. If you are here for a longer period then it is something you might consider.

UTILITY BILLS

Utility bills in Thailand are likely a lot cheaper than your home country. Electricity, water, internet, phone bills, TV packages and other utilities are pretty straightforward in Thailand. Most utility companies have English-speaking staff who will be able to help you.

Electricity

If living in a condo or house then in 99% of cases you will pay your electric bill directly to the Metropolitan Electricity Authority (MEA). You can pay your bill in a range of local shops, banks or online using the MEA app or your Thai bank's app. Bills will be posted to you monthly and you will be given a two-week period to make payment. Using a few hours AC a day and a few other appliances should cost around 1,200 baht a month for a 35sq metre condo. A three-bedroom house using two or three air conditioning units a few hours a day will spend around 3,000 baht a month.

If you live in an apartment, you will pay your bill directly to the building, which should be at the official MEA rates. However, this is a new rule and some apartments might try to charge more for electricity.

Water

Water bills are usually paid to the office of the building in both apartments and condos. Houses usually pay directly via banks or 7/11.

Water bills are unbelievably cheap in Thailand. Having two or three showers a day and running a washing machine every day will still set you back less than 300 baht a month.

Internet

Apartments usually have the most convenient internet as you just need a code to log in. The problem is that many rooms share the same, usually very weak, connection so you might not have reliable internet. Price-wise you will pay a reasonably high amount for poor service. 300 baht a month is the norm in most apartments. You will probably also be limited to connecting two devices at the same time.

In condos and houses you will have to call in outside companies to set up your internet connection, which can take up to a week. These days a 50MB connection with around 100 local TV channels included is around 700-1,000 baht a month. 30MB packages without TV are around 550 baht a month.

The main companies who offer internet are True, AIS, TOT and CAT. They all offer similar services and price-wise are very similar. It is worth noting that True and AIS offer mobile phone packages and if combining them with internet can lead to extra discounts and promotions. You can find these companies inside any mall in Thailand.

TV packages

As mentioned previously you can arrange a TV package through one of the internet providers or the alternative is to do things independently, which might work out better.

In my opinion the packages offered by the internet companies in Thailand are pretty terrible unless you either speak Thai or live with a Thai partner. The variety and quality of the programming is sub-standard and the top-level packages cost over 2,500 baht a month. The only positive I can think of is that they include news channels and a few others that you might find interesting.

The alternative is to do things yourself. Netflix offers packages in Thailand for between 250-450 baht a month, which provides much better TV and movies than even the top-level packages from True and AIS. On top of this you can purchase a yearly subscription from BeIn sports for all football matches which costs 1,599 baht a year. My total TV bill is 600 baht a month for the top-level Netflix 4K package and all UK and European football matches live and on demand in HD.

If you are a fan of other sports or channels you can use VPNs to access them from Thailand. There are also other streaming services offered but most of these are illegal and should not be used. A lot of expats in Thailand have lost money from buying yearly packages only to see the owners shutting down the service after threats from copyright holders.

Home phone

It is very rare for Thai people to use a home phone; most calls are made on mobiles. However, if you really want a home phone line it can be arranged via the main operators True, AIS and TOT.

FURNITURE

Most places come at least partly furnished. International shops such as IKEA can be found if you want to buy some extra pieces. Local stores also carry a wide range of furniture at all price levels.

If you are really stuck then head to your nearest supermarket which will have a range of cheap furniture which should last a year or so.

APPLIANCES

A lot of places come with basic appliances, which may not fulfill your needs. A trip to one of the big supermarkets or a mall will give you plenty of options when it comes to buying those extras you need. Prices are usually cheaper than in the west but not by a huge amount.

MAIDS

If you are making a decent salary, probably over 50,000 baht a month, you can start looking at the possibility of hiring a maid to clean, iron or cook for you. Those with higher salaries can even look at live-in maids.

Maids can be hired at an hourly rate of around 200-400 baht and will clean your one-bedroom condo in a couple of hours. Many agencies offer discounts if you book the maid at least four times a month.

Live in maids will expect free accommodation and meals as well as a monthly salary starting at around 10,000 baht. Maids who also offer childcare or have a lot of experience and language skills charge in the region of 15-20,000 baht a month. Live in maids typically work six days a week.

NANNIES

Like with maids, you can get a professional nanny to look after your children in Bangkok for a reasonable price. Going through an agency, which is probably the safest way to do things, you are looking at hourly rates of 300 baht. Again, discounts are offered for full day bookings or live in maid/nannies.

Agencies often have nannies from neighboring countries so a Burmese nanny will probably be cheaper than a Thai nanny and also speak better English.

LAUNDRY

A lot of cheaper apartments and condos won't have a washing machine in the room. You have the option of washing your own clothes in the self-service laundry rooms or using a laundry service.

Most condos will have a self-service laundry room which charges around 30 baht per load. You will do everything for yourself but bear in mind the cleanliness of these machines is questionable. More expensive condos and houses will usually have a washing machine in the kitchen. I even negotiated to get the owner of my first condo to buy a washing machine rather than ask for a discount on the monthly rent.

Laundry services are pretty reasonable in Thailand. For around 15 baht you can get a shirt washed and ironed. Many places do packages for a certain number of garments.

Finances and Budgeting

The idea of a cheaper cost of living is one of the main draws of Thailand. "Live in Thailand for less than 1,000 USD a month" is a pretty common web article out there but is this really the reality? In this section we will look at the various costs of living here in terms of your move, settling in and then day to day life.

If you're reading this book then it is likely that you are still in your home country and not actually in Thailand yet. Maybe you have travelled here before or spoken with some people who have but you aren't really aware of the day to day costs. The cost of being here on vacation doesn't really give an accurate impression of how much you need to live in Thailand.

Moving itself is an expensive process and something which you really need to consider. Your initial airfare is a big sum and then add to that the cost of temporary accommodation; as such setting up your life will end up costing you more than you imagine. Most guides will give you a figure but to be honest they usually underestimate costs. In this section I've given my figures to show you how much I live on. All of our interviewees have also been asked to give recommendations for how much you need to live here.

My Move Finances (first month in Thailand)

Airfare UK to Thailand – 25,000 THB
Accommodation – 15,000 THB
Travel – 12,500 THB
Transport – 6,000 THB
Entertainment – 12,000 THB
Food and drink – 17,500 THB
Clothes – 6,000 THB
Others – 9,000 THB
Total – 103,000 THB

I had planned to spend a lot less than this but the excitement of being in a new place together with not knowing how much things should cost meant I overspent.

I planned to find a place for less than 10,000 baht a month but upgraded to a fancy apartment near Lardprao MRT. I ate in shopping mall restaurants every night and bought Western food from supermarkets. I had to update my wardrobe to suit the Thai climate. I made the most of my free time and hit the beach twice in the first month. I also went out and partied most nights. It was just a few beers but it added up quickly!

There were many extra costs I hadn't thought of too. Trips in taxis added up quickly and there was also a visa run to extend my stay before my first job. In short, you will most likely spend more than you imagine in your first few months; make sure you have enough money to cover this.

When it comes to moving to Thailand you will need to think long and hard about where you will live. Take a look at the previous chapter about accommodation and areas to read up about specific locations. In this section we will look at the budgeting and set up costs of your condo or house.

ACCOMMODATION FURNISHINGS

Although most places come furnished there will probably be a few finishing touches that you want to add. When you hit the shops, you might need to buy bedding, cutlery, decorations and kitchen electronics to make your new place livable. Even if you head to a supermarket, the cheapest place to buy all these items in one place, you will still probably be spending several thousand baht to get even the most basic items. If you splash out on a good blender, decent bedding and fancy cutlery then you could be looking at around 6,000 baht. If you go all out for the best of the best then your budget will skyrocket.

RENT OR BUY A PLACE

A big question to ask yourself is whether you are going to buy or rent a place. There are certainly positive and negatives to both but a lot of this will come down to how long you plan to stay in Thailand.

Renting

The main benefit of renting is that you have more flexibility in terms of your location and the place where you stay. With rents starting at around 3,000 baht a month it is certainly a cheap way to live but when you look into it you might end up paying a lot more.

First things first, 3,000 baht a month places are horrific and not somewhere that people would really choose to live in. They are small studio rooms often in old apartment blocks with very minimal facilities. These are the type of rooms that Thai people who work for minimum wage (350 baht a day) live in. Often you will get friends and families sharing these rooms as they are the cheapest options.

Spending 6,000 baht gets you a nicer version of the rooms mentioned in the previous paragraph. Maybe the apartment is a little bigger and perhaps there might be something like a shared fitness area but all in all you aren't living in any kind of luxury. To give you an insight I would say these 6,000 baht a month places are equivalent to a two-star hotel.

When you get to around 10,000 baht a month you start getting more quality and a place that you will enjoy spending time in. If we are talking about Bangkok this means a big studio or very small one-bedroom condo away from the central zone or sky trains. In other tourist locations such as Chiang Mai, Pattaya, Phuket or on the islands we are probably talking about a decent size one-bedroom condo or small house away from the central areas.

12-18,000 baht gets you a good one-bedroom condo or small/medium sized house away from central areas of pretty much every part of Thailand.

If you are looking towards the higher end, condos in central areas or houses in prime locations then you can expect to spend 20,000 baht a month or more. Prices for luxury two or three-bedroom condos in prime Bangkok locations go for around 50-75,000 baht a month.

When you move into a property in Thailand you will need to pay first and last month's rents and a one-month security deposit. For example, a 10,000 baht a month condo means you will need 30,000 baht to move in. It is normal for most contracts to last one year and for around 500 baht to be kept from the deposit to cover cleaning when you move out.

Buying

Buying a property is a big step whether it's in your home country or abroad. Buying in Thailand is probably not as straightforward as in your home country but it is possible for certain types of buildings.

Condos are the easiest purchase option and cost from around one million baht for a simple small studio room all the way to over 50 million baht for a penthouse in the most stylish areas of town. Most condo developers are used to dealing with foreigners so you will be able to get advice and assistance from them. If buying a used condo unit then you need to rely on the seller knowing the process or hire an agent to assist. Agents usually charge a fee of around 3% to help with property matters.

If you purchase a condo you will be liable to pay a monthly / yearly maintenance fee. This fee is based on the size of your unit. The total amount is not too high. The average amount seems to be between 40-75 baht per square metre per month. This fee covers upkeep of facilities, cleaning of communal areas and waste disposal. As an owner it is possible that you could be liable for extra charges if major work or redevelopment was done in your building.

Condo insurance is cheap, major firms offer good coverage from 2,500 baht per year.

When buying a property, our first step is normally to go to a bank and see how much we can borrow. In Thailand it is almost a certainty that the bank will reject you, as a foreigner, even if you have a great job and have lived here many years. The only way they will lend to you is if you put the property in a Thai person's name and you act as a guarantor.

One of the key points when buying a condo in a foreigner's name is that all money for the purchase must be sent from overseas into Thailand. This means you can't use Thai savings to purchase a place without sending the money out of Thailand first.

Land in Thailand cannot be purchased by foreigners. This makes buying a house very difficult. You can buy the physical building but not the land it is on. There are a couple of ways to get around this by leasing the land but it isn't a route most people like to go down.

If you are married to a Thai national then you can put property in their name if you wish.

Is it worth buying?

What I will say is look at the cost of buying somewhere versus how much you could rent it for a year. My current condo is 20,000 baht a month to rent and cost the owner 5.5 Million baht. This works out at 23 years' worth of renting. As a renter I wouldn't have to pay for any refurbishments or issues although the rent could increase. In my view the flexibility makes it worth renting unless you found somewhere you fell in love with and could see yourself living in forever.

The major benefit of buying for many people is that once a place is paid for then you never need to pay rent again. The feeling that comes with this is something a lot of people appreciate, especially those retiring here.

UTILITY BILLS

Although a great part of Thailand is exploring the outdoors and experiencing everything this country has to offer you will also need to think about budgeting for when you are at home. Phone, electricity, water, internet and TV are just some of the bills you will need to budget for.

When buying a phone in Thailand it is important to know that normally you can't get one on a contract but have to buy the phone and pay monthly for a package of calls, SMSs and internet. There are a few companies who offer phone packages and the main three are True, DTAC and AIS. All three are quite similar in terms of package and offer a wide range of options. My current package of 100 minutes, 10GB internet allowance and free SMS to same network costs just over 300 baht a month.

If your phone is region locked (only able to be used by your carrier in your home country) then take it to any mall and find a mobile phone stall. They will unlock it for you in a few minutes so you can use a Thai sim card.

Internet options again are dominated by a few firms, True, AIS, TOT and CAT. All of these are very similar in terms of pricing. A 50MB private connection will cost around 750 baht a month. If you take out a joint Internet and TV package you will get a package costing around 1,000 baht a month but will mainly consist of Thai channel with a handful of English language shows.

Electricity and water are unlikely to set you back more than 2,000 baht a month unless you run the AC 24/7 or live in a large house.

Many people also use online services such as Netflix and Bein Sports. Netflix provides the best international TV shows from 250 baht a month. Bein Sports covers European football leagues for 1,599 baht per year.

Paying utility bills

It is now easier than ever to pay utility bills in Thailand.

Water bills are usually paid directly to the front office at your condo or housing estate.

If you receive a paper bill with a barcode then take it to a 7/11 and you can pay it there in cash. They will charge you a 15-baht fee. You can also do the same at your bank or supermarket. Check the back of your bill and it will normally list the stores where you can pay.

For electricity, your phone and internet you can download the specific app for your provider and pay online. This saves the effort of going to the branch or paying a 15-baht fee to another shop to handle the payment. The apps work well and are a great option if you aren't in the country on the due date.

You can set up bill payment via your bank. This can be complex to set up and might take a while. Personally, I don't do this as I know of a few people who spent months trying to get their bank to set up payments without success.

Finally bank apps now allow you to scan bills and pay directly from your account. Again, these sometimes come with fees so do check first.

FOOD AND DRINK

One of the first things many people think of when it comes to eating in Thailand is street food. 40-baht dishes of food eaten by the roadside. Cheap eats that will fill you up three times a day. Do this for every meal and you will spend around 4,000 baht a month.

In reality if you eat street food three times a day everyday then all I say is good luck to you! Street food has its place and most expats do indulge in it but after a while you will hit some problems with it. Firstly, it is limited to Thai food which, although great, does become a little tiresome after a while. Secondly, the hygiene isn't great and it has been the source of all my food poisoning and related illnesses in Thailand. Finally eating by the side of the road sucks.

Shopping in the market

Another popular image of Thailand is the local market. There are local markets everywhere around Thailand. Some are small whereas others could take you hours to walk around. They sell a wide range of local produce. You get many stalls selling pre-cooked meals and others selling the original ingredients.

A lot of Thai people like markets because the fruit and vegetables are cheaper than the supermarkets. Bunches of bananas starts at 20 baht, cucumbers 10 baht and a large box of strawberries for under 100 baht.

You can also get snacks such as donuts, cookies and muffins for around 10 baht each. There certainly is a wide range of items at the market and it won't hurt your pocket.

In my opinion there are a couple of downsides to the local market though. The first thing that will hit you is the smell. In general, a lot of markets sell a wide range of meats, none of which are kept in chilled environments so it creates a stink. Chok Chai 4 (an area in Bangkok with a famous market) smells from around 500 metres away. It's grim. A lot of other fresh markets do have a whiff that is very off-putting. Then you have the un-refrigerated meat which to me is a big no-no. I wouldn't ever buy food other than snacks and fruits/ vegetables from the market as the food hygiene is terrible.

After a while you will crave eating somewhere inside to avoid pollution, rain and noise. Many restaurants offer air-conditioned comfort and great food for around 50-100 baht a dish. At this point you can see that if you want to eat in a better place you will be looking at a budget of at least 200 baht a day for meals. 6,000 Baht a month is still quite cheap for eating a whole month.

Food is one of the cornerstones of life in Thailand. You will spend a lot of time in restaurants eating and socializing. If you go to a good restaurant then it is quite likely you will spend between 300-500 baht each time. Add on alcoholic drinks and you can almost double that.

Thailand has a large number of international restaurants. Tourist hubs are the best places to find genuine tastes from home but there are fast food restaurants all around the country too. International food is rarely under 100 baht a dish and in tourist areas is probably closer to 200 baht. There are a number of fine dining choices where you can get world class sushi, seafood and steak and these meals normally cost over 1,000 baht per person.

Cooking at home can save you money but in the end the savings come if you cook for a big group of people. If you are living alone or with a partner then the average cost per meal is probably about the same as eating out in a decent restaurant.

Cooking at home does mean that you can make your favourite dishes from back home the way you like them. Do bear in mind that a lot of imported products will cost more than you pay in your home country. A trip to the local supermarket can be great value if just buying local produce but can easily skyrocket if you spend too much time in the imported food aisle!

Supermarkets and 7/11 stock lots of drinks. Soft drinks are cheap, a 1.5 litre bottle of water is around 15 baht. A can of Pepsi is 14 baht. Local beers (Singha, Leo, Chang) are around 35-60 baht for cans / bottles. Imported alcohol can be very expensive due to tax. A decent bottle of wine will be over 500 baht and more likely closer to 1,000 baht. Imported beers are normally at least 100 baht in the supermarket.

If drinking at a restaurant or bar then expect to pay around 100 baht for a local beer and 250 baht for a glass of wine. Some bars do have happy hours with prices starting at around 60 baht for a small bottle of beer or perhaps buy one get one free on wine and cocktails.

With all this you can see that unless you want to stick to street food and water then you will spend a fair amount on food. I budget between 12-15,000 baht a month for food and drink which works out about right to get a good mix of local food, imported products and eating in mid to high level restaurants a few times a week.

HEALTH INSURANCE

Being left with a high bill after a mishap in Thailand is becoming more common. As an expat you really need to consider the cost of health insurance when budgeting for living here if it is not provided through your work. If you're from a country that provides free health care then you need to be aware that Thailand is the opposite, everything will cost you.

If you are working in Thailand, you will likely get some form of health insurance but it may not be very comprehensive. Standard social security payments do allow you to use basic services at government hospitals but the standard is likely way below what you are used to and the waiting times can be horrific. Many mid-level companies will provide a form of private health insurance but with heavy limits such as a 4,000 baht per injury claim and a maximum number of claims per year. The top jobs offer insurance with international companies such as BUPA or AXA which offer full coverage and treatment for you and your registered dependents.

If you aren't working here then you will have to look at privately funding an insurance policy or paying for treatment as needed. A single policy for full coverage with minimal deductions will cost around 25,000 baht a year for a 35-year-old with no previous conditions. You can see that if you are insuring your whole family then the cost is going to be high. Also note that many insurance policies do not cover accidents caused whilst on a motorbike.

Some people choose to not take out an insurance policy and pay for treatment as and when needed. The good news is that treatment for basic illnesses is cheap and easily accessible. An appointment with a doctor at a local clinic will cost in the region of 500 baht.

If you decide to go to a private facility you can easily spend a small fortune even for something quite basic. Private hospitals often give endless tests and a variety of medicine to bump your bill up considerably. Check out the chapter on getting sick in Thailand to find out more about the health service here.

SCHOOL FEES

If you are moving here with children then school fees could quickly add up.

If you are employed by an international company then you might get international education for your children included. If not then you will need to budget accordingly.

The top international schools charge fees from 300,000 baht to one million baht per year. These schools have internationally trained and qualified teachers from western countries. The schools have facilities similar to those you would expect in your home country.

Bilingual schools offer English programs and fees are usually around 60-100,000 baht per year. You will get teachers from Western countries but they aren't always qualified to teach in their own country. Many of these schools also employ Filipino teachers. The facilities are better than Thai government schools but probably not up to the standard of your home country.

Government schools cost around 10-25,000 baht a year. There are some western teachers but most lessons are in Thai. If your child cannot speak Thai, this won't be an option for you.

TRANSPORT

Whether you decide to use private or public transport there will always be a cost to consider. Saving money by walking is perhaps possible but the horrific state of sidewalks means that you are likely to get some form of injury over time or have to walk on a main road.

Buying a motorbike or scooter seems to be a form of Russian Roulette, not if you will have an accident but when! Everyone I know who has a motorbike has had some form of accident at some point. Is it worth risking your life on a bike in the second most dangerous country in the world for road death accidents?

If you do take the plunge and get a bike they can be rented for around 2-4,000 baht a month. You will then be responsible for the gas. Purchase prices start at around 30,000 baht for a very basic model up to around 100,000 baht for a good scooter and much more for imported bikes and superbikes.

There are also motorbike taxis which run in most towns and cities in Thailand. They will take you short distances and fares are normally between 10-50 baht.

Cars in Thailand are expensive due to the high import taxes levied on them. A cheap new car will cost at least 600,000 baht but most models are closer to a million baht. Finance is available if you meet the bank's terms (usually a hefty deposit and visa showing commitment to Thailand). Monthly payments will likely be around 10,000 baht for basic models. Insurance prices range from 8-25,000 baht per year.

Driving license

Regardless of what people might say, it is mandatory to have the correct license to drive a car or motorbike in Thailand. Please note there are two types of license, one for cars and another for motorbikes.

You can get a Thai license very easily if you are qualified to drive in a western nation. You need to show your home country license, have a medical exam and do a couple of vision tests and you will get a car license. For a motorbike you will also have to do a quick practical test too.

If you don't have a license from an approved country then you will need to do a theory and practical test before getting a license. There are driving centres in all major towns and cities.

Finally, a Thai driving license can be used as a form of ID and used to get Thai price at some attractions.

Taxis are considered expensive by Thai people but, in reality, they are very cheap. In some locations they use the meter in others they don't. A 30-minute taxi trip in Bangkok will cost around 150 baht whereas it could cost 600 THB in Phuket, as meters aren't used there. Grab Taxi is a popular company who offer online taxi booking with transparent pricing, which is becoming more popular. You can use Grab in most tourist locations such as Bangkok, Chiang Mai and Phuket.

Buses are a cheap way to travel but there aren't many which use air-con. Single bus trips in most towns cost between 10-25 baht. Inter-city buses are a decent option to get around for three or four-hour trips. For example, the three-hour bus between Chiang Mai and Chiang Rai costs around 250 baht.

Minivans, which carry between 12-15 passengers, are the choice of many people to get from town to town. It seems almost every road accident in Thailand involves one of these so I wouldn't recommend them unless there is no other option.

Seven Deadly Days of Songkran

Songkran is the Thai new year. It has a deep cultural and religious background but these days it is best known for the huge water fights which take place around the country. Almost every street will be lined with people throwing water at each other from buckets or squirting you with a water gun. The idea behind this is that Songkran is usually the hottest time of the year and it's nice to get cooled down. Khao San Road, RCA, Chiang Mai, Pattaya and Silom are the main areas for people to enjoy huge water fights between the 13-15th April each year. The less well-known side of Songkran is that it is the time of year with the most road fatalities.

The period April 11-17 is when people from all over the country return to their families and then head back to work after. A total of 390 people died in road accidents during Songkran week in 2017 with a further 3,808 injured. In 2016 the death toll was 442.

A mixture of tired van and bus drivers and partying drink drivers makes it a truly deadly time to be on the road. If you want my advice don't travel by road at this time of the year....

Converted pickup trucks with seats in the rear are called songthaews. They are available in almost every town in Thailand and are the choice of many Thai people on a budget. The fare is usually less than 10 baht, except in tourist areas where the price is maybe 20-30 baht per person.

Tuk-tuks are three wheeled motorbikes and are a famous symbol of Thailand. They are found in tourist destinations as well as some local communities. They are not regulated in terms of fares so you will need to negotiate a price. Tuk-tuks in tourist locations will charge a fortune so should be your last resort.

If you are traveling between major cities within Thailand then take advantage of the cheap low-cost airline carriers. If you book far enough in advance return trips within the country to major destinations will be around 2,000-3,000 baht.

Finally, there are trains which travel (slowly) around the country. In my opinion they aren't really worth it if you are travelling for more than three or four hours. For example, the cost of a return ticket from Bangkok to Chiang Mai by train is almost as expensive as a flight. However, if you are going from Bangkok to Ayutthaya then the 20-baht ticket price for a three-hour trip isn't bad value.

TRAVEL IN THAILAND

Weekends away, day trips to the beach or adventures in the jungle are just some of the fantastic travel options you will have whilst here in Thailand. Whilst it is true that you can keep costs down it is very likely that you end up spending more than you would think.

A single person travelling alone to somewhere like Phuket for three nights will find it almost impossible to spend less than 10,000 baht when you include flights, airport transfers, hotels, food and activities. Travel with your partner and that creeps up to 15,000 baht and with a small family it could be 20,000 baht or more.

Staying in hostels can bring the price down but a lot of people want somewhere private and decent to stay in. You should budget at least 1,000 baht a night for a semi-decent hotel and 2,000 baht if you want something resembling three or four-star quality.

Internal flights can cost as little as 1700 baht return if booked far enough in advance but you will see prime locations can cost 3-5,000 baht even if booking a few weeks before you travel.

ENTERTAINMENT

Thailand offers many forms of entertainment, some well-known others less so. Drinking is the choice of many here it seems and although a night out is relatively cheap it can quickly add up if going out too often.

Below I have put an example of a few common types of entertainment here and the costs.

Example costs

Cinema ticket (weekend) – 220 baht
Large bottle of beer in supermarket – 55 baht
Large bottle of beer in average restaurant – 110 baht
Round of golf (weekend – caddy fee included) – 3,000 baht
Ice skating (60 minutes) – 200 baht
Massage (60 minutes) – 300 baht
Thai lesson (60 minutes) – 300 baht
Gym membership – 500-2,500 baht per month
Scuba diving – 1,500 baht for one dive and equipment

For a lot of people in the west, TV is a major form of entertainment. As you can see in this chapter the cost of TV packages can be low so if you are a homebody then you can be a couch-potato cheaply here!

If books are your thing then Asia Books is your best option for getting international titles in English. They have stores around the country as well as a great website.

Video games in Thailand are becoming more popular among locals and a number of new shops have opened recently to meet demand. Hardware itself is normally more expensive than other local countries but if you buy software through online platforms such as Steam or the PlayStation Store it will usually be cheaper than in the west.

If you are a fan of card games such as bridge or poker be careful. Groups of expats have been arrested playing these games as police officers suspect illegal gambling is taking place.

Photography is popular in Thailand. There are many great places to take photos. Equipment can be expensive but there are camera shops in pretty much every mall in the country. If you are into flying drones to take pictures then make sure you register your drone or you will be liable to pay a large fine.

Thailand also has lots of entertainment for children (and big children!). There are a number of water parks in Bangkok, Pattaya and Phuket. Bangkok also has 2 theme parks which are not at the level of world-famous parks but great for kids or anyone seeking an afternoon of thrills. You can use a work permit to get Thai price at these places, expect to pay around 500 baht for adults and half price for kids. Bangkok and Chiang Mai have a few zoos if you are into that kind of thing.

Shopping malls have a wide ride range of entertainment for the whole family. There are arcades in most malls with a range of games, the majority in English. There are also soft play areas for children. Thailand doesn't really do outdoor playgrounds so bring your children to the mall to get them to run around for a few hours!

Sports are popular in Thailand. Read more about sporting options later in the book.

SHOPPING

As previously mentioned a lot of imported goods are quite expensive. If you plan on buying imported food or need the latest Adidas shoes then your budget will need to be high.

Anything considered a luxury will actually be comparatively more expensive here. High end brands often have stores in the top malls but you can get the products cheaper in your home country.

Talking of malls, you cannot go more than about 5 minutes in Bangkok without seeing one! All around the country, malls are a focal point, perhaps due to the free air-conditioning. I find myself spending more time in malls in Thailand than I did back home. If you are the same then prepare to spend more on impulse purchases.

In the UK I always used Amazon for my online shopping but they don't operate in Thailand. For my online shopping needs I use Lazada and Ali Express (based in China) which both deliver to Thailand. Lazada are faster but Ali Express has more choice.

WHAT KIND OF LIFE CAN YOU LIVE ON...

At the start of this chapter I mentioned that there are a lot of articles saying that you can live in Thailand on $1,000 a month. In all of the interviews in this book we have asked people how much they recommend you need to live on here in Thailand so feel free to see what our interviewees think. Below I have given my opinions on life at different budgets in Thailand based on my experience.

Around $1,000 a month (c. 33,000THB)

To be honest with you this isn't really living at this level, it is just surviving. This works out at around 33,000 baht a month and means that you can live here in Thailand but you will be missing out on many things and always worrying about making expensive purchases.

You will be living in a low / mid end apartment outside of the central areas and probably a fair distance from public transport if in Bangkok. Your studio apartment will start to feel like a prison cell and you will have to think long and hard whether you can really justify spending 300 baht on a pizza. You will be miserable and most likely better off staying in your home country. When Skyping your family back home they will honestly be wondering what happened to you and that things must be so bad living in such a crappy environment.

The major downside to being on this kind of budget is that you are unlikely to be putting anything away for a rainy day. If you are working in Thailand then you need to think very carefully if the benefits of being here are worth it when you can barely save 3,000 baht. If here on retirement then you maybe don't need to save but remember you will be paying for healthcare, which certainly isn't cheap. Forget about a trip back home, the flight alone is likely to be close to $1,000 for many people and then you need spending money on top of that.

The type of people who live on this type of salary are gap year English teachers and those who don't know any better. It isn't uncommon for people who live on this kind of salary to say things like "I live a more simpler life" or "I've adapted to live how Thai people live" but in all honesty, they are cutting back on something that they would like to do.

Around $1,500 a month (c. 48,000 THB)

Now you're looking at around 48,000 baht a month and things do get a bit more interesting and your quality of life will be a vast improvement on those scrimping by on their 33,000 baht a month.

You can just about afford a big studio room or perhaps a small one-bedroom apartment in a reasonable location. Sure, it won't be luxury but around the three-star standard. It's the kind of place where you might actually invite someone over to without fearing they will think less of you.

You will be able to splash out now and then and eating Western food won't feel like it will destroy your bank balance. Savings and trips back home are still a worry for most people at this level of income though.

Around $2,000 a month (c. 66,000 THB)

At just over 60,000 baht a month, things take another leap in terms of your quality of living.

Decent apartments in central locations can be had for around 12-20,000 baht which means a one-bedroom condo, or perhaps even a small townhouse isn't out of the question. We are looking at buildings with pools, fitness centers and a nice feel to them. You'll be able to get a good internet connection, run the AC when you're in without worrying over the monthly 2,000-baht bill and splurge on Netflix and a sports package to watch.

Eating out will mean you're able to visit local, international and, occasionally, fine dining options in Thailand. You can travel locally on this wage and enjoy being in Thailand.

You can put away at least 5,000 baht a month which should be enough to cover a trip back home and some spending money.

Around $3,000 a month (c. 100,000 THB)

This is a very important number for a lot of people living here. This is the level where you will be able to support a partner and child to a good standard. Forget about doing that on 33,000 baht a month and even at 66,000 baht you will be missing out on lots. At almost 100,000 baht a month you have the means to buy imported products for your child and live in a good, safe environment.

The budget for two adults and a child to eat a wide variety of healthy food in Thailand will come in at around 25,000 baht a month in most expat areas. In the sticks you can do it for less but when it comes to things like baby milk and food you probably don't want to scrimp on it.

You will probably want to get a place with at least 2 bedrooms when you have a family. Two Bedroom condos start at around 16,000 baht in the outskirts whereas a place in a good location in a tourist area will be minimum 20,000 baht but more likely approaching 30,000 THB. If you are living outside tourist areas, you can rent a decent two or three-bedroom house for around 12-25,000 baht a month. In the sticks it is possible for around 8,000 baht a month.

You will be able to afford the fees for a bilingual school and have a few little trips locally too. Flying a family back to your home country might be difficult on this salary alone but if you're partner is earning too then it is possible.

If you are a single person at this salary then you can live a fantastic life here!

Around $4,000 a month (c. 135,000 THB)

If you are an expat from a Western country being relocated to Thailand by an international company then this is the kind of salary you should really be looking at. It isn't unrealistic but many people here have a negative attitude towards asking for what they are really worth.

At 135,000 baht a month you are going to have a really nice lifestyle. You can eat out every meal if you want and go to fancy bars to socialize without having to worry about the tab at the end of the night. Forget using public transport you can travel by taxi or Grab everywhere.

The nice thing about this level is that you will be able to save a decent amount at the end of each month. A single person on this salary who goes out a few nights a week, travels once a month and lives in a good one-bedroom condo should be able to save at least a quarter of their income pretty easily. This means that trips home or to other countries are possible and buying things like new laptops or phones isn't an issue either.

Around $5,000 a month (c. 160,000 THB)

Pretty similar to the $4,000 section above but the same can be said for small families. Savings are possible and you can do a lot here without worrying too much over money.

Over $5,000 a month

At this level you have pretty much no worries at all. You can travel and stay in top hotels and visit other countries in the region without any difficulty.

You will be the sort of person high level condo developers target and could rent one of the more luxurious rooms in the 50,000 baht a month range. Depending on how much over $5,000 you have then you could look at a penthouse in one of the key areas of Bangkok with private pools and elevators. These cost in the region of 100,000 baht a month.

My 2017 Average Income and Spending

Below you can find information on my monthly income and spending in 2017 as well as monthly average with a breakdown of the costs.

For my full monthly breakdown over the last two years check out my website – lifeinanewcountry.com

Month	Income	Spending
January	70,000 THB	103,500 THB
February	59,000 THB	57,000 THB
March	67,000 THB	57,000 THB
April	82,000 THB	100,000 THB
May	62,500 THB	55,000 THB
June	71,500 THB	58,000 THB
July	132,500 THB	57,500 THB
August	134,500 THB	57,000 THB
September	100,000 THB	73,800 THB
October	80,000 THB	55,000 THB
November	64,500 THB	62,500 THB
December	112,000 THB	72,000 THB
Average	86,292 THB	67,358 THB

Accommodation – 20,000 THB

I live in a two-bedroom condo at the end of the MRT line in Bangkok.

Transport – 2,500 THB
Taxis, public transport and Grab Taxi.

Utility Bills – 3,000 THB
Netflix, electricity, water, internet and phone.

Food – 15,000 THB
Restaurants and cooking at home. Includes snacks and drinks.

Entertainment – 5,000 THB
Cinema trips, beers out and playing sport.

Travel – 13,000 THB
A few little trips a year and a couple of big ones including back to the UK for Christmas.

Shopping – 5,000 THB
Clothes, electronics etc.

Other – 4,000 THB
Gym membership, haircuts etc.

Average saved per month – 18,934 THB
This money is either invested here in Thailand or sent back to the UK to pay my student loan.

RETIRING IN THAILAND

A lot of people move to Thailand to retire. With a warm climate, many cheap activities and a decent level of medical care Thailand is a good option for retirees. The information in this book will help you to prepare for your retirement here but below are a few specific points for retirees.

Firstly, when it comes to pensions you will need to check if your country will make payments to Thai bank accounts or if you are required to keep it in your own country and then transfer. Some countries also freeze pension increases when you leave the country.

As a retiree you will not be eligible to benefit from many schemes aimed at retired Thai citizens. Public transport offers discounts to Thai OAPs but refuse to give the same to foreigners, even those with yearly retirement visas.

More retirement homes and assisted living facilities are opening in Thailand. Chiang Mai is the hub for these facilities. The Care Resort Chiang Mai and Dok Kaew Gardens are two facilities which get good feedback. Costs range widely but there are packages starting at around 45,000 baht a month for accommodation, meals and basic care. There are also other packages to look at with more comprehensive care.

If you do require constant medical attention then you might consider hiring a private nurse. A full time live in nurse who is qualified and speaks English would charge around 35,000 baht per month. If you just need basic care on a part time basis then you could find a nurse to help with this too.

Thai people's impressions of foreigner's wages

Thai people are quite intrigued by expat wages and it won't be uncommon to have people ask you how much you make. Whilst it is probably considered rude to ask this question in your home country it seems to be an acceptable thing for people to ask here. Students, taxi drivers and people from the village are likely keen to know how much you're getting paid.

You'll probably be quite shocked at their directness but you can easily brush it off if you do not want to talk about it and they won't hassle you. I often have fun with this question and say something outrageously high or low which stops the line of questioning.

I've also experienced potential dates asking this question with one lovely lady saying she wouldn't date a foreigner unless he was making over 100,00 baht a month. Just a bit of a red flag I'm sure you'd agree!

TWO PRICE THAILAND

Something to be aware of is that many attractions in Thailand have a two-tiered pricing structure. One price for Thais and another for foreigners. Sometimes this is obvious when looking at the ticket prices but, on some occasions, establishments display the rarely used Thai symbols for numbers to avoid showing foreigners the difference.

This issue enrages some expats whereas others don't care too much. To be honest if you are here in Thailand on a proper yearly visa and have either a work permit or driving license then you can often get the Thai price. The only real exceptions are at temples and national parks where they will charge you the foreigner rate regardless.

My Wage Progression

Over four years in Thailand my salary has increased and I have seen a huge improvement in my quality of life. Below I will tell you how I lived at different salary levels during my time in Thailand. You could use this as a guide to show potentially how soon you can move up pay grades here in Thailand.

Months 1-3 Living off savings

My first three months in Thailand were spent completing my CELTA (teaching certificate) which meant I had a month of studying with a few weeks either side for settling in and travel. I was in holiday mode and threw money around like it was nothing. I estimate I spent close to 80,000 baht a month and didn't think anything of it.

Months 3-6: first Job 34,000 baht a month + free accommodation

My first paid job in Thailand was working at a Thai government high school. The agency I worked for were useless but I was sold the dream by them and the promise of free accommodation meant I took up their offer.

   The accommodation was horrible. I spent my evenings sitting outside drinking beers until midnight with the other teachers from my school just to avoid the 20sq metre studio room I had. I found myself spending all my money on trips to Bangkok to avoid the boredom. 34,000 baht was enough to get by on because there was literally nothing to spend my money on in that area apart from beer.

   After my weekend splurges on a hotel and partying in Bangkok I was left with nothing at the end of the month. I quickly realized that if I was going to be here long term I needed to up my salary.

Month 7 to year 2: 55,000 baht a month

I changed jobs and got a nice increase in salary. 55,000 baht a month meant my life improved a lot. The first thing I did was to move into a great 44sq metre condo which cost 13,000 baht a month. It actually scared me to pay so much but in reality, it was a great decision and helped change my mindset that I wasn't going to scrimp on everything.

My savings were normally around 5,000 baht a month which wasn't great but it helped. I was able to go on a couple of small trips a year to local countries during this time.

Year 2 to year 4: c.75,000 baht a month

I was still at the same job but took on a number of part time roles and outside projects which pushed up my earnings. I had gotten to know a few more people and from them was recommended for outside work.

It was at this time I purchased a condo as I was more secure in my financial status. I actually sold it after about 18 months due to changing jobs and needing to be in another part of Bangkok.

Year 4 onwards c.85,000 baht a month

A change of job again pushed my basic salary up to around 80,000 baht a month. I then have the choice of taking overtime at around 1,000 baht an hour if I so choose.

I moved to a 20,000 baht a month condo and was able to start using taxis more often to travel around. Every week involves going out a couple of times.

Hopefully this shows that it is possible to progress your career whilst here. I didn't do anything special and I don't have amazing contacts. The process involved getting more experienced and finding new opportunities to improve.

Setting Up Your Life in Thailand

Moving to a new country involves jumping through many hoops and dealing with unexpected situations. You will have undoubtedly tried to read up on things and hopefully by the end of this chapter you will feel a lot more confident when it comes to setting up your new life in Thailand.

Also, note that visa regulations change very often in Thailand so this section is a guide based on the beginning of 2018. Many of the experiences and information here will provide you with an insight of how things work in Thailand but do check with official sources and websites as to current procedures when you come to move to Thailand. You can find official website links in the "Useful Resources" section at the end of the book.

WHY AM I HERE?

You need to really think why you are moving to Thailand. Moving to a new country is not a decision to take lightly. You need to be sure that it is the right time and the right place for you. You must be prepared for the stress, the mistakes and the annoyances that moving overseas brings.

There are many good reasons to be here but also an equal number of bad ones. Sure, you had a good holiday here but that doesn't mean living here full time will be the same. I can tell you that the dream of sitting on the beach every afternoon with a cold beer is not something that most expats get to do. It is easy to get to the beach every so often but working on your laptop under a coconut tree, no chance!

Moving to be with family is a popular reason to be here. Long distance relationships can't last forever so a lot of foreigners take the plunge and move here.

The sexpat in my condo

I recently met an American guy in my condo. As I live out of the city centre there aren't too many foreigners in my area so we had a little chat and agreed to meet up for a beer later that week.

Within a few minutes of drinking I realized I was in for a recital of the different women he had slept with and bars he had been to. He'd been in Thailand for 9 months and had lived in Pattaya and Bangkok over that time. He was recently divorced and had taken early retirement.

I'm obviously not naïve about what some people get up to here in Thailand but sex was his life. He was hitting on every woman who walked past us in the local restaurant. He said he spends every day chatting to women on websites and in his words "forgetting that bitch I left in America".

Whilst he is obviously enjoying his life I am not sure he will have long term happiness in Thailand. Without a job, social network or meaningful relationships I think he is someone who will be here for the short term.

Telling friends and family

Moving overseas not only impacts your life but also your family and friends. The chances are they likely have a lot of questions and concerns. You can help this process go smoother by having as much information to hand as possible.

Hopefully this book will provide you with lots of things you can tell them but let your family know there will be surprises and bumpy patches too.

Is moving to Thailand career suicide?

Looking online you will see a lot of people saying that moving to Thailand is career and financial suicide. To be honest I don't think there are many places in the world which don't have cutbacks, pay freezes and low interest rates right now. It is quite depressing listening to friends from Europe and the US talking about how bad things are.

My post tax average salary in Thailand of 86,292 baht works out at a pre-tax salary of 30,000 GBP. The average UK salary is around 28,000 GBP so I'm already ahead of the game. Then consider Thailand is cheaper than the UK to live in. Certainly, this isn't financial suicide.

In terms of my career, I have managed to move up the ladder over my time here. I am at a progressive company and have plenty of training and development options. In the next couple of years I am aiming to have an average monthly salary of 100,000 baht.

There certainly is the opportunity to progress in Thailand if you have a positive attitude and are prepared to work for it. A lot of people here don't put in the effort or try to look for promotions. I'm not trying to tell you that progress is easy but it is possible.

If you plan to head back to your home country after a couple of years in

Thailand then it won't be an issue. You will have gained valuable experience here. If you sit around on your ass doing nothing then it will look bad.

VISAS

When you know that Thailand is the place you want to be you need to think about your visa options. There are many visa options; we cover the most common ones below for expats.

You can apply for the visas by yourself or use an agency to help you.

Tourist

There are several types of tourist visas in Thailand. Some you can get on arrival, others you need to apply for in advanced.

Many countries get a 30-day visa on arrival which is free. You can also get 60 or 90-day visas before traveling from Thai embassies which will cost around $90.

In the past many expats have just stayed in Thailand on tourist visas and left the country when it was due to end. After a few days overseas, they would come back to Thailand with a fresh 30-day visa. Nowadays the authorities are trying to stop this. People with multiple visa stamps may need to prove why they are coming to Thailand and show finances that will be used to support them.

Some expats do arrive on tourist visas as they will hunt for a job and change to a different visa when in Thailand.

Non-Immigrant (Non Imm) – B / O

A non-immigrant visa basically gives you 60 extra days in Thailand over the standard tourist visa and it allows you to obtain a work permit or apply for a yearly extension. This visa is usually obtained at a Thai embassy located outside Thailand. Penang in Malaysia or Vientiane in Laos are popular options for many who have initially arrived in Thailand on a tourist visa and need to visit a Thai embassy overseas to get a non-imm visa.

Retirement, marriage and work are the three main types of yearly extension expats get here in Thailand. Below you can see a little bit of information on these three extensions. Please note that there aren't work visas, retirement visas or marriage visas, they are all extensions of a non-immigrant B / O visa.

Many expats use the phrases work / marriage / retirement visa as an easy way to describe them.

There is also a dependent extension which allows you to bring a spouse or child to Thailand based on you having one of the extensions or visa types mentioned below.

Retirement Extension

This extension allows the individual to stay in Thailand for one year. The visa must be applied for annually. At the time of writing you are required to show a bank balance of 800,000 baht in a Thai account or a monthly income of at least 65,000 baht from outside the country and be over 50 to be eligible for the visa.

Marriage Extension

If you are married to a Thai citizen you can apply for a marriage extension. You have to show a minimum income of 40,000 baht a month from overseas or a bank balance of at least 400,000 baht. Also note that Thailand does not currently recognize same sex marriages.

Work Extension

A lot of people arrive in Thailand on a tourist visa and find a job. Once they have the job they will leave the country to get a non-immigrant visa. The paperwork can be complicated and you will need many forms. Your employer should be able to compile all the necessary documents for you.

Once this is completed you will go to your local immigration to get a yearly extension and then your company will organize a work permit for you. If you are working for a good company then they should send a representative with you to the immigration centre in Thailand.

Education Visa

If you are coming to study in Thailand this is the visa you will get. Your school should arrange this for you as part of their service.

For those who don't wish to work this is also the visa of choice for many who aren't married to a Thai citizen and aren't old enough for a retirement visa. Many schools advertise this as a way to get a visa and don't put too much stress on the education side of things. Immigration might do a test though to see how much you have learnt during your time in the classroom!

90-day reporting

Quite possibly the most annoying part of living in Thailand is having to complete a 90-day report. This is to show immigration that you are still in the country and residing at the same address. You either need to go to immigration yourself to complete the forms or can post them. There is a website to complete your 90-day report but it hasn't been working reliably for the last 18 months.

Work permit

If you are planning to work in Thailand you need to obtain a work permit. Even volunteers are technically required to have this document.

Your employer will provide you with all the paperwork to support your application. It is probable that you will have to complete a criminal background check too, especially if you will work with children.

Work permits are quite expensive to obtain so some employers ask people to work on a 30-day tourist visa. This is illegal and I would recommend finding a new job if this happens to you.

MOVING YOUR STUFF

You need to think about how you will get your belongings to Thailand. If you have a few suitcases then it will be easy to bring them on a flight and you can buy anything else here. If you are moving your family, or not planning to return to your home country then you will need to find a relocation company to help you get everything to Thailand.

One key point is that Thai customs will want to see proof of a long term stay in Thailand before releasing your possessions. This could be through a job offer letter or a retirement visa. If you are travelling with a Thai partner then it might prove easier to process the move in their name.

Most companies will have online tools to help you see what services you require and how much they cost. The more expensive companies will send a sales rep to your place and help make a plan. There are restrictions on certain items being brought into Thailand so do check with your chosen company. In the same vein, it is possible that you will be charged duties on some items, again ask your moving company to assist.

A lot of companies will use a Thai agent to get your belongings from the Thai port to your new home. These Thai companies are well versed with the complex laws and regulations when it comes to getting your possessions into the country and to your house.

Once you agree to go ahead with a company you will be asked to give a valuation of your possessions for insurance purposes. This can be difficult but common sense comes into play. As always, the company will be able to provide assistance.

Most companies state that items will be shipped to Thailand in around six weeks. As such you can plan the shipping date to be just after you arrive into Thailand. I would recommend making the arrival date around one or two weeks after you arrive so you can get the basics set up first. When your items arrive, the local agent will contact you to take your documents and deal with customs. This process normally takes around five working days.

As your items have probably travelled a long way it is possible there might be delays or damage. The whole process can be stressful and take time so do bear that in mind when taking this option.

BANKING

Setting up a bank account in Thailand is one of those things which seems easy but there will probably be something that makes your blood boil during the process. There is a hell of a lot of paperwork and each branch seems to have a different way to interpret the rules for a foreigner to open a bank account. At the time of writing you need your passport and proof of residence in Thailand (work permit, retirement extension or similar).

In theory those with work permits find it easier to open an account as it is the document that bank staff are expecting to see. People on other long-term visas extensions sometimes have to provide additional documents such as proof of income or address but this is randomly asked for at different banks. A common saying about banks in Thailand is that if one branch won't help you another down the street probably will!

Banks in shopping malls tend to have staff with the best English. If the bank staff can't understand you they will contact their call center and allow you to communicate with staff over the phone. Overall Thai banks have a lot of information on their websites in English to help. There are many banks in Thailand but the most popular with expats are probably Siam Commercial Bank (SCB), Bangkok Bank and Krungthai Bank.

These banks all have very good banking apps which allow you to transfer money within Thailand, check your balance and pay utility bills.

When setting up an account you will have to pay for a debit card. This is usually around 300 baht. There are some free accounts but they often have drawbacks such as being blocked for online shopping or international payments. Many accounts have a yearly fee too but often include some benefits such as insurance or discounts at certain restaurants.

Pin codes are used for ATMs but not when purchasing items from a shop. You will soon notice when paying with a card in a shop that staff don't check signatures when signing for items. You will likely get an SMS confirmation of your payment before you have even signed your receipt. It is highly recommended to have your bank's phone number saved to cancel your card if it is lost or stolen as security is lax and someone could have a shopping spree at your expense.

When using your card to buy items online the bank will send you a six-digit pin code via SMS which you need to enter onto the website you are using to confirm the purchase.

As well as an ATM card you will also be given a small bank book which records all of your transactions. It is updated in a small printing machine in your bank branch. If you forget or lose this book then expect the bank staff to act like the world is ending. This book is needed for depositing, withdrawing, transferring and making changes to your account at the counter of the bank. If you lose it they ask you to contact the police to get a report before they replace it. Because of this a lot of expats stick to using machines to deposit and withdraw and using the online apps for bill payments and transfers.

ATMs

It is pretty easy to find an ATM in any town or city in Thailand. In the countryside it may be more difficult. If you are struggling to find an ATM then just ask where the nearest 7/11 is and you will find at least one ATM there.

ATMs have multiple languages including English and Chinese. In tourist areas many have Russian, Japanese and French languages too. At the ATM you can withdraw money, transfer cash between your accounts or even pay a bill.

If using your bank's ATM in another province you might be charged between 15-30 baht per transaction as a fee. If using another bank's ATM anywhere you may also be charged as well.

If using a non-Thai card then you will be charged a fee of between 150-200 baht. It really is worth getting a Thai account.

Finally, there are also Cash Deposit Machines (CDMs) which allow you to deposit money directly into your account. These CDMs count notes and will give you a receipt to confirm what has been paid into your account. They are a good option if you don't fancy joining a huge queue in the branch.

Online banking

All of the Thai banks offer some form of online banking. The issue is that the features are somewhat limited, especially when it comes to international bank transfers. Bangkok Bank are recommended for making international bank transfers. They get good feedback and their fees are around 300 baht (plus whatever your home country bank charge). Bangkok Bank's online banking site has a section to transfer money internationally and it remembers your recent transfers too.

These days most people use banking apps rather than the website itself for internet banking.

Banking Apps

Most banks also have apps you can download on your phone or tablet. My favorite is SCB as it is simple to use and the English is perfect. These apps are the future and hopefully they will keep developing them to make them easier to use.

There are many great features to these apps including getting an overview of your account balances, being able to transfer to any account in Thailand and reviewing past deposits and payments.

A useful aspect is that you can scan the barcode from your utility bills within the banking apps and pay them directly without having to go to a shop.

Credit cards

Credit cards are not easy to obtain for many expats in Thailand. A lot of companies will ask you to deposit a sum of money equal to the credit they will give you which kind of defeats the object of a credit card.

KTC will give credit cards to foreigners providing they have an income of more than 50,000 baht per month, have a Thai work permit and have been working for the same company for more than two years. Bangkok Bank also gives credit cards to a select group of foreigners who have a history with the bank. It is worth checking with a local branch but be prepared to be rejected even if you have a large bank balance and a history with the bank.

Thai credit cards have a number of great rewards schemes. You can earn miles for local airlines, get discounts at restaurants and cashback on a monthly basis depending on the card you choose.

Most credit cards have apps similar to those described in the banking apps section.

Transferring money

Living in Thailand means at some point you are going to be faced with either transferring money back to your home country or sending it to Thailand.

If you are relying on income from overseas whilst in Thailand you are going to be hit with hefty fees unless you play things smart. Services such as TransferWise or Smart Currency Exchange can help reduce costs. You can also use cryptocurrencies such as Ripple or Litecoin to complete low-cost transfers if you have accounts in your home country and Thailand. BX.in.th is the best Thai crypto exchange.

Thai banks are quite nosey and will ask why you are transferring money out of the country and can make things awkward. As mentioned before Bangkok Bank gets the best feedback from my friends here in Thailand for international money transfers.

There are also the options of using Western Union, MoneyGram and PayPal too but these have higher fees if transferring high volumes.

Investments and savings

These days there are many different saving and investment options in Thailand. Whilst some options here in Thailand are reserved for Thai nationals there a few open to foreigners.

Most banks offer fixed rate deposit savings accounts. These are normally in terms of 5,12,24,36 and 72 months. The interest rates are currently pretty poor, not higher than 2.5%. There are also Long-Term Equity Funds (LTF) and Retirement Mutual Funds (RMF) which are open to foreign nationals. The main benefit of these is that they can reduce your personal income tax if working here. Check with your work's accounts team to get more information on these.

A lot of people still choose to invest in their home country. Sending money back home is possible but there is the possibility that the transfer fees will negate the higher interest rates you get in your home country.

Property would be many people's first investment choice in their home country. In the UK property prices have historically always risen at a decent rate. Buying a condo in Thailand could prove a good investment but with the huge supply of new units you are unlikely to see dramatic rises and, in reality, you might have to accept a loss to make a sale.

For those interested in Cryptocurrencies then there are currently two Thai exchanges which have English language versions. BX.in.th is probably the easiest to use to use for foreigners with a Thai bank account. The other choice is Coins.co.th

If you plan to be a long-term expat working in Thailand then you will need to consider your retirement. There are Thai retirement funds out there you can join and if you work for an international company then you might be eligible to join their provident fund.

As soon as Facebook realizes you are an expat in Thailand you will likely be hit with hundreds of adverts from companies offering expat savings accounts. It may well be these are an option for you but in my experience, I am yet to find a reliable choice.

Loans and mortgages

As mentioned in the Finances and Budgeting chapter it is very unlikely that a Thai bank will give a mortgage to a foreigner. It is possible to get a loan for a car but business loans or general loans will not normally be approved.

Banks do allow foreigners to act as guarantors on loans for Thai nationals. This means if you are married you could be the guarantor on a property for your partner but you would have no legal right to that property. If you were to break up with your partner you would still be liable for the loan or mortgage.

WORKING

Whilst there are a large number of retirees who move to Thailand there are also others who need to work. As you can see from our interviews there are a vast range of career options open to foreigners, not just teaching English!

There are a number of foreigners working for international companies, in the tourism sector and for NGOs. However, many jobs are reserved for Thais only and others only for citizens of AEC nations. Most job adverts will state who is eligible for the position.

One thing to consider is whether you should apply for your job before you arrive or once you are in Thailand. A lot of the true expat jobs with high salaries, free flights and all the added extras are normally advertised internationally and won't be local hires. If you arrive in Thailand on an international contract with great benefits then it may be possible to get these if changing jobs.

You can get a job whilst based outside of Thailand but there are some downsides. If you haven't been here you might not know about the area and end up somewhere you hate. There is also a lot of paperwork and your visa is linked to your job. If you want to leave, it could mean exiting the country too until you find new employment.

The major benefit to finding a job before you arrive is the peace of mind it will bring. Moving to a new country is stressful enough without worrying where your first paycheck will come from. You can also use it as a stepping stone to a better position after a few months in the country.

If you do decide to wait until you are in the country to find work then there are some real benefits. You can network easily and get good connections to find jobs not advertised online. You can visit the company and area to see if it is a good match.

The downside is that people might take advantage that you are desperate to work. This could involve paying you a lower salary or not providing a work permit and proper visa.

Life as a teacher in Thailand

Teaching, especially English teaching, is the most common job for foreigners in Thailand. There are many different types of teaching jobs in Thailand so I have broken them down into sections to tell you them in more detail.

Government school teacher

State education in government elementary and high schools is the easiest way to be employed as a teacher in Thailand. Throughout the country there are government schools and they each aim to have foreign teachers to teach languages.

English is the main language learnt but Chinese and Japanese are common too. Some schools offer French, German and Spanish but this is rare. The government aims to have native speakers to fulfil these roles but this doesn't always happen.

Away from the most popular areas (think central Bangkok, islands and other tourist locations), government schools fail to attract enough native speakers to fill positions. The list of native speaking countries are USA, Canada, UK, Ireland, South Africa, Australia, and New Zealand. As such people from the Philippines, India and other countries with high levels of English are offered positions in government schools but at lower pay than native speakers. Non-native speakers will need to show a TOEIC score of 600+.

Talking about salaries, government high school teachers make between

25-40,000 baht per month. Non-native speakers usually make 15-25,000 baht per month.

To work in one of these schools the requirement is that you have a degree in any subject. You are then able to work in a government school for up to two years without any other qualification. Should you decide you want to stay longer you will need a Thai teaching license which means taking exams and becoming qualified as a teacher with an MA in Education, teaching license from your own country or equivalent.

Expect to be in school between 8am-4pm Monday-Friday and teach around 21 hours a week. There is a trend not to pay teachers over holidays in some government schools therefore you may find yourself without a paycheck for one month of the year. Don't expect air-conditioning in your classroom.

Bi-lingual schools

These schools often have better facilities than government schools, including air-conditioned classrooms. They also employ both native and non-native speakers. The major difference is that often teachers can teach subjects other than languages. If you are not qualified as a teacher but have a degree in science then you could be employed as a science teacher at a bi-lingual school.

Salaries for native speakers are usually around 40-60,000 baht per month. Non-native teachers should expect between 20-30,000 baht.

After a couple of years you will need a Thai teaching license to remain in your job.

International schools

International schools are expensive to attend and have facilities similar to western schools. They will usually only employ teachers who are qualified to teach in the west.

International schools come in many standards. True international schools will pay teachers over 100,000 baht per month, provide housing allowances, medical insurance and flights home every year. A lot of teachers are employed from their home country rather than in Thailand.

Some schools use the name international in their title but often aren't up to this high standard. The pay is normally lower, around 70,000 baht.

Top international schools provide the best financial package for teachers but often come with a lot of stress and the most demanding parents!

Language schools

There is a high demand for foreign languages in Thailand. There are many companies who set up language schools where children and adults can come to learn. There are a vast range of schools catering to every budget.

The cheapest will employ non-native speakers and pay around 150 baht per hour. They require a degree and TOEIC score to employ someone. Mid-range language schools pay 300-500 baht per hour. The best ones will only employ native speakers and pay around 1,000 baht per hour. These schools ask for a CELTA qualification (see later in teaching courses section) and often some experience teaching.

Language schools are normally busiest on weekends and in the evenings. It means working whilst most people are off which might be a problem for some people. Some language schools offer fixed hour contracts whereas others are part time which could greatly affect your pay.

The major benefit of a language school is that you don't require a teaching license so you can work for many years without having to become officially qualified.

Private tutoring

It is possible to pick up private teaching in Thailand. Depending on your background, the rates do vary a lot. Most qualified native speakers charge around 500 baht per hour for private classes. Some people do teach online too but it is a grey area when it comes to the legality of this.

Corporate teaching

There are positions available as English instructors for companies. This is especially true in the hospitality and tourism sectors. It is not easy to find these positions and pay varies greatly.

Teaching courses

I would recommend taking a short teaching course to help in your journey as a teacher. Basic four-week TEFL courses can be taken in Thailand and cost around 25,000 baht. They may not be recognized by some schools and are only suitable for those looking to work in government schools or low-level language centres.

If you want to aim for a bi-lingual school or high-end language centres, you should take a CELTA which is offered by Cambridge University. It is internationally recognized and a four-week course in Bangkok will cost around 60,000 baht.

Finding a teaching job

I found all of my teaching positions on the website Ajarn.com. You can also go visit schools and language centres to give them your CV and ask about open positions. For international schools visit job fairs and look online for adverts.

Finally, you could use an agent to set up a position at a government high school. The agents take a cut of your salary and work with rural schools to help them fill positions. Agents will guarantee you a position but they are in it to make money so be aware that there have been mixed reviews on teaching agencies in Thailand.

Is teaching for me?

When I arrived in Thailand I had never taught. I did my CELTA and have progressed well, take a look at my career journey in the Finances and Budgeting chapter.

Teaching in Thailand can be a fun and rewarding career. There is the chance to develop if you put work in and take opportunities when they come. That being said you don't need to be a serious teacher when here. I know plenty of people who are teachers in Thailand because it is fun and gives them the chance to live in the country. As long as you don't let your students down it isn't a problem if teaching isn't your passion. As you can see through our interviews in this book, plenty of people arrive as teachers and then move on after a few years, there's nothing wrong with that.

How to find work

Whilst this is not a complete list there are several key ways to find a job in Thailand. For more information also check out our useful resources page at the end of the book.

Internet – There are lots of Thai jobs websites including monster.co.th and jobsdb.com. These are probably the best place to start. Teachers check out Ajarn.com.

Social Media – There are a lot of jobs advertised on LinkedIn. This has proved a good method for me and I usually get an email every few months offering a full-time position or freelance work.

Networking – It can be easy to find the right job if you know the right people. There are lots of networking events where you can meet influential people.

Knocking on the door – It doesn't hurt to hand your CV in to companies you are interested in. A lot of the time businesses will have a need for foreigners but don't always advertise it.

Wages

Wages for foreigners in Thailand do vary a lot.

People from AEC countries such as the Philippines should expect salaries similar to Thai people. This would be around 20,000 baht a month for an office worker.

Teachers make between 15,000-150,000 baht per month depending on their school and position. See the previous section "Life as a teacher in Thailand" for more information.

Some people work in commission-based sales jobs in Thailand. These might be in property, retail or insurance. The starting salary for a lot of these jobs is around 30,000 baht with the chance to earn more based on performance.

If you are working for an international company then you should expect a similar salary to that you would get at home for the same job. International companies will usually pay internationally recruited staff more than local hires though. Often internationally recruited staff get better benefits such as yearly flights home.

How easy is it to find work here?

One of the main benefits of finding a job before you arrive is the peace of mind it will give you. If you know the company and location then chances are you will be happy with your job. On the other hand, you could be taking a leap in the dark by taking a new position somewhere you have never been before.

Personally, I took a job in Thailand before seeing the place and it turned into a nightmare. A quick Google search didn't reveal much about the location or company. After a month I was planning my escape!

I did a lot of research into the next company I worked at. I visited their office and scouted the location in detail. I ended up staying there for three years before a better opportunity came up.

Something that you will see through the interviews in this book, and in my personal experience, is that it can take time to find your dream job here. If you are flexible and happy to take a job for the short / medium term you can find something better in the long run. Finding a job here isn't too difficult and you shouldn't be worried that there will be nothing here for you, especially if you are planning to work as a teacher.

Tax and social security

Tax in Thailand is lower than most western countries. Below are the 2017/2018 tax rates as a guide – note these are subject to change.

Income	Tax Rate
0-150,000 THB	0%
150,000 – 300,000 THB	5%
300,000-500,000 THB	10%
500,000 – 750,000 THB	15%
750,000 – 1 million THB	20%
1 million – 2 million THB	25%
2 million – 5 million THB	30%
5,000,001 THB +	35%

Thailand also has double taxation treaties with many countries to ensure that you don't pay tax twice if you are paying overseas.

You will also have 750 baht per month taken from your salary each month. This social security payment covers healthcare at a government hospital and goes towards a pension which foreigners can claim if working for more than 15 years in Thailand.

Volunteering

One of the most disappointing aspects of life in Thailand is that it is difficult to volunteer. There are lots of opportunities but you need a work permit to volunteer here legally. If you are caught volunteering without a work permit then you could be kicked out of the country. This stops a lot of people from giving back. Many people would love to offer a few hours a week teaching English in schools or helping in the community but they are prevented from doing so.

There are of course some major projects where volunteers are needed and are given work permits but this is quite rare.

Unfortunately, it seems volunteer tourism is the way most charities and organizations want to go in Thailand. Lots of people are prepared to pay a fee to come to Thailand and wash elephants and teach English for a few weeks.

As a fee is paid it qualifies as a service so a work permit isn't needed. It makes money for charities which is a good thing but it is sad there aren't ways for expats to help out without fear of being deported.

BRINGING PETS

You can bring your pet from your home country provided they meet quarantine standards. Your pet needs to have the relevant documents and injections and can be with you on your flight.

THAILAND FOR FAMILIES

Coming here with your family means you need to consider what their life will be like. You also need to think about the practicalities of family members being here.

International nurseries, schools and universities can be found throughout the country. The price of these is not cheap so you should be aware of the cost. Check out more about these in the finance and budgeting chapter.

Daily life with a child can be difficult in Thailand. In general safety standards are most probably lower than in your home country. On average around 60 people a day die on the roads in Thailand. Sidewalks are normally bumpy and cracked, making it hard to take young children out. Public transport, especially buses are not really suitable for young children.

There are a number of activities here which your child can enjoy. From sport through to music there are many clubs and facilities. Thailand may also offer opportunities not found in your home country. The cost of joining clubs and doing activities might also be much lower than in your home country.

For more information on life with a child in Thailand read the interview with Kathy in this book, she gives some brilliant tips and links to resources.

BOOKING FLIGHTS

The good news is that Bangkok is a major hub in Southeast Asia. You can get into Thailand easily and directly from many locations. There are also many deals throughout the year meaning that flights can be inexpensive.

There are a number of local airlines here which are much of a muchness. Websites are available in English and booking is straightforward. There are many routes covered and multiple flights a day between major cities and tourist destinations. The easiest way to find the cheapest flights is to use a flight comparison site such as skyscanner.net.

INITIAL ACCOMMODATION

Unless you have been to Thailand before you should not sign a rental contract until you have been in the country a while. Maybe you have a plan to stay in a certain area but even so you should really explore a little first.

Booking at least a few days in a hotel or service apartment will give you time to sort yourself out. Check out the Accommodation and Areas chapter for more information on different areas you could live in in Thailand.

TECHNOLOGY

A lot of technology is quite expensive in Thailand due to import taxes. The latest phones tend to sell well here but you will pay a premium. Many people choose to unlock their phone and bring it to Thailand to use.

Laptops and computers are around a similar price to those in your home country. There are also specific IT malls such as Pantip Plaza in Bangkok where you can buy specialist IT products.

Most electronics stores hold sales two or three times a year where you can get large discounts on appliances such as TVs, fridges and washing machines.

SIM CARDS

You can get a sim card at the airport but bear in mind these are aimed at tourists. The deals are normally based on a 7-14-day period. You will be better off going to one of the malls to the phone shops directly or even at 7/11.

Expect to pay between 200-400 baht a month for a package with a large internet allowance and a few free minutes of calls.

APPS

When you have your sim card there are a few must-have apps to download.

LINE is the go-to messaging app of choice for Thai people. It works very much like Facebook Messenger and WhatsApp. LINE is easy to use and allows you to make free calls, send unlimited free messages and use interactive stickers. You will quickly learn that Thai people don't call phone numbers but make calls via the LINE app. It is also used for chat groups such as between co-workers or members of a club.

Once you have your bank account set up you should download their app. The major banks all have decent apps which allow you to check balance, transfer payments and pay your bills. Also, the MEA electricity app is great for paying your electricity bill.

Grab Taxi will cover your transport needs if you don't feel like dealing directly with taxi drivers. They recently took over Uber's operations in South East Asia so they have plenty of experience.

Food is important in Thailand so get Eatigo for discount restaurant prices and Food Panda for home delivery.

LEARNING THAI

You don't need to speak Thai to be able to live here but at least learning a little will help you a lot.

Basic phrases and important things such as numbers can be learnt quickly, even before you arrive. Thai numbers are not too difficult to learn and realistically you only need to learn up to 10,000 for most things you will do.

Before arriving here you can use a number of resources to help yourself. A quick search on YouTube will bring up hundreds of videos teaching basic Thai words and phrases. There are a few apps to download to your phone to help. Also, a look on Amazon will show a few decent books to help, including Steve's books, which are also available in local bookstores.

Once in Thailand you will soon learn new phrases and key words. If you live somewhere with tourists, the chances are you can avoid Thai in 99% of situations unless you actively want to use the language.

There are several Thai language schools around the country. They vary a lot in terms of price and quality. Some offer education visas to allow foreigners to stay in the country without a job. There are also many freelance Thai tutors who advertise on Craigslist and Facebook. Finally, a lot of Thai people enjoy hearing foreigners speak Thai so chances are you can find a language exchange partner or someone who doesn't mind helping you with your Thai.

HAIRCUT

This may sound like a little thing but it can be difficult to find someone in Thailand you trust to cut your hair. Maybe you are like me and aren't too fussy about the look you get but many people want a certain style.

In general hairdressers and barbers in Thailand don't speak much English. Maybe in tourist locations you might find someone who can but otherwise expect to use a lot of hand gestures and pointing at pictures. Be careful as Thai haircut styles are different from western ones.

You can always go to a mall and find the classiest looking salon but chances are they aren't much better than a much cheaper option. For men the cheapest barbers cost around 50-80 baht whilst women should expect to pay at least 200 baht at a local salon.

Most people choose the middle ground of a basic salon in a shopping mall which will cost both men and women between 200-300 baht. You'll get your hair washed and hopefully have an experienced person to cut your hair.

FITNESS

A lot of mid-range or higher end condos and housing complexes will have at least a basic fitness centre. Some will also have swimming pools. However, if you are a fitness nut then they may not fulfill your needs. The good news is that there are a variety of health clubs out there.

Fitness First is the best known in Bangkok with several branches. A monthly membership will cost at least 2,200 baht. It isn't cheap. The alternative is Virgin Gym which is pretty much the same price. The benefit of these two is that they have English-speaking staff and classes. Both Virgin and Fitness First offer yoga classes as part of their package prices. All over Thailand you can find yoga schools.

Chiang Mai has Fitness Thailand which has a lot of Western members and a monthly cost of around 1,000 baht.

Outside these big chains there are a lot of independent gyms with membership normally under 1,000 baht a month. The quality of English and equipment varies so take a look before you sign-up.

Finally, a lot of local districts have health clubs which cost less than 100 baht a year to join. You then can pay per activity such as 10 baht for the gym, 20 baht for swimming or 50 baht for an hour's badminton. This is a good option if you have a Thai partner who can help you with the language and signup process.

SPORT

Sport is cheap in Thailand. If you are happy to play during the day you get great discounts on court rentals but even in the peak evening hours prices are low.

Expect to pay around 150 baht an hour to rent a badminton court while a tennis court will cost around 250 baht. If you don't have a swimming pool at your place you can normally find a place to swim for less than 100 baht.

Football is popular with Thai people. At your workplace you can normally find enough people interested to get together a game of five a-side. Expect to pay around 100 baht a head for an hour on a decent floodlit 4G pitch.

Golf is popular with many expats. Prices do fluctuate throughout the year. 18 holes at a low-end course costs around 1,000 baht including a mandatory caddy fee. International standard courses charge around 3,000 baht for a mid-week round including all fees. Expect to pay around 30-50% more on week-ends. You can also find deals and promotions online. Driving ranges are cheap. Normally 100 baht will get you 100 balls to hit.

If you fancy playing a team sport then head to your nearest expat bar as you can normally find a team to join. In Bangkok for example there are rugby, lacrosse, cricket and baseball teams you could join via expat bars.

Thailand is also a great place for those who love the water. Scuba diving is a popular hobby for many here. There are many world class dive sites where you can see some incredible marine life, corals and also take training cours-es. Prices start at around 2,500 baht for a couple of dives and equipment. Be careful if renting a jet-ski in Thailand as they are often the cause of scams. It isn't uncommon for people to be made to pay thousands of baht for "damage".

Getting Sick

It's pretty much a certainty that you will get sick at some time during your stay in Thailand. Sure, you can solve your sniffles with a quick trip to 7/11 to pick up some medicine but the time will come when you need to visit a doctor.

You might be a bit worried about the medical facilities here in Thailand but it is likely that you will be pleasantly surprised.

HOSPITALS

Hospitals can be found in all areas of Thailand but you may have to travel further if you live outside of the big towns and cities. Popular expat destinations such as Bangkok, Phuket and Pattaya have many hospitals so you will have one within easy reach of wherever you decide to stay.

There are two main types of hospital, government and private. Government hospitals are aimed at the lower income citizens of Thailand and are rather basic. Private hospitals are up to international standards and cater to people with health insurance or those with a lot of money to cover themselves.

Government hospitals are rather basic but are fine for simple issues such as sickness or sprains. The facilities are likely a little old but they do tend to be quite clean. Waits can be lengthy and the staff will struggle with English. Many of the doctors will have had basic English training in university. A lot of doctors in rural government hospitals will be newly qualified as it is a stipulation of their degree funding that they go to outer provinces for a few years.

Private hospitals are normally more modern in design. They will be a lot more welcoming and have better facilities throughout.

Hospital Service

Most hospitals in Thailand rely on an army of staff to guide you. Upon arriving you will go to a reception desk where your information will be taken. Make sure to bring your passport with you if you need to go to a hospital or clinic. The idea is that your information will be kept on file should you return again.

If you are with a Thai partner it is likely you will be ignored and the medical staff will speak in Thai with your partner. In some ways this is understandable as they want to clearly find out what is wrong with you. On the other hand, it can get annoying and frustrating for you, even if you speak Thai.

You will then be guided to the different wards and despite all your information being taken beforehand, will probably need to give it out again each time! Then comes the issue of English. Away from the main reception a lot of staff struggle to communicate apart from in the top private establishments.

I'm colour blind and despite trying to explain in English and broken Thai it took a good ten minutes before the nurse understood. This was in a mid-level private hospital.

Doctors tend to speak good English although outside common expat and tourist areas they might be out of practice. One thing all doctors are good at is giving medicine. You will likely be offered a range of pills and sprays to overcome your illness. It is a bit over the top in all honesty. The reason for this might be because they want you to get better sooner but another might be because they make a huge profit on each item they sell. The same medicine purchased in a local pharmacy might be up to ten times cheaper.

CLINICS

Clinics are like doctors' surgeries. They usually have between one to five doctors and a lot of nurses. They can do simple things like blood tests and diagnosing common illnesses. These clinics are the go-to place if you are living in a rural area without a hospital. The quality varies quite dramatically and outside the main districts you shouldn't expect anything fancy.

They are only equipped to deal with certain medical conditions so don't be surprised if they do refer you to a specialist at a hospital.

PHARMACIES

There are pharmacies dotted all around Thailand. In the malls you will find them as well as on local streets. They usually have the medical cross sign on them which makes them easy to spot. If you are just looking for some aspirin or paracetamol then head to 7/11 which will have all you need.

Pharmacies are usually a lot more liberal in Thailand compared to other countries. It is possible to get many types of medicine without a prescription. The price is very reasonable and much less than a hospital would charge.

Many pharmacists speak decent English as this is a mandatory part of their university studies. If you are looking for Western medicine then the best option is to use the pharmacies in the branches of Boots and Watsons which are in pretty much every mall. However, it seems the pharmacists in these malls are often not available and you won't be allowed to buy any medicine until they return.

ALTERNATIVE MEDICINE

In Thailand there are lots of places where you can get alternative medicine. There are a lot of people in Thailand with Chinese heritage so it is no surprise to see traditional Chinese remedies available.

SOCIAL SECURITY

Foreigners working in Thailand will have a 750 baht a month social security payment taken from their salary. This covers many things but the most important is the access to local healthcare at reduced rates. This will more than likely be at a government hospital. You will need to register at a nominated hospital but can change this once a year.

Not all companies are up to speed on this matter so make sure you check with your HR department to get this covered. You need to make sure you get your social security card to take with you to your chosen government hospital.

HEALTH INSURANCE

For those who do not qualify for social security or who do not wish to use government hospitals then you will need to arrange health insurance. There are a number of famous international companies offering this service in Thailand such as AXA and BUPA. You will also find many local firms.

Do your homework and see what you need before agreeing. You can find more about the costings in the Finances and Budgeting chapter.

MEDICAL CHECKS FOR VISAS, ETC.

One of your first trips to a hospital or clinic will probably be to get a medical checkup for your visa extension.

Actually, a lot of things require a medical check in Thailand. Getting a driving license, joining a gym or starting a new job all require medical certificates. The standard checkup will cover the following:

Syphilis (third stage)
Elephantiasis
Leprosy
Alcoholism
Blood Type
Mental Illness
Weight/ Height/ Blood Pressure
Vision Test

For medical checks you will be given a form by your employer / gym / driving centre which you can give to reception. Most clinics and hospitals are very familiar with the process when they see the form.

I normally go to a clinic for a medical check as they are cheaper and do things very quickly compared to hospitals. The first clinic I went to just asked me my blood type and didn't even bother to take my blood.

Other clinics have made me do the blood test. My first "medical check" cost 100 baht and following ones have all been under the 250-baht mark. One company did request a medical check at a hospital which came to 990 baht but they covered the fee which is quite normal in such a situation.

The Expensive Bill

To give you an idea of the difference of cost between private and government hospitals I want to tell you about an American woman who I worked with and her experience.

We lived in the same apartment block and she didn't turn up to work one day so I decided to check in with her in the evening. It turns out she had food poisoning and her condition had deteriorated quite badly during the day. Our location in Pathum Thani, around 20KM north of Bangkok, meant we had to rely on a local government hospital. A couple of other friends and I rushed her to the emergency ward. Because we arrived at around 9pm, she had to stay overnight to recover after having an IV and being given medicine.

The following morning, we heard she had checked herself out and was on her way back to the apartment. She arrived and said she wasn't happy with the quality of the hospital. To be fair it wasn't exactly five-star quality but it was clean from what I had seen. She was also insistent that she was better, but this seemed like an excuse just to avoid being in hospital. Her bill for this overnight stay, medicine and care was 2,500 baht.

Two days later she was still suffering. She couldn't eat and was constantly throwing up. It was at this point I received a call from her mother who asked me if I would mind taking her to a private hospital in central Bangkok.

Later that day we arrived at one of the best-known hospitals in Bangkok which looked like an exclusive resort. My colleague stayed there for three nights and was much happier with a private room, cable TV, Western food and a floor dedicated to foreign patients. She wasn't so happy when the bill was presented to her at the end of her stay – 90,000 baht.

DENTISTS

Thailand is a cheap place to get your teeth checked. From around 500 baht you can get a checkup and clean. If you go to one of the more upscale places then the bill should still be way under 2,000 baht.

Dental work is cheap and the dentists are seemingly pretty skilled. Most in the major tourist destinations will speak English to a decent level. Orthodontists are skilled as it seems a lot of Thai teenagers get braces. For around 30,000 baht you can get braces and aftercare.

Dentists also provide teeth whitening and other cosmetic services for a reasonable price.

Hospital Shopping Malls

Many private hospitals in Thailand look like they are slowly becoming shopping malls. Places which are designed to make people better are often filled with Hi-So coffee joints, dessert restaurants and at least a couple of 7/11s.

This adds to the feeling that you are in a lifestyle center rather than just a hospital.

OPTICIANS

Glasses can actually be very expensive in Thailand. If you chose branded eyewear then it will be hit with a luxury tax. The price will certainly not be any cheaper than in your home country. Local brands are reasonably priced.

Contact lenses cost around 450 baht for a month's supply. You can buy at opticians and also at many of the malls. Many expats stock up on lenses when they are in their home country.

LASIK surgery is becoming more popular in Thailand. For a high-quality operation expect to pay between 70-80,000 baht.

Social Media Sickness

It seems like the first thing people do here when they arrive in hospital is to update their social media. Checking in, taking a selfie and putting a load of sad stickers on a Facebook post is a common thing and it attracts a load of sympathy. Looking at the picture it looks like your friend is on death's doorstep but a quick translation of the message will normally say something like "have the flu" or "hurt my leg falling over". I quickly learned to scoff at these attention seeking posts and think a little less of the poster.

PREGNANCY

Hospitals in Thailand offer a wide range of pregnancy packages. Basic packages cost around 35,000 baht. However, you will probably end up spending more to get extra treatments, scans and medicine. A budget of around 100,000 baht will be enough for a mid-tier private hospital pregnancy package. Read our interview with Kathy for more information on pregnancy in Thailand.

SEXUAL HEALTH

The rate of HIV and Aids in Thailand is growing. This isn't just in the sex industry but in all walks of life.

Condoms can be easily found throughout the country. 7/11 and pharmacies in the shopping malls carry a wide range of sexual health products from international companies.

The contraceptive pill is also easy to find at all pharmacies, including in shopping malls.

The Red Cross and other international charities have sexual health clinics in the main areas of Thailand. Here they offer checks and medication for STIs and other sexual health concerns. You can also visit some local medical clinics for tests.

COSMETIC SURGERY

Cosmetic surgery is big business in Thailand and the country is often promoted as a medical tourism destination. There are a huge number of clinics which offer all manner of cosmetic procedures. The quality is variable so make sure you research somewhere first.

There have been stories of unlicensed doctors performing surgeries resulting in serious injuries and even death. That being said a large number of health-tourists come to Thailand and are happy with their treatment.

WEIGHT LOSS

Beauty and weight loss clinics in Thailand have a lot of customers. Walk around any mall in Thailand and you will see a large number of these types of shops. They also have a large team of promoters who will walk around and approach potential customers. As a foreigner they won't come to you and my experience is that if you are walking with a Thai partner they will not disturb your partner either.

Although Thai food seems healthy it is possible to gain weight whilst here. A large amount of sugar in dishes with the temptation of snacks means your diet might not be as healthy as you might imagine.

MENTAL HEALTH

It is sad to read in Thailand about the number of foreigners committing suicide. Being away from home and family can certainly cause stress. If feeling depressed or if you need someone to talk to there are a number of resources. Your doctor can refer you to an English-speaking counselor or psychiatrist to help.

Food

It is almost impossible not to fall in love with Thai food. There are so many fantastic flavours and smells. You could eat something different every meal for a week and still have many other dishes to try. However, you will miss food from back home at some point. The good news is that you can get pretty much everything you want here but, it might come at a cost.

As an expat you will have plenty of dining options which cater for all budgets. In this chapter we will look at all food related matters including restaurants, cooking at home and vegetarian/vegan options in Thailand.

SUPERMARKETS

Supermarkets in Thailand are plentiful and stock a wide range of products. They are similar to Walmart in the USA in that most supermarkets sell a wide range of items, not just food. You can find your favourites from back home and a wide range of local produce too.

The two most common supermarkets are Tesco Lotus and Big C. You can find these in pretty much every large town or district within a city. They are normally located on the outskirts of a town and are part of a complex with many restaurants and other shops such as pharmacies, electronic shops and banks.

If you are looking for a wider range of foreign products then you should look at Villa Market, TOPS and Gourmet Market. These three supermarkets tend to be more expensive but will give you the food you miss from back home. They are usually located within a shopping mall rather than standalone stores.

Makro is another option but is less common around Thailand. Makro is worth visiting for the range of frozen food which is cheap and includes a large range of products you would see in your home country.

A lot of the supermarkets also do online shopping and delivery. This means you don't even need to go out to get your groceries. Whilst the online delivery service is pretty good, I have experienced a couple of small issues with incorrect or damaged products being delivered.

Is it Worth Cooking at Home?

Thai people rarely cook at home unless they live with a big family. This is partly due to time constraints but another key factor is the cost.

When you can get food outside from 40 baht or eat in a semi decent restaurant from 70 baht it seems pointless to cook your own food. When you look at the time and effort of cooking you have another reason why most people don't cook here.

Perhaps you love cooking and that is a fair reason to make your own dinner. However, if living in a condo or apartment you will have limited facilities and space.

Personally, I only cook at home when making international dishes which are hard to find here or aren't cooked to my preference in local restaurants.

CONVENIENCE STORES

There seems to be more 7/11 stores in Thailand than any other shop! You will sometimes see a couple of 7/11s within spitting distance of each other. Family Mart is the other major player in this market and they are also quite easy to find.

Both Family Mart and 7/11 offer a range of basic products but lack a lot of fresh food which you might find in the convenience stores in your home country. You can pop in to buy water, snacks, toiletries and cleaning products at reasonable prices.

You will also hear the term "mom and pop shop" which refers to an independent Thai convenience store usually run by a family. They normally have a more limited range of products and will charge around two baht more per item than 7/11. The benefit of these places is they won't worry too much about selling alcohol after midnight when 7/11 stops.

STREET FOOD

You have most probably heard of the famous street food in Thailand. The numerous stalls which open up along the roadside offer tasty, cheap eats. From around 40 baht you can get a simple dish.

Most of the time it is the less well-off Thais who eat at street food joints. The food can be good but the atmosphere makes it less appealing compared to basic restaurants. Street food is normally not that healthy and as such it is not recommended to rely on it for your complete diet.

It seems that in Bangkok the authorities are cracking down on these road-side eateries in order to create more space for pedestrians. This move has been controversial with critics stating street food is necessary to support the poor and is also a cultural icon of Thailand.

FOOD COURTS

Food courts are like big school canteens where you have a large choice of dishes and you eat in a large communal dining hall. They are usually found in shopping malls or supermarkets. They are pretty much the same as street food but are located inside. You normally get an electronic card to deposit money on, which the vendor will then scan to deduct payment. At the end you go back to the cashier to reclaim any unspent funds.

You should budget around 50 baht per dish and around 20 baht for a soft drink. The standard of food courts varies a lot but there is one standout. Terminal 21 in Bangkok has a fantastic food court, great design and good quality food. It's worth trying out!

FRUIT CARTS

All around Thailand you will see people pushing glass carts full of fruit. Pineapple, mango, papaya and watermelon are common. For around 15-30 baht you can get a fresh portion of fruit. These carts can be found at all times of the day and are a great way to get one of your five portions a day.

COOKING AT HOME

One way to get that taste of home is to cook at your place. Also, it is true that many dishes cooked in restaurants in Thailand are not particularly healthy. By cooking yourself you can control what goes into your food. Many stores now sell organic products.

Cooking equipment is easy to find although international brands tend to be pricey. The only issue you might find is that many condos and apartments have poor quality, small kitchens.

PRE-PREPARED DELIVERY

There are a couple of companies who cook healthy food and deliver to you. Paleo Robbie is the most famous of these businesses in Thailand. There are also local Thai options but communication could prove a problem.

VEGETARIAN AND VEGAN FOOD

There are a lot of vegetarians in Thailand and finding good food is possible. There are more and more vegetarian or vegan restaurants opening all the time. Be careful though as the term vegan is not widely known in English by most Thais.

The Thai word for vegetarian is pronounced "J" which makes it easy to ask. If in a food court there will normally be at least one stall with vegetarian options.

HALAL FOOD

With a large number of guests from Arabic countries it is now possible to find Halal food. Tourist areas cater for this although you might need to try a few places first.

THAI SNACKS

Thai people love snacks. There are now a lot of people eating Western snacks but there are some Thai options which are fantastic.

Pla Muk Ping is a grilled crispy squid which is popular. It is normally sold via street vendors on a cart. Roti Sai Mai is a thin sweet bread filled with a thick candy floss which is famous across the country. Crispy seaweed is another popular option and is sold in sheets from 7/11. You will often see a cart with a person ringing a bell, this is Thailand's version of an ice cream van. Vendors often serve ice cream with bread, nuts or sweetcorn.

Everywhere in Thailand you will see stalls selling deep fried meatballs and sausages. These come with a spicy sauce and are served in a plastic bag. Curry puffs are a savoury treat which can be filled with chicken, pork or taro.

RESTAURANT STYLES IN THAILAND

A la carte is still the most common way to eat in Thailand. Ordering from a menu is pretty simple and as a foreigner you can either tell them what you want in Thai or point to menu items as a last resort. Most waiting staff in tourist areas will speak English. After a short while you will learn the vocabulary needed to order in Thai.

Buffet restaurants have been growing in popularity here over the past few years. The chance to eat as much as you can is a temptation a lot of people can't turn down!

Hot Pot is a style of cooking where you get a pot of boiling soup and use it to cook a variety of meats and vegetables. It is popular here and many chains have become successful out of this idea of letting their customers do the cooking.

BBQ restaurants are similar to hot pot places in that you cook your own food, the only difference is that it is grilled not boiled. Prices can be very cheap and in many restaurants it's an unlimited buffet. Be aware that raw meat is left outside and can be mixed with other meat.

Fast food is popular and many chains have opened up. These can normally be found in shopping malls or retail parks.

Sharing is Caring

Something that you will quickly find out when eating with Thais is that they like to share food.

If you order from a menu be prepared to share if it is traditional Thai food. The idea of ordering just for yourself is pretty rare here unless you go to an international restaurant or order something like a burger.

MARKET

The market is usually the focus of small towns and districts in Thailand. It is a place for people to sell their goods and meet up. As an expat you can take advantage of great value fruit and vegetables. There are also normally a wide range of snacks and treats to buy too. You can also buy meat but it will be outside unrefrigerated which is a concern for many expats.

As a quick warning some of these markets can smell horrific. Meat and fish are often left out in the sun and you can smell the market from far away.

NIGHT / TRAIN MARKET

In the last couple of years night markets (sometimes called train markets) have become a place to go out. They are nothing like the traditional day markets. These places are full of bars, boutique shops and a vast array of food stalls. Basically, hit the food stalls and get a few things to eat and take it to the bar you like the look of and you can chill out with a few beers whilst you eat.

A lot of bars have live music and the food is more like snacks and finger food which make it great for sharing.

INTERNATIONAL RESTAURANTS

The good thing about Thailand is that once you have grown a little tired of Thai food it is very easy to find international food.

In tourist areas such as Pattaya and Phuket you will see international restaurants on pretty much every street. From French style cafes with fresh bread to Ethiopian restaurants you can find it all.

If you aren't in a tourist area then there are a few international chains which can be found pretty much everywhere. KFC, MacDonald's and Pizza Hut will cover your fast food cravings. They also do delivery if you aren't too far away for a 40-baht surcharge.

Japanese and Korean food is loved by many Thai people. You can't move in shopping malls for Japanese buffet restaurants. The quality is pretty inferior unless you go to a specialist high end Japanese restaurant.

Finally, many expats swear by the buffets offered at international hotels to get their fix of foreign food. These restaurants often offer discounts and specials otherwise expect to pay around 1,000 baht per person. Take a look at the app Eatigo to get great discounts at many restaurants in Bangkok and Pattaya.

THAI STYLE INTERNATIONAL COOKING

A lot of bigger restaurants will offer international food. Pasta and steak are popular here but don't be expecting an Italian style spaghetti or a New York steak. The quality does vary a lot and you might end up disappointed. For the best results head to a specialist restaurant run by someone from that country.

BARS AND PUBS

If you want that feeling of food from home in a familiar surrounding then head to one of the many international style bars and pubs in Thailand. Mainly located in tourist areas or expat hot spots these places will give you a taste of home. They are also your best bet for getting a traditional Christmas / Thanksgiving dinner.

British and Irish pubs are quite common in Thailand. For around 300-500 baht a dish you can get a reasonable taste of home. They normally have international beers on tap.

There aren't too many North American style bars in Thailand. The exception is Hooters which has a few branches across the country. If you are looking at a taste of American / Canada then check out the many burger joints which offer a wide range of dishes including poutine, chili fries and wings.

There are a few Aussie bars in Thailand too which attract expats and tourists. The Kiwi bar in Bangkok is a popular place to get local food and watch rugby on the big screen.

If you are looking for something fancier then there are an increasing number of sky bars in Bangkok. Some have featured in movies but be aware there is often a dress code – no shorts or sandals!

Let's go for a beer!

Back home Friday night was always beer night. Heading out for a beer or four with friends was quite normal. Here in Thailand it still happens with expat friends but not so much with Thai people.

The idea of going for just a beer is strange for a lot of Thai people I know. Sure, Thai people drink but it is normally always linked to eating. They will go to a restaurant and have a beer with it, drinking isn't the main event.

You do see groups of Thai men drinking but normally it is whiskey and usually outside a house or by the side of the road.

COFFEE SHOPS

Coffee shops can be found everywhere in Thailand. From international chains through to locals selling on a bike there are all types of coffee joints here.

Quality varies a lot and a lot of places seem to open up and shut down after only a few months.

You can also find international chains like Starbucks in almost every town now. One of the main selling points of coffee shops here is that they have fee Wi-Fi and air-conditioning.

Tea of all varieties is popular in Thailand. Milk tea and bubble tea are the most popular. In shopping malls you will see many stalls selling these.

FOOD HEALTH AND SAFETY

Maybe you have had problems after eating Thai food or heard of people who have. In general, a lot of restaurants in Thailand would be shut down if they were checked by Western inspectors. You will see things here that will make you cringe. On the flip side you will also see things which make you think people worry too much about food standards in the west.

By paying more you might presume you are getting a better quality of kitchen and therefore higher food safety and hygiene standards but you are probably wrong. Many fancy restaurants will still have a basic kitchen out the back in the same condition as cheaper places.

Things such as having a hair in your food would be considered a major issue back home but here in Thailand you will probably get a quick apology and a replacement dish. In cheaper restaurants you will get cutlery and dishes which look extremely worn and battered. Some very cheap food stalls re-use straws and ice.

If you really care about food standards then you should cook at home.

Interviews with Expats
in Thailand 1-6

Interview 1: The Bar Manager

Max Rapkin is a British manager of the Sportsman Bar on Sukhumvit Road in Bangkok. Max is also a co-founder of Live Lounge BKK – Thailand's newest poetry, comedy and performance arts venue.

Tell us a bit about your background and why you came to Thailand.

In a nutshell, in 2009, there was a catalyst or spark for me moving out here and that was the financial recession, which had a knock-on effect on my dreams and ambition of becoming a news reporter. I was doing sports and news reporting in London and as a consequence of the recession, I was told I would not get a permanent contract. I did various sales jobs as they were the only type of jobs hiring and then, in 2011, I came out to South East Asia for the first time. I travelled around Laos, Cambodia and Thailand for a few months and fell in love with Thailand.

I completely fell in love with the culture and the people. I was in demand over here as I was an English man with an English degree. I was so open-minded at the time, I had no commitments back in England. I met people and built relationships very quickly. One of the people I met was a girl who had a friend who was a teacher, an Irish guy, and the girl said "Let me introduce you to this guy, if you are up for staying here, he's got an opportunity for you. He's been talking about it; his school needs a teacher". I ended up meeting this guy, one thing led to another and I ended up in a classroom.

Did you have any background in teaching? If not, how did you get into it?

I didn't have any background in teaching. It was a government school in Nonthaburi. This Irish guy said it's 40,000 baht a month, 12 classes a week, it's a breeze. He basically sold the job to me although I was very keen on it anyway as I had already fallen for the charm of Thai people. I really felt it was something I could do; I had developed a lot of self-confidence when I worked in sales. I walked into this teaching job with a lot of confidence. There were 45 to 50 kids staring at me, I was ready and it was "let's do this".

I also got to design my own curriculum and the school was laid back. They arranged my work permit and didn't insist on having an education degree to teach. I was working in the elite English programme where parents were spending more money to send their kids. I had the top 4 classes in each year, I was teaching the students who were excelling at English. It was just a dream start to my teaching career, I couldn't have asked for more.

Was your salary enough for your lifestyle?

I lived in Nonthaburi which is a beautiful, peaceful province. I had met a few other expats and they put me in contact with someone who was leaving Bangkok and had a house to rent. It was only 5,000 baht a month and it was literally opposite my school so I could not have asked for more. My electricity was about 1,000 baht a month and my other expenses were peanuts so I was living a beautiful life out there on my salary. I was very happy and I stayed there for three years even though I changed jobs. My new job came through a friend I played football with. He said it would come with a 10,000 Baht pay rise which was great and it would give me more of a challenge. It was a step up in terms of professionalism. They were more rigorous with the interview process, more rigorous with having the right qualifications.

Do you think learning Thai is important?

There's a lot of expats here who will tell you that 'you don't need to use Thai language out here because everyone knows English and Thais need to improve their English anyway'. You meet a lot of expats who believe that but what they don't realise is that they will never, ever, penetrate the culture. They will always remain on the periphery and they will always live in their own bubble outside of what is really happening. They will never be able to form close relationships, they will always have to devolve responsibilities or jobs or anything that involves Thai language to someone else. For me, the moment I started using Thai language, I sussed this out; the first time I said "<u>Sa</u>-<u>wàt</u>-dee <u>krúp</u>, <u>sa</u>-baai dee <u>mái</u>" and saw the Thai person's eyes light up, saw them smile, I just knew this is a place where they are receptive to you making the effort with the language. I aggressively learnt the language more and more and continued to get an amazing reaction from it and I still do to this day. Even though I don't think I speak it that well or, at least, not as well as I would like to, I still appreciate that I do speak it.

For example, I wouldn't be able to run this bar and have a good connection with the staff without speaking Thai. Their English is good but not good to the point where they can have a heart to heart conversation or how they are feeling in the job or what the nature of their dispute with another staff member is. And the kitchen staff cannot speak a word of English so yesterday, for example, there's a kicking off between the lady chef and one of the bar staff who comes to me teary-eyed and says the chef has called her this and that. I would not have been able to have the conversation I had with the chef and go in there and talk to her face to face if I didn't speak Thai. So what would I have done? How could I be an effective manager? Would I have sent someone else in there to have the conversation? That would have no impact whatsoever. What had the impact was me going in there and speaking to her in Thai. So I ended up saying "<u>mâi</u> <u>dtâwng</u> <u>kui</u> <u>gan</u> <u>gâw</u> dâai, <u>mâi</u> <u>dtâwng</u> <u>bpen</u> pêuan <u>gan</u>"…'you don't need to be friends, just be polite and work together'.

What were you expecting when you came here and did it turn out to be different?

I had very high expectations when I came here as friends had told me great things about Thailand. People were telling me how beautiful the place was and talking about the south of Thailand a lot. My friend had been here before so I sort of had a semi guide and he showed me the Thai dishes and he had been to Koh Pha Ngan before and he knew the good places to stay. I had an amazing experience when I came and did the island hopping and it was just absolutely sensational and far outweighed my expectations, to be honest. What I had not expected was the warmth of the people and how receptive they were. When I first came, I was mainly in tourist places and I just connected with the people wherever I went...cynics would say that they are only smiling because they want something from you but they don't understand Thai culture, that they are naturally happy people.

Do you think your experience would have been different if you had lived in Bangkok rather than Nonthaburi?

Yes, I think so. Actually, my friend, based on my recommendation, lived in Phloen Chit and it was a very high-end place but it had no soul. We sat down after six months and he said that he wanted to move and he suggested I move to Bangkok from Nonthaburi. This was after four years of being a teacher and he suggested I get a job at the Sportsman bar. I was here quite frequently because I started a football team here, the Sportsman Football Club, about six years ago. I used to come here, play football, play pool and the owners really impressed me and I just felt at home here and so came here all the time. When he suggested me getting a job here, it was a lightbulb moment.

Shortly after that I proposed the idea to one of the owners here who was a good friend of mine. He said "we don't need anyone right now but I'll let you know if we need a manager" and so I continued being a teacher and eight months later, he called me and said "I've just had to sack my manager, are you still up for coming and working here?" I got the job because I always brought people to the bar. I was a good customer and had built up a relationship with the owners over time. I've always behaved impeccably in terms of not making trouble and I'm very reliable as well as consistent so he could see all these qualities. I said to him I want to learn how to run a bar.

What were the main challenges (beyond any mentioned already) in setting up your life here and were there any pleasant surprises?

One of the main challenges was learning how to be disciplined here. More than any other place, this is a land where anything can happen if you want it to happen. The culture is so laid back and there is so little enforcement of things that you can really run wild here. You can make your wildest dreams come true. You'll pay a price for it though! For me, I've got all the partying out of my system so I've got that discipline now. I'm on a different path now. I always used to be a big clubber and was really into it back in the UK but I've never really got into it here. With me working weekends and having commitments, I just can't go wild on a Saturday night because if I don't turn up on the Sunday, it will cost the bar revenue. If I come late and the customers want to watch the sport and I'm not here to deal with any issues, they will just take their business elsewhere. It is temptation town around here but over the years I've developed a stop button. So, going back to the original question, when I first came here, alcohol was so cheap so reining that in was a real challenge.

Another challenge was communication with Thai people. I encountered a lot more problems because I didn't speak Thai, just daily problems with interactions where I would encounter an obstruction or block and I would retreat into my shell of "I'm saying it the right way, they know exactly what I mean, why are they pretending they don't". The more time I spent here the more I realised it was me, not them. I had tried to say something in Thai and they didn't understand it because it's a tonal language and so their look of confusion was very real. It wasn't like, you know, any act of malice on their part or any lack of motivation to talk to me, it was simply they just didn't get what I was trying to say. I had a lot of these awkward interactions when I first came to Thailand.

The warmth of the people was a pleasant surprise. There were times when I was living in the village in Nonthaburi when I didn't have much money and they would ask me if I had eaten already and ten minutes later there would be a plate of food outside my door. Acts of kindness like that were commonplace. They expected nothing back and went out of their way to make me feel like a family member. The local shop and my neighbours would have parties and invite me for food and beer. A lot of the time I would say no because I was trying not to drink too much but it was difficult to say no.

Me and my friend researched where the best place to learn Thai was and we found out it was Chulalongkorn University. They had the best intensive Thai language programme; it's a nine-stage programme and you do these six-week phases that you can pick up and put down whenever you want. We enrolled in the Chula programme and we, very quickly, made friends. Chula is a university with very educated, really cool Thai students who are on another level spiritually. They worked really hard and spoke great English. Studying in the Arts faculty at Chula opened so many doors to friendships I've got now.

What has changed over the years in terms of your life in Thailand? What have you learnt about life in Thailand that you did not know back then?

There are so many opportunities in this city. There's various different career prospects, like the recruitment industry, which is booming at the moment. Several people I know are full time in recruitment and are making good money. For any foreigner who can learn and master the Thai language, the sky is the limit here for them. Any successful Thai company would love to have an educated and smart foreigner who speaks fluent Thai. All the foreigners that I know here who speak fluent Thai are all in really, really good positions. I know a couple of guys who are assistants to CEOs in major companies in Thailand; they have been accepted into Thai culture. The most important thing these guys have all done is aggressively networked and the fact that they can speak Thai is so important.

I think the only way to ensure longevity in Thailand for a foreigner is to do what I did and learn about the culture, study the language and get a feel for the place. I didn't go to many networking events but if I had done, it would have probably sped up my progress. There are opportunities around every corner so networking is key if you have skills to offer and can speak the language because you can then not just be interesting for foreign companies but also Thai companies too. What I have learnt about Thailand is, it is a developing country and they are big on going international – they're big on the word 'international'. If they're from a wealthy background, they love sending their kids abroad and they love to have a foreigner on their books in Thailand.

So, assuming you have learnt the language and so on, how do you actually network with these Thai companies?

You could apply online through the job websites but the best way is probably just to network. It's the oldest piece of advice you could give anyone but it's just to put yourself out there and meet people and good things will come of it. If you put the right energy out there and you are genuine, you will get it back and things will escalate very, very quickly. You can sit there tapping at your keyboard or you can go out there and make it happen and speak to the right people. There are millions of expats here and there are loads of opportunities and many of these expats are doing really, really well. I know expats who are making ridiculous money, ten times what I am making.

What about your top tips for settling in Thailand? And conversely, what are your top things to not do?

Focus on what you're good at. So, for example, if that is communication skills, go all out for a job where you're going to be using that skills such as, say, bar management, recruitment or teaching. Don't hold back and just throw caution to the wind and go all out after what you are good at. Just go for it and don't do it half-hearted.

In terms of what not to do, don't hang out with a group of cynical expats, don't hang out with criminals. There's plenty of them here. Surround yourself with the right people is the bottom line and don't let those people poison your mind. I remember going to this wedding and meeting a foreigner who said I shouldn't trust Thai people. I totally disagreed with that. There's loads of these poisonous people out there. Don't live this way, in a sort of foreigner bubble and develop a negative attitude toward Thailand.

Another thing to do, if you want to understand Thailand and Thai people and how they operate is to learn about Buddhism. It's a Buddhist society here and 90% of people here are Buddhist; some practice it more than others but it doesn't matter, it's still what underpins the way they behave. If you learn about it, you'll understand why Thai people are so calm, why they are so peaceful, why they smile. Buddhism teaches you to be true to your inner self and go with the flow of life. As such Thai people are less resistant to things and less dogmatic and more open-minded.

To what extent have you integrated into Thai society?

There's small differences to where I am from, things like eating together and sharing food. This was a foreign concept to me when I came here. Where I'm from, you get a plate of food, you eat it. However, with any of the staff here, if I show any interest in what they are eating, they will invite me to share their food.

But there are more serious cultural differences. Thailand is still quite old skool so, for example, in terms of sex before marriage, Thailand is quite conservative. And even marriage, as a concept, has diminished back home whereas here, it is still quite rigid and strong.

In terms of how Thai people treat me, the only reason they speak to me as an equal and relate to me directly is because I can speak Thai. I have also become quieter and humbler since I have been here. If you are loud and opinionated and overbearing, egotistical or argumentative or whatever, you are just not going to fit in here. American people maybe more than other nationalities have to adjust their cultural ways. But going back to how Thai people treat me, say, for example, my girlfriend's friends or whatever, again, it all goes back to speaking Thai. If you can't speak Thai, you'll just be sitting there and you'll get frustrated…and so you should be really. It does require effort – her friends are beautiful people but it does take effort because they are not the most confident of people, especially if they do not have good English skills so you do need to make them feel comfortable.

What do you think of other expats in Thailand?

In my position, I meet a lot of people, a lot of expats and generally they're a good sort. But then you get some who haven't connected with the culture, or angry expats or just haven't had a great experience. I've got quite an acute sense for people and I've got no time for anyone who does not respect the culture. I most certainly avoid those sorts of people.

What are your plans for the future?

I'm going to marry and have a family here for sure. I absolutely want to bring my kid up here and be here long term. I'm taking my girlfriend to the UK for Christmas but she's got no particular desire to live there. She's very close to her family and I don't think she could move away from her mum. I'm really looking forward to bringing up my kid in Thailand. It's a beautiful place. Marriage is not far away, which is great.

How much do you need per month to live in Thailand?

I would say 40,000 baht is enough if you can land a residence which, say, is no more than 10,000 baht a month. It's enough to have a happy, comfortable existence. If you can live a life of simplicity and discipline, 40,000 baht a month is more than enough. But if you crave indulgences, luxuries, high-end food, you better double that.

Interview 2: The Retiree

Jean Armignon is a French retiree who initially settled in Bangkok and recently moved to Chiang Mai. Jean spends a lot of him time studying Thai in his never-ending quest to become fluent.

Tell us a bit about your background and why you came to Thailand.

I'm 67 and have been in Thailand since I was 63. I was a civil aviation engineer in France working for the government. I've always been interested in exploring other cultures and I was more interested in foreign women than French women. I first married an American woman and had 2 children and divorced after 20 years. My second marriage was with a Filipina and again I had two children before we divorced. I then found myself alone in France but wanted to be in Asia. I saw Thailand as the safest, easiest country to live in. The health system is good, prices are low and the visa isn't too difficult to get.

Had you visited Thailand before you moved here?

Yes, I visited Thailand twice before. The first time I met a Thai woman and nearly married her but my divorce wasn't finalised at that time. The second time with my Filipina wife, we had a vacation here.

Why didn't you choose the Philippines to move to?

I didn't choose the Philippines because of bad memories and for safety reasons; it's a little bit more dangerous. They have kidnappings there. Also, people say Philippines is not really Asia, it's not part of the mainland. I prefer the countryside and mountains; Philippines has a lot of beaches!

How often do you go back to France?

I try to avoid going back home. I went back twice for administrative reasons including my divorce. I like France, it's very beautiful, but I just don't want to go anymore. I think it would just be boring now, I don't feel the need to go back.

Where in Thailand have you lived?

I have lived in Bangkok for four years and Chiang Mai for three and a half months. I bought a car three and a half years ago and I've been traveling around the country too.

Where did you live in Bangkok?

I wanted to live in a mostly Thai neighbourhood so I chose a nice place near the end of the BTS line in Bang Na.

What do you think are the good things in Bangkok for an expat?

I chose Bangkok because I like big cities. I remember when I was in Paris I enjoyed it because you have everything. Also, I am a bridge player and wanted to meet and play against others and thought Bangkok would be my best option to do this. Also, it's quite central, you can go anywhere easily from the city.

Is there anything you didn't like about Bangkok?

The traffic makes getting anywhere difficult. A seemingly short journey can take several hours. It makes you feel tired sometimes just going out of your house.

Is there a reason you chose a condo rather than a house?

I don't like houses, there are too many things to take care of. I arrived here without any furniture and didn't want to buy anything so a fully furnished condo was perfect. You also get good security and sports facilities in a condo such as a swimming pool.

Did you choose to rent or buy a place and why?

I chose to rent because I wanted to be able to move anytime quickly and I don't want to re-sell. I didn't want to rent my place out because there are too many problems. I had no plans to stay in Bangkok forever. Even here in Chiang Mai I have no plans to buy.

Why did you choose to move to Chiang Mai after four years in Bangkok?

I chose Chiang Mai because I'd visited before and after travelling around the country found it the most attractive place and very quiet. Also, at the time I was there the climate was good, and still it is cooler than Bangkok. You can also find everything you want here.

Is there an area of Chiang Mai you think is best for living?

It depends on your taste. I like to be inside the city. A lot of my friends live in the countryside and seem to be happy there. As for me I want to use my bike to travel around, especially here inside the big city square. In this area there are lots of restaurants, shops, temples and fewer cars.

When you arrived what were your impressions after the first couple of months?

I didn't feel discouraged after my first few months. I knew the language would be difficult to learn and the weather would be hot.

How's it been building up a social network?

I'm not really looking to make foreign friends here. I have a few acquaintances who I know though. I meet people through playing bridge but outside competition we don't really socialize. Most of them have a Thai girlfriend or are married and I'm single so I don't want to bother them! I enjoy being alone as I was raised as a single child, maybe that's why I'm still single!

What resources did you use to help you plan and prepare for living in Thailand?

I only cared about the visa so I had to explore the internet to find out how to get a visa. I just followed the instructions and I didn't have time to look for anything much. But I had experience travelling around the world before so I wasn't scared.

What was your experience of getting a visa?

I followed the official procedure and found it easy. The only thing is sometimes I found different opinions and advice on the internet which were wrong. I was puzzled by the different opinion I could see but in fact it's not difficult. I do everything by myself every year without any problems.

How was the process of buying and registering your car?

I had the idea of buying a second-hand car but people discouraged me from doing this because I might run into problems. I decided to get a new car and the process to buy it is very easy. the only difficulties came through the language barrier. Having a car is a huge benefit for me, especially now I am outside Bangkok. Here in CM I use it almost every day. I could have bought a motorbike but I had to choose between a bike and car and I felt it was too much to have both so I opted for car because you can carry people and things. It's more relaxing as I'm older and less dangerous than motorbikes at my age!

After four and a half years have your feelings about Thailand changed?

No, I'm still trying to understand how people function here.

Do you think if you'd stayed in Bangkok you might have become unhappy?

If I had stayed I wouldn't have been unhappy as I enjoyed living there. However, now that I am in Chiang Mai I do prefer my lifestyle here.

What advice would you give for retirees thinking of living in Thailand?

It's difficult for me to give advice because it's so personal. Everyone has different expectations. I like to take care of myself which is why I cook for myself. In fact, Thai food is not very healthy in general. You have to take care of your health, what you eat and how much you exercise.

What do you think about Thai culture, were there any surprises?

I don't know enough yet. I suspect that the people say that some Thai people are lazy and Thai women are more serious than the men. You see the same things everywhere in the same proportion so I couldn't say that Thai culture is so different from other cultures. They marry they divorce they do everything like we do. The main difference is that families live together in a more traditional way.

What would be your typical night out in Bangkok?

I liked to go out and practice my Thai. Firstly I would go to a restaurant and then speak with some bar girls after. Sometimes I liked to go to a massage parlour. There are two types of massage shops, traditional and not traditional, I like both. I like traditional places because they're relaxing and you can still talk to the women, most of them are nice. Non-traditional massage for other reasons but you can still talk to the women. I had in my mind to meet a woman on my nights out.

You met them in bars or via other ways?

I was inclined to meet women at bars or massage shops as it was easier. There was also less pressure on me. Dating normal women was possible but I didn't like that it was harder to breakup with them. A lot of the bar girls had many jobs in their life and worked in the bars to top up their salary. Many sold clothes, worked in restaurants or had other businesses. The idea of working in a bar is not liked by many Thais but it is accepted.

Is it easy to meet Thai women in social situations?

Overall, yes, it is. You can easily meet nice Thai women on the bus and get their numbers. In restaurants I can exchange contact details with women of all ages, it is simple to do if you make the first move. A lot of Thai women of all ages play bridge so I could meet them through there. Thai women of all ages like to talk with foreigners, especially those who live here, not just tourists.

Would you go on a traditional date or just at the bar?

I met some women in the cinema but we had problems due to the language barrier. In the end I prefer bar girls because they have a basic level of English and it makes it possible to communicate in meaningful conversations.

Is Chiang Mai more suited for retirees?

I think it is better here for sure. There are better facilities for retired people such as great hospitals.

Is Chiang Mai cheaper than Bangkok?

Yes, it is cheaper. Here I can afford to eat out more often than Bangkok. My bills and rent are also less than Bangkok for a similar place.

How much do you recommend you can live on in Chiang Mai?

20,000 baht is not enough. I think with 30,000 baht, if you exclude bars, girls and massages, you can live easily here. On 20,000 baht you really have to buy at the market and never eat in restaurants. My budget was 55k in Bangkok and here I can spend the same, I find it easy now in Chiang Mai. I'm used to the low cost of living so find it easy to live here based on my budget.

I also don't worry about spending a bit more sometimes. I know this is also a tourist area and somethings are overpriced.

Anything else?

In Chiang Mai there are a lot of activities you can do, more so than in Bangkok. I do yoga and paint watercolours in my spare time. There are also lots of classes you can take such as in dance or cooking.

One thing that is more expensive here is the price of drinks and for the girls compared to Bangkok. You only have touristy areas in Chiang Mai for bargirls. In Bangkok you could find local style bars where prices were lower, I haven't found these yet here.

Maybe in the future I will get married again. However I know that if I do marry a younger Thai woman she will expect money from me. I know of people who give their Thai wife between 10-30,000 baht per month. In the end it is like an agreement, the man gets a wife who looks after him and the woman gets financially rewarded.

Interview 3: The (Working) Mum

Kathy Rougier is a British insurance executive who moved to Thailand for work. Kathy has spent a lot of her time in Thailand setting up a website on the process and costs of having a baby in Thailand.

Tell us a bit about your background and why you came to Thailand.

I was living in Singapore as an insurance broker in an international broking company. My boyfriend was living in Bangkok and we were commuting between Thailand and Singapore. It came to crunch time, in terms of where we wanted to settle down, and Bangkok seemed more suitable than Singapore. We reached out to our contacts in the Insurance industry to see whether I could find a job and thankfully I did easily. That was nearly four years ago. Life then changed, my husband (then boyfriend) got a larger condo and we looked to settle down in Thailand, get married and start a family.

When you first arrived, what were some of the obstacles to living in Thailand and what was easier than expected?

I think the visa and work permit process in Thailand is more complicated than it needs to be. One of the hardest things to navigate is transferring between the different visa types, especially needing to leave the country each time you have to do that. The most worrying thing about being here (unless you're on a retirement visa) is that if your work permit is cancelled, your visa is also cancelled straight away. Having changed jobs once and finished my most recent employment whilst I was pregnant, therefore transitioning onto a dependent visa, I can advise that it is worrying and difficult, and requires good contacts and local speakers to navigate the system.

But there is a lot that makes Bangkok an easy place to live. You can get everything, and anything, delivered. If you ask in the right way then pretty much anything is possible here. Things you couldn't get in Singapore, and certainly not in the UK, so I think once you get under the skin of living in Thailand you realize that it is quite easy.

How did you settle into life here in Bangkok during your first few weeks and months?

Fortunately for me I had a job straight away. Within the first few days I was walking into the office. I had a phone given to me by my company so that was easy. I do recommend getting a phone as quickly as possible so you get Google maps, getting around is chaotic, make things easy for yourself, get 4G! To get a bank account, you have to trust someone to help you. I trusted in a Thai colleague to assist me with translation and form filling. I guess the lack of English here, even in formal environments, is one thing I am still surprised at.

It makes us laugh (and sometimes worry) about the amount of times we sign something without really knowing what it is.

Now, you're not working?

I stopped work when I was pregnant which was lovely. Thanks to Thai employment laws I was able to have a little bit of money in my back pocket when they decided they didn't want to keep me on anymore. Thai Employment Law is very much in the employees' favour. Termination payments are regulated by statute depending on how long you've been working, ranging typically from the equivalent of 5 months' salary to over 1 year's salary in lieu. When negotiating employment contracts, I would personally always go for a Thai based contract (with expat type privileges as a side agreement, extra holidays, international health insurance etc)

Now I'm a stay at home mother and blogger, but mostly a stay at home mum! I don't get much time for the blogging!

How did the blog come about?

babyblueinbangkok.blogspot.com came about due to frustrations with the health care service here. The healthcare service is technically very good, they have hospitals that are internationally rated 5*, and even the government hospitals have a good reputation. But, the customer service style, ethos and approach to patient involvement and consent is very different to back home.

Just a recent example, a doctor (in a well-known hospital) prescribed a cream for my daughter. I was verbally told how to administer the cream but that was the only direction given. There was no paperwork, no instruction leaflet, no advice as to side effects or contradictions, I was just given a tube of cream in a bag. I still kick myself at times like this because I should say more at the time (especially after promoting that in my blog) but it's not until I get back home that I often think about it.

During my pregnancy I also frequently had things done to me in hospital that I had not directly given consent to. Don't get me wrong I wasn't violated or upset, but I wasn't told about them before they were done. Often, I didn't find out until I got the bill! On one occasion they took 17 vials of blood from me and didn't say what is was for, on seeing the bill I noted they did the same tests several times.

Was that a language thing?

No, my doctor was fluent in English.

Was it to pad the bill?

Most definitely. Even doctors have admitted to me that their salaries are directly related to the revenue they generate from patients. They have confirmed to me that procedures requiring express consent in countries like the UK are often carried out here as a matter of course due to culture, and more worryingly, revenue.

Which medical system do you prefer? UK or Thai system?

As I've mentioned previously, the hospitals here are 5*, so technically I have always felt in good hands but the culture and general ethos make the systems polar opposites in my opinion. It's a money-making business in Thailand. It is big, big business. You see it on every billboard.

From a patient's viewpoint is it worth it? Would you prefer more of an English system?

Probably yes. Here you go straight to the premium level, with the cost associated to that. In the NHS they would give you the cheapest option, only escalating your treatment and/or tests if that was inconclusive or required further intervention. In Bangkok they typically only offer premium level tests and treatment, which may not be necessary and therefore you are normally always subject to large medical bills.

Do you think that's because they know many expats have good health insurance?

Absolutely. Having an insurance background, it's something that I'd love to look into it more (if I had the time). I've had both Insurance Companies and Hospital Management admit to me that the cost of private healthcare is driven by access to Health Insurance, and consequently the cost of Healthcare Insurance is directly proportional to the prices charged by private institutions. They've all admitted it and said that it's a problem.

Speaking to a lot of people in health and child care industries from around the world (midwives, doula's, GP's, Lactation Consultants etc) they all describe the healthcare industry here as incredibly paternalistic. There is a general belief that doctors know best. Patients accept the doctor's actions and doctors can get quite upset if they are challenged. I have friends whose doctors have reacted very badly to being questioned or challenged, when in reality my friends have simply wanted to know more about the diagnosis, prognosis, alternative treatments and side-effects. I don't mean that the doctors here are wrong, it's never done me wrong but I have paid a lot more money than I needed to, before I got wise to it.

Even now, after being acutely aware of the cultural differences, I recently took my daughter to St. Louis hospital. The doctor wanted to do a physical examination and before I knew it the nurse had taken my baby and started undressing her, without asking me and almost blocking me from my baby. I like to think that this would never happen in the UK, consent underpins the healthcare system and consent for a baby has to come from the mother, no one should touch or undress a baby without first properly consulting the mother. Again, I don't want to be too negative; you just have to find your own way.

What support groups are there for expats expecting children in Thailand?

There are some amazing groups here that can help you navigate becoming parents in Bangkok.

BAMBI (bambiweb.org) is just amazing; helping mums-to-be and mothers. They set up playgroups all over Bangkok. There is something going on with BAMBI every day of the week. What is also amazing is that they are supported by professionals (midwives etc) who can't technically practice here but that volunteer instead. There is also a well-established Doula network in Bangkok (https://www.facebook.com/bangkokdoulas/), whether you plan to have a Doula present at your birth or not, these ladies are some of the most knowledgeable and influential women when it comes to all things about child birth and babies. They have invaluable insight into the best doctors and hospitals according to your needs and requirements. Other resources include The Mummy Club Bangkok Facebook Group (facebook.com/groups/TheMummyClubBangkok), and BKKKids (bkkkids.com).

Having found these resources I can say that the support network, outside of the official healthcare network, is amazing. You have to go looking for it but once you find it, it is incredible and I don't think you'd find that back home.

What are your thoughts on your daughter growing up in Thailand?

I have no concerns. In terms of schooling there's a lot of choice. I'm in the process of researching costs as it's obviously expensive, although there are cheaper international options as well. It seems from what I've seen that there's a range of different teaching styles as well. There's everything you would need here. We're perfectly happy to educate our daughter here in Bangkok.

Are you planning to stay here for the long term?

Yes, but for us it depends on visas and work permits. My biggest concern is how the system links your visa to your work permit. If you stop working, they cancel your work permit, and therefore your visa immediately. Technically you can apply for a 7-day extension and then you must leave the country. That's scary. We've got 2 cats and a baby, and it's less than ideal to have to exit and re-enter the country on different visa types in order to carry on your life here. But assuming everything goes well, we'll be back to being on a permanent status here soon.

We have discussed whether to go home but the UK is bottom of the list at the moment It's the last thing we would do right now. The lifestyle you build here can be amazing and much easier than back home. I don't have a nanny but I have a maid who comes in every morning, I wouldn't have that it in the UK. We find ourselves doing things we would never do back home. For example, hiring a car and a driver for a few days. Here it seems likes nothing. There's always a way here. You need to know how to find the way and you may need someone to explain the Thai way, but there is always a way.

I think you build yourself a lifestyle that can't be achieved back in Europe right now.

To what extent have you integrated into Thai society, if at all?

Through work I have some Thai acquaintances, but they do tend to be more internationally minded. I haven't properly integrated with many Thais. I personally think it is hard on a friendship level.

What budget would recommend for expats with and without children to live a comfortable lifestyle?

We recently calculated what we needed to live as we were going down to one salary. Our cost of living is approx. 90,000 baht, that's 2 adults 2 cats and a 7-month-old baby in a 3-bedroom condo, just outside the centre of Sathorn. The condo is 55,000 of that. Through choice we shop in markets and keep costs down. We don't have a car and I have a maid five days a week in the mornings.

In terms of salary, from my personal experience and speaking with friends, to really enjoy yourself as a single person then anything less than 100k baht a month is difficult. If you want to enjoy yourself, go for a beer, nice restaurants, holidays and don't want to be in the arse end of nowhere then I think you need at least 100k. I appreciate it sounds a lot but as people live here longer they often spend less, but it's that initial splurge, the craziness when they first arrive. You're in the land of sunshine and smiles, you want to enjoy it. We know from being here longer that you can get decent condos, for a single person, for 15,000 baht but people don't do that when they first arrive they spend 30-60k minimum to live somewhere, it's a big chunk of cash. If you're looking at it from a family perspective you need to be bringing in at least 200,000 baht to run a family for the first year of being here. But then again, in our experience the expat packages are getting harder to come by.

Interview 4 – The Middle-aged Man Who Married a Bargirl

David Neil is a British ex headteacher who has spent his whole career in education. Having spent twenty years in Asia recruiting Asian students for scholarships to study in the UK, he is now approaching retirement. David has been married to an ex bargirl for the last twenty years.

Tell us a bit about your background and why you came to Thailand.

I was head of a college in London. I had been the head for 16 years and the numbers of local students wanting to study with us but that number began to decline. In 1986 I came out to Asia to a British Council exhibition, recruited 19 students and they proved to be very, very bright. After this we basically said let's go back to Asia and get some more! I started off in places like Japan, Singapore, Taiwan, and did very well. It wasn't until 1993 that I first came to Thailand, again to a British Council exhibition.

I came to Thailand, and at that time, my first marriage was going through a difficult patch, mainly because I was away for two to three months a year recruiting, so naturally, this put a great strain on the marriage.

So, roundabout 1996, because we realised the great potential of getting students from Asia, I decided to resign and come out here, based out here to be a full-time recruiter. I started off in Vietnam, lived there for two years but of course, all the time, I was travelling around these other countries and coming, maybe, three or four times a year to Thailand. I never stayed in any place f o r more than about six days so I always came on a simple tourist visa.

Anyway, on one of the trips to Thailand, I met my present wife in Bangkok. We started a relationship and I then got married a second time and started a family. So, obviously, having met my wife and gotten married, I decided to move from Vietnam to Thailand to live here. I started off living in my wife's village. We built a house there – a small bungalow – and it worked very well, except it was very difficult for my work, from two points of view. One – for travelling, it meant I had an extra leg of the journey to get from the village to the airport. The second reason was there were no facilities – there was no Internet, no WiFi, the post was pretty poor and so on. So we decided to settle in Nakhon Ratchasima.

So when you got married, did you come and stay here on a marriage visa?

The first visa I had was a marriage visa and I did that for four or five years before I twigged onto the fact that the retirement visa is much easier. I had no problem with the retirement visa and have not had to this day –it takes me twenty minutes to go down to the local immigration office and renew it.

Can you tell me a little bit about what Thailand was like back in the late 90s?

As far as social life is concerned, Thailand was much the same as it is now. When I used to come here on business trips before I lived here, I used to stay in the Nana to Asok area because all the British Council exhibitions were held in   the old Queen's Hotel on Soi 2. What happened was, at   my very first exhibition in 1993, we had a sort of…pre-exhibition drinks evening and I met this lady who happened to be working for the Swiss Embassy in Bangkok. I'm not sure quite why she was there but anyway, after the drinks, she said, "Look, I'll take you around some of the nightspots here in Sukhumvit." She took me and we looked at some go-go bars and I took a fancy to this girl who was dancing on stage. That's how I met my wife!

What did you think of Sukhumvit nightlife?

I definitely saw it as a pleasure paradise. I could see the seedy side of it – you know, you would see these huge, old guys with beer guts out here with these little Thai girls who may have been underage. So, yes, I could see that unsavoury side of it.

Did you commit to your then future wife or did you continue to see other girls? And if you did commit, how did you manage to resist the lifestyle, since you were staying in that area anyway?

I was committed to my wife from day one. I was 56 by then so I knew what life was about and I knew the economic circumstances of these girls. I got talking to the girls and I knew what the background was, why they were there and why they were doing it. One of the first things I spotted was when I went to the post office and I could see all these girls, one or two of whom I recognised from the previous night. They were all queuing up so I asked my wife what they were all doing and she said "oh they're all sending money back home". That's when I got interested in the social side of it – why was it all happening. By then, I had twigged another important fact that the vast majority of these girls were not Thai at all. Ethnically, they were Laos, they were all from the North-East.

I was 56 then and she was only 20 so there was a big age difference and of course, I felt very flattered. But obviously being mature and switched on, I realised that she was interested in me because of the financial support I could offer. Eventually I realised that there were two types of girls – there were the ones who wanted to milk as much money as they could and the others who were more genuine.

There was one girl who had five guys on the go and they would all come to Thailand at different times. She would tell each of them when they could come and they were all sending her money. I learnt all of the tricks of the trade like, you know, 'my brother's had an accident and broken his leg' or, 'our buffalo has died' was another popular one. These girls, they were basically milking the situation – all of these guys, mostly middle-aged, like me, were often going through some personal crisis such as going through separation or divorce, they had money and were flattered by the attention they were getting from these 20-25-year-old girls. I suppose most of them realised the economic implications. My big problem was deciding whether this girl I was having a relationship with was just in it for the money or was there the chance of a long-term relationship. As it's turned out, 21 years later and with three kids aged 18, 16 and 9, it has proven to be a long-term relationship.

Have you faced any judgement from other expats when you tell them 'my wife used to work in a bar'?

Very rarely because the expats you come into contact with, on the whole, have been through a similar experience. The only people where eyebrows might be raised is if I am talking to a bunch of people who have come over from UK universities for an exhibition. They might ask "Why have you lived here all this time? Where did you meet your wife?" and if I tell them, then it becomes a different attitude altogether. How do I deal with it? I deal with it like I deal with most things – I ignore it. Other people's opinions don't matter to me, unless I think they are valid opinions.

One of the other interviewees has said 'don't marry a bargirl', in terms of advice to potential expats. So, given your experience, what would you say?

As you said, there are some pitfalls if they go with the wrong type of girl so what would be your advice to other expats who may be coming here and meeting girls and so on? Well, the biggest advice I can give is to control your finances carefully. Don't hand over any financial control to your girlfriend. Be prepared to lose something. Within a very short space of time – when I started – in 1999, what happened in my case is I bought her out of the bar. I paid 10,000 baht and that bought her out. I went to see the mamasan and said "Look, I want my wife to give up her job and we are going to go and live in a village." She was happy with that and she was happy to get away from the business. She had been in the business since the age of 18. She had left school at 12 and went to work for her uncle who had a grocer's shop for six years and then obviously got recruited to work for one of the bars. She was making quite good money, around 30,000 baht a month plus tips, gifts and gold etc.

What was the transition like for her and indeed, for yourself, to move to a village in Thailand?

She was absolutely delighted as she is a village girl at heart. She is one of those girls that has never outgrown the village life and she sees that as where she would always like to be. She was not particularly happy in Bangkok although she was obviously happy with the money. Out of this money she was earning, she built a concrete house that cost 30,000 baht, which was quite a bit of money back then in 1999. She was also sending money back to her parents, her two brothers, their families and various other relatives.

As for me, the change in lifestyle wasn't a big problem. I have always been very adaptable because I always analyse situations, always think about them and always see them in perspective. Coming from the UK wasn't a problem for me as it was a decision I made and I was happy to come out here and take on this new role. I was actually very keen to come out here to live. I was more interested in the relationship with my wife and not so worried about living in the village or the reaction of the people in the village. I tried to suss out what they wanted, which is fairly obvious – they wanted financial support. I was ok with that, partly because you were talking about a miniscule amount of money compared to what I was earning at the time.

The first thing I did when we moved to the village is have a 2-bedroom extension built, which was much more 'upmarket' than what they were living in. I got some decent furniture, wardrobes, decent bed and a toilet with a sit-down basin and so on. All of it only cost me about 8,000 baht so it was incredibly cheap.

I could speak a little Thai back then and could hold a basic conversation. Also, the relatives and neighbours were very curious in having a foreigner come to live with them. The immediate family were delighted because here was somebody who was going to pay the bills. These bills were very small, but for them, they were huge. For example, I got satellite TV installed and bought a huge TV and all the village kids would come and watch films on it – it was like the local cinema!

Did you find you had to resist being cynical about the fact that you were seen as the provider for the extended family or did you openly accept it?

Yeah, I was happy to be the provider, really, to keep my wife happy I suppose. Also, soon, there was a baby on the way. The first kid was born in 2000. The only problem was my job – I required a lot of Internet time because there was a lot of e-mail communication and it just wasn't convenient in the village.

Because of this we very quickly decided after six months to move to Korat and had the second and third child, bought a car and settled down.

What were you expecting when you came here and did it turn out to be different?

It was only when I moved to the village that I saw real Thailand. Previously, I was just staying in hotels in Bangkok. It was only later that I realised that there was a big divide between what was the village in Isaan and Bangkok, which was what me and my friends call the 'High-Thais'. The High-Thais don't really like the people from the village at all, they look down on them as an inferior race. I found that very revealing and it led to me being a little negative about the High-Thais. However, all the time I was dealing with both sides so I did not have any problem; I was just aware of this big racial divide between Bangkok itself and the rest of Thailand.

The big advantages for me were the weather, the food and the cheapness of life. Once we were out of Bangkok, transport was very easy. For example, if you were to drive to my wife's village, you could drive 4 or 5 miles and not see another car, albeit that was back then and there are a few more cars now. I really fell in love with the Thai countryside. I could see that they weren't exploitative at all. People would say "Oh, they're just after your money". I realised they were after my money, yes, but that was because they didn't have any money themselves. They were subsistence farmers, and if there was a bad harvest or there was flooding, which there was quite often, they would be left with nothing apart from a few sacks of rice. Because my work often involved giving money to those who didn't have enough – scholarships and so on – coming here and seeing people needing help was just a natural extension of what I was doing anyway.

What has changed over the years in terms of your life in Thailand?

Well, my life hasn't changed that much because I have been doing the same job for the last twenty years. Also, don't forget, I was out of Thailand maybe 12 times a year. So, for example, I've been to China 67 time, Vietnam 90 times, Myanmar 70 times so I was out of the country a lot, all of which impacted on family life as well. As such I've not really aware of the changes over the years.

To what extent have you integrated into Thai society?

Well, speaking Thai certainly makes a difference. I often have long conversations with my neighbours over the fence and am able to talk about quite a lot of things, except the intricacies of Thai politics. The other thing to bear in mind is my status is probably quite different to a lot of expats who settle here. First, because of my age, I am treated differently.

Secondly, because I was a head of a school, that counts for a lot in Thailand. Even an ordinary teacher gets a lot more respect than they would get in European countries. In the eyes of the villagers, it wasn't so much about me being a headteacher, it was more that I was supporting them. Here, in the city, all my neighbours are Thais and I get on fine with them. They treat me in a very friendly way. I've never had a problem. But I can imagine, say, a particular type of farang who did not really speak Thai well, they would treat him differently.

What do you think of other expats in Thailand?

On the whole, I try to avoid them because I know their stories. I know if I sat down next to one, their story will pretty much be the same in 90% of cases. Divorced, got problems in life, out here and met a girl. I am a bit of an intellectual sort of person and have been in education all of my life so I tend to not relate very well to people who have not had higher education.

What about your top tips for settling in Thailand? And conversely, what are your top things to not do or to avoid?

The first thing to do is to be very careful about your relationship. Being the sort of person I am, I did a lot of background research into 'farangs' marrying Thais, in particular, marrying village girls. You don't see many High-Thai girls with farangs because I don't think your typical high-class Thai girl could take a farang home to meet their mum and dad. As such Thai – foreigner marriages are often only in circumstances where you have families that need economic support.

If it is a relationship based just on sex and money, it's not going to last. It's got to be based on the more permanent aspects of life – marriage, children and complete commitment to stay here. It's also a question of really getting to know what makes them tick. I realised quite early on that my wife wanted gold because gold, for them, is easily convertible into cash.

Then there is property because you have to be prepared to lose it if things go bad. And that is because it has to be in the wife's name.

The main thing is to decide, are you going to stay here or go back and come back again. I did that for six years but once I met my wife, I knew I was going to stay so I did my research into visas and so on.

Do you feel safe in Thailand?

Well, I've always felt very safe here. Apart from the odd driving-related fine, I've always had a good relationship with the police. My personal driver for many years was a police captain. When I lived in the UK, – the house I lived in for 16 years – we were burgled five times. I've lived here for 20 years and not had a single burglary although we often leave the windows open or whatever.

I don't see a lot of crime on the streets. I know there is an appalling record of motor accidents, mainly because of the way Thais are taught to drive. I, personally, having experience of driving in many other Asian countries, think Thailand has some of the worst drivers in Asia. They don't use their indicators, their lane discipline is non-existent and they turn corners very slowly because they are dead scared of confrontation. The one thing all Thais try to avoid – all Thai drivers – is having an accident, even a minor accident. Because it involves not just loss of face but all sorts of hassles. So, if you look at Thais, most are very, very cautious drivers and you can get quite frustrated if you are stuck behind a Thai driver. On the other hand, you also see quite a few who drive recklessly.

What is your estimate of how much you need to lead a decent life in Thailand?

I'm spending roughly 500 baht per day on food and that is for a family of five and that includes a bottle of wine for the week for me. My food is a bit more expensive because I shop in Tesco's because I buy some imported things such as Earl Grey tea or Australian wine.

Actually, I've got a full month's expenses here…in September, my income was 87,000 baht and our expenses were 85,000 baht. The biggest item is the rent, which is about 20,000 and the utility bills are about 5,000. I'm giving my wife about 7,000 a month and 10,000 is for repayments on a new car. I'm paying 6,000 a month for school meals for the kids and a TV bill of 2,500. Transport for the kids is 1,900 and extra classes for the kids 3,500. So, with food and a few other bits and bobs, it comes to over 80,000 baht for a family of five with e few handouts to my wife's relatives. I am sure that we could live more cheaply, say on 55-60,000 a month, which is what I will have when I retire.

Are you thinking about staying in Thailand or going back to the UK?

I've never considered going back to the UK, it has never been in my plans. I spent 55 years in the UK, which is long enough for anyone! I much prefer it here. If I try and identify what it is about here that keeps me here, it is the easy-going way of life. Also, you can enjoy a much higher standard of life here on a much lower income. How is it better? Well, firstly the people – they are always very, very pleasant. They have an inbuilt politeness and kindness. I don't think I've ever had a harsh word with anyone in Thailand whereas constantly in England, you're witnessing or getting involved in a dispute or argument or you have kids shouting out at you in the street or on a bus. You would never hear kids shouting obscenities here or being disrespectful to their elders in any way. So, it is a very, very different lifestyle here. I'll be here forever now, however long that is for me.

Interview 5 – The Ajarn

Phil Williams has been in Thailand for 27 years. With a background in teaching as well as various other jobs, he has been running Thailand's number 1 site for teaching English for the last 15 years.

Tell us a bit about your background and why you came to Thailand.

Like a lot of people, I fell in love with Thailand when I came here on a package tour (Bangkok and Pattaya) with an old schoolfriend. I had grown disillusioned with life in England at the time (although I was doing ok financially and career-wise) so I thought I would have a complete change of scenery and came to Thailand 'permanently' in 1990.

I did nothing for about a year except travel because as silly as it sounds, I came over with too much money! Not a great amount of money but enough so that I did not have to work. After a year, the bank account started to dwindle so I put an ad in the Bangkok Post Classified section, which not a lot of job-seekers did at the time.

I had some amazing offers such as 'can you come and run a hotel in Pattaya' and I had no experience of hospitality whatsoever; I was basically just a foreigner looking for work!

I was then contacted by an Indian gemstone company based in Bangkok. They were looking for a salesperson to go around to all the Thai jewellery manufacturers and sell semi-precious gemstones. The company said if they used Indian salesmen, those salesmen generally got shown the door. They needed a clean-cut foreigner I guess.

I ended up doing that job for 18 months. The company had an office in Jaipur so I got a few trips to India out of it as well (wonderful times). Unfortunately, the job wasn't quite making me enough money so I quit over unpaid commission and decided to get into teaching.

I did very well at teaching initially and so the first language school I applied to offered me a full-time position in Central Bangkok. The days were long and sometimes I wouldn't leave school until well after 9pm but I really loved teaching, And I ended up teaching on and off for fourteen years!

In 2002, I was offered a job with a company selling educational software. They said they were looking for a sales guy and my name kept cropping up. So I went for an interview and they offered me the job on the spot. Basically, my job was to go around schools, universities and companies in Thailand and Malaysia, selling CD-ROMs to put on their servers and intranet systems.

I did that job for a couple of years and hated every second of it. My finances were the lowest they have been in Thailand before I got this job but even though I made good money from the software sales, the job was too stressful.

Flying down to Malaysia once or twice a week, being alone in strange hotels in unfamiliar neighbourhoods, the heavy business lunches, the endless small talk – it just wasn't for me. I'm not actually that much of a people person. Put me in a room full of students to teach them presentation skills and I'm in my element; invite me to a professional networking evening and I'll look for any excuse to cry off.

So I gave up the sales job in 2003, went back to doing a little bit of corporate training on the side but also got to take over the running of Ajarn.com, which has now become the biggest teaching website in Thailand.

When I took Ajarn over in 2002, the guy who had started it two years earlier (who also worked at the same place as me in the educational software company) had simply got tired of managing the website and wanted to move on to other things. He also had a job offer in China.

I instantly recognised Ajarn's potential and the site grew in popularity very quickly.

I actually had experience in running websites. I wrote all the content for a website called bangkokmouth.com back when I was one of the original Thailand bloggers. There were only three or four of us blogging back then in the late 90s.

Bangkokmouth was a really popular website but it was basically a rant. A way to get things off my chest because the late 90s were not the happiest of times in my life. There was too much uncertainty. Sometimes I couldn't see a long-term future here.

But I did get a kick out of once getting on the Bangkok skytrain just after it was built and sitting next to a guy who had printed off entire sections of my Bangkokmouth website. So it was kind of weird to see my face and ramblings on printed paper. Nowadays of course, the world and his uncle is a blogger.

The most important period in my life in terms of making money was 2003 to 2007. I had taken over Ajarn.com and that was ticking along nicely but I was contacted by a friend who was working in Kuwait. He had gone there to work as the academic director for the largest training company in The Middle East. The oil was running out in Kuwait and the Kuwaitis had to get back to work and my pal said "We need to train up 10,000 security guards. Can you write a training manual for a 120-hour training programme, nothing complicated? Basic stuff like 'May I see your ID card; the toilets are over here, the office is over there'. Can you put together a course?"

I had two people in mind to help me. Both top professionals when it came to putting together training manuals so naturally I asked my contact in the dunes how much he was willing to pay? He showed me the figures and I said "we'll do it! we will most definitely do it!"

I put my small team together and we produced the book, delivered it to the company in Kuwait and they were absolutely over the moon with it. They said "it's better than we expected and you have delivered it way before deadline. How many more of these training manuals can you do?"

126

So our team of designers and materials developers and graphic artists got bigger and bigger and we just knocked out training manual after training manual (English for firefighters, English for drilling specialists, you name it) – and we all made a small fortune, at least by English teacher standards.

The training manual stuff was a once in a lifetime opportunity. I knew that from the get-go. So most of the money I squirrelled away in various low to medium-risk investments with one eye on the future. The investments haven't all done well though but I guess that's another story for another time.

I've always said you need to have 'fingers in pies' in Thailand. The smart guys have several things going on at the same time. A lot of the people I know through social media do a bit of teaching and a bit of this and a bit of that – and it can all add up to a decent monthly income.

So, since you have been here for so long, can you talk a little bit about how Thailand was different, say, in the 1990s to now?

I've always lived in Bangkok so I can only comment on living in the big city. In the 90s, there was simply less to spend your money on. Your needs were fewer – and I think this is a point people often miss when they are reminiscing about the past. There was no technology, no smartphones or laptops. There was one McDonalds on Silom Road, opposite Patpong, and you went there perhaps once a month as a special treat!

You paid for your accommodation, your daily transportation, put food in your belly and some money went on the occasional weekend trip away and that was pretty much it. It was possible to live well in Bangkok on 30 to 40 thousand baht a month. I earned about 35,000 baht a month when I was 'just a teacher' and it was more than enough but it was a different ballgame then.

Today, we're sitting here drinking 70-baht cappuccinos. Bangkok has become a lot more expensive in the last five years, particularly if you want to jump up to a 'Western' standard of living. You can still live comfortably at the Thai level but it's difficult for a Westerner to 'live like a Thai' for any extended period.

To come back to the question about how Bangkok has changed, the skytrain has made it so much easier to get around the city of course. Before the skytrain came along, when you arranged to meet someone, you would say "I'll be there sometime today!" – and you were only half-joking.

Traffic was so bad back then and it always will be I guess. Cars are a big status symbol here. People won't give them up even if it means spending hours stuck in traffic jams. You'll never get my wife on the skytrain. She hates the idea of using it to commute to and from work.

And in the good old days, let's not forget that you had to negotiate taxi fares because there were no meters in taxis. Meters were introduced around '93 or '94.

I used to always negotiate in Thai though. I studied the Thai language in England for a year before I came here to live so I was already capable of holding a decent conversation when I settled here permanently. After I came here on that initial three-week package holiday, I went back to the UK for a year with the prime objectives of saving money and studying the Thai Linguaphone course.

In the early days, I struggled with my listening comprehension because my ears were not attuned to Thai but now my listening comprehension is probably better than my speaking ability.

What else has changed? Look at all the shopping malls you have now! In the 1990s, you had Mah Boon Krong (MBK), Siam Center and that was about it. You wanted to go shopping, you went to Siam Square, whereas nowadays there is a swanky shopping mall in every suburb of the city. Has this been a change for good, this Westernisation of Bangkok? – or has Bangkok lost a lot of its character and what made the city uniquely Thai? I can understand both sides of the argument.

Overall, Bangkok is a better place to live now compared to back then. There are more things to do for a foreigner – cinemas, malls, coffee shops and so on but sometimes you get up on a Saturday morning and look for something to do and it's very often the shopping mall. I just become so bored of walking around them without any real objective other than to window-shop.

Yes, Bangkok has become a nicer place to live and an easier city to get around in but it's become more expensive as a result.

What were your first impressions of Thailand?

I'll never forget that first ever day in Thailand and it's a great shame you can never really recapture the magic.

I stayed at some run-down, three-star joint on Sukhumvit Soi 15. The three weeks I spent here were just unbelievable. I think to come to Thailand for a package holiday is one of the greatest travel experiences you can imagine. I never ate anything for five days! I was just surviving on adrenaline. Bangkok just blew my mind!

In 1990, to come to Thailand was a big deal. It was exotic, it was a dreamscape and mystical culture on the other side of the world.

Nowadays you go back to England for a family visit and every new neighbour you chat with has been here, many of them several times.

What were the main challenges in setting up your life here and were there any pleasant surprises?

Finding a nice place to live was tough because when you haven't got a car and you don't speak the Thai language that fluently, you're totally reliant on Thai friends that you might have made. You hadn't got the skytrain to get you around either so you would have to choose a neighbourhood, strap on your best walking shoes and walk up and down sois looking for apartments to rent. It was bloody exhausting.

I've lived in some really crappy places though. There wasn't a lot of choice back then. What apartments were available (especially to those on a budget) were often in the 3,000 baht a month range and attracted a very working-class Thai resident, so you had problems with neighbours playing loud music, people cooking in the corridor, couples fighting, card games and all sorts. You didn't have so many apartments in the 7,000 to 10,000-baht range, as you do now, so you lived at the lower end of the housing market and put up with all the social problems that go with it.

I can't think of much else to be honest, in terms of challenges or problems, which is probably quite positive really. I have mellowed though over the years and I have to be honest, having a bit of money behind you certainly helps.

Do you think that the reason you cannot think of many challenges was because meeting your wife made a big difference because she could manage those day to day interactions or she could say complicated things in Thai on your behalf?

Truthfully, I hate my wife helping me. I always try and manage most day to day situations myself and rely on my own spoken Thai.

Sometimes a Thai waitress for example will say "yêe sìp hâa" and my wife will turn to me and say "25" as though I might somehow have lived here for almost three decades and still not know my numbers. I suppose she's just trying to be helpful.

Sure, but it often helps having a Thai wife in certain situations such as when sorting out your visa at immigration...

The annual visa renewals are often a nightmare here. I'm sure you've heard that from everyone else. It's a constant source of frustration for foreign expats.

I've lived here 27 years. I've been married to the same Thai woman for fourteen of those years. She's got a great job and comes from a very respected family and yet my visa renewal this year was the most difficult one yet. I won't go into the gory details but trust me it was difficult.

Immigration have the power of God, though don't they? It's their country. We are only ever guests. I can have a Thai wife and a dozen half-Thai kids, I'm still only ever a guest. And with one stroke of a pen, they can kick you out of the country at any time.

My wife rarely accompanies me to immigration but she's of the opinion that civil servants are there to serve the public and we are paying for the service. So she tends to gets right in their face while I stand awkwardly in the background. She's not nasty to them or anything but she's very straight-to-the-point. She doesn't suffer fools or put up with any bureaucratic nonsense.

And that's probably why I prefer to go on my own :)

I used to do a one-year visa extension based on marriage to a Thai woman but now I'm over fifty, I get the one-year 'retirement visa'. The retirement visa is a lot easier to apply for and requires far less paperwork.

I'm one of life's great over-thinkers though. Even though I've done the annual visa renewal many times, I still worry about what could go wrong (but in truth rarely does)

Talking about getting things done here, how do you compare getting things done here compared to back home?

There's always a place nearby to get something done here. In the UK, it can be difficult to find somewhere to get even basic tasks accomplished. I only go back to the UK for holidays so I never really need to run errands but my good friend moved back to England a couple of years ago (after living in Thailand for fifteen years) and he said "nah, trust me, Thailand is much, much easier to deal with".

Why do you think foreigners love Thailand so much?

I just think it's such a 'go-with-the-flow' country. I feel so safe here – so why ever contemplate going back to England to live.

I may be over-cautious but when I'm in the UK, perhaps in a city centre pub or walking the streets late at night, I always feel like something is going to kick off or trouble is never far away. England's become quite a depressingly violent society. It was never like that back in the eighties. They were good times!

People talk about Bangkok being a dangerous city. That is complete rubbish. I have never ever felt in danger here. You just feel like you are surrounded by people who are looking for a peaceful life. I think that's what I love most about Thailand.

What have you learnt about life in Thailand that you did not know in the first few years? What has changed in terms of your development as a resident of Thailand?

Living here is very different to coming for a holiday. You need to get that straight.

Marry a good Thai woman, someone who is going to make a good partner and most importantly, not be a financial burden. You don't even have to be madly in love. You need someone who is going to be your soul-mate and best friend. I definitely found one!

Learn to speak Thai! It sounds like obvious advice but so many foreigners live here for donkey's years and can barely put a sentence together. Life is a lot more fun here when you can speak the language and no one takes the piss out of you either.

Getting to a decent level of spoken Thai can be a tough old slog. It takes motivation and self-discipline. When I first came here, my Thai improved steadily for the first three years, I reached a certain level and then bang! – for the next 20 years, I did absolutely no study at all and my Thai just stagnated. And then one day I got into a taxi and had the usual chat with the taxi driver and just as I was about to get out, he said to me "Considering you've been here 23 years, your Thai is not very good is it?!"

I watched him drive away and I thought 'you're absolutely right mate'. That day I got back home and signed up for an on-line course. Now I continue to do my half hour of Thai study a day, religiously. Even if I can't get in front of a computer, I'll have conversations with myself about what's going on around me.

So, over the last three years, my Thai has improved exponentially and my life has become more fun as a result. My advice – learn Thai and be serious about it. It pays off, it really pays off.

What are your top tips for settling here successfully and what are your top things to not do?

I do like the advice I have heard from so many people, which is make your money in another country and come here to Thailand and retire. I think that's sound advice.

I had a good friend back in Birmingham called Tony. Tony was a milkman and like me, he loved Thailand. It was his dream to live here for the rest of his days.

Tony was a good fifteen to twenty years older than me and his employer had offered him voluntary redundancy so he took his lump sum and a golden handshake – about 13 to £14,000 – and came over here.

That kind of money, although considerable back then, wasn't really enough to last Tony the rest of his life. He needed to do something to gain a bit of income but all he knew was how to deliver milk.

Eventually he decided to sink most of his redundancy pay-off into a 50% share of a bar down in Hua Hin. But Tony had no social skills. He didn't know how to engage customers and keep them glued to a bar-stool. He had none of the skills that a pub landlord really needed. The customers naturally drifted away and the business went rapidly downhill and closed. The last I heard Tony was back in London and sleeping on a friend's sofa. The money was all gone.

Tony should have made his money in England and retired here to do nothing except perhaps sit on the other side of the bar.

With Thailand, you've got to have a plan if you're going to make a success of it out here. Thailand can be brutally unforgiving if you find yourself down on your luck with nothing in the bank and a visa that's about to expire.

So in terms of what not to do, I guess not having a plan can put you on a very slippery slope if you're not careful.

To what extent have you integrated into Thai society?

I've always been a loner. I was a loner when I lived in England. I am always happiest when I am at home alone (or with my wife).

I've never seriously mixed with Thai people. I've picked up a few Thai friends along the way – folks living in the same apartment building or people that I have taught English to. But they have never become lifelong friends. That's probably my fault as much as theirs.

I read someone who said that you can live in Thailand 30, 40 or 50 years without ever making one true Thai friend and I happen to believe that.

I think Thais are culturally too different to Westerners. Even with my wife, we sometimes disagree and it is a cultural issue but with Thai friends, you can't be as honest with them. The conversation is always going to be superficial, flowery or rather dull. Can you eat spicy food? How about Chiang Mai?

My wife and I had a house built just outside Bangkok. My mother-in-law actually lives next door but sometimes I can go a week without seeing her. She's a wonderful lady. She's given me so much support and help over the years. She's one of the few Thai people I have a decent conversation with. She doesn't speak any English so I have to communicate fully in Thai and I always find it a little fearsome – she's very middle class so I'm always careful I don't pronounce a word with the wrong tone when I speak to her.

My wife's sister is also a great person and she was actually my Thai teacher for a while.

What do you think of other expats in Thailand? Do you consciously try to hang out with them or do you try to avoid them?

I have nothing against them but I don't actively seek out other ex-pats. I have no interest in sitting in Sukhumvit bars and trading war stories. Most of my expat friends are people on-line who I've never met. I probably prefer to keep it that way.

When you are with your wife and you go to places like the hospital or a restaurant or whatever, do people speak to you directly or do they treat you as...?

That drives me mad.

When I ask a person something in Thai and they immediately look at my wife for a 'correct translation'.

My wife doesn't stand for any of that nonsense though and she will say 'he's speaking in Thai to you. Don't you understand him?'

Any other scary, funny, embarrassing or dangerous anecdotes in Thailand?

Well, I've been in prison here. I was put in the immigration detention centre for five days back in the early 90's for overstaying a visa. I was living in a dodgy area of Yannawa near Lumpini Park at the time and was getting by on visa runs. In this one particular instance, my visa was about to expire but I had booked a flight to Singapore the day after and it was my intention to just pay a one-day overstay at Bangkok Airport. It's what many people did at the time if they had let their visas run out by a day or two.

So, Saturday morning, I was just about to go to work at the gemstone company and there was a knock on the door. I opened it to find half a dozen plain-clothed immigration officers doing a random passport check of all foreigners in the building. They looked at my passport and immediately noticed I had overstayed by one day. I showed them my flight ticket to Singapore but they weren't interested. It was my fault. You can pay an overstay fine at Bangkok Airport but you are in trouble if immigration police catch you first, as they did on this very unfortunate morning. So I ended up in the detention centre for five hot, sweaty days with about two hundred other prisoners in a large holding room designed for half that number. It was so cramped that when half the prisoners wanted to sleep, the other half had to stand up. So we all slept on a sort of rotation system.

It goes without saying that I've never overstayed a visa since.

Over the years, my parents have been to visit me eight times in Thailand but unfortunately, they are not healthy enough to make the long journey anymore but the second time they came, I took them to see The Erawan Shrine and a few other places in the Chidlom area.

Showing people around Bangkok is always an arduous task and I was hot and tired and my mum and dad were flagging as well. I suggested getting a tuk-tuk back to their hotel and having a relaxing afternoon around the pool or something.

I then made the stupid mistake of approaching a mean-looking tuk-tuk driver for a ride back to their hotel and predictably he quoted us some grossly inflated fare. I just refused the offer and laughed in his face. Then as we pulled away in another taxi that I had flagged down, I gave our tuk-tuk driver friend the middle finger. It was a heat-of-the-moment, stupid thing to do and I regretted it instantly.

Anyway, we've driven down Wittayu Road and just about to turn the corner by Lumpini Park. To my horror, I realised that the angry tuk-tuk driver (furious at being given the middle finger) had jumped into his vehicle, sped to overtake us, and was now flagging our driver to stop. I ended up with a couple of slaps around the head while my Mom and Dad went into panic mode over their son being physically assaulted in broad daylight. I gave the tuk-tuk driver my best wâai, apologised and it thankfully diffused the situation.

Totally my fault. I made a Thai lose face and when Thais reach breaking point, it's a case of stand back and light the blue touch paper.

It's funny really but apart from that one incident a long time ago, I never seem to have the problems with taxi drivers that other expats seem to have. I don't know if it is because of the area I live in now but I think the Bangkok cabbies are a great bunch of lads. I enjoy the banter with them and generally I find them to be courteous and polite.

Would you go back to the UK to live?

To live? No, I don't think so. I do love going back to England for an annual visit but I find it rather grey these days. England has moved on. Times have changed. It's not the place that I left behind in 1990. When I go back, people sometimes ask me if England still feels like home and my response is 'no, it's like a foreign country where I just happen to know the language'

I wouldn't want to move to another completely new country either. I've invested so much time in Thailand. I've become savvy about the culture, I've learned the language to a decent level. I don't fancy the thought of moving somewhere and starting all over again. There's probably not even a conversation in it because my wife would not move away from her family anyway.

Interview 6 – The Entrepreneur

Karsten Aicholz is a half-German, half-English, pro-gamer turned entrepreneur who has set up several very successful businesses in Thailand. He is also the owner of Thailand Starter Kit, possibly the best site to check for specific information, once you have read this book.

Why did you come to Thailand?

I originally co-founded a company in Germany that mostly catered to international clients. About a year in, we figured it wasn't the best location in terms of talent, cost, and other factors. My business partner at the time had done an internship in Bangkok and when we were looking for a place to move our company to, Thailand was an option that offered good business conditions, low costs and at the same time an acceptable lifestyle (a.k.a. not in the middle of the Turkish desert)

Had you visited Thailand before and if so, how many times?

Once, for a weekend trip while I was traveling with friends who worked with Lufthansa German Airlines at the time. So yes, I went to Thailand for a single weekend from Germany (thanks to Lufthansa's cheap employee tickets) and that was all I've seen of the place before I committed to moving here. I did travel however to India and Japan before and figured that it would be roughly somewhere between the two – not only geographically speaking. There's only so much you know and are aware of at the tender age of 23, so I'm trying not to be too hard on myself about the decision-making process :).

What were your first impressions when you did move here and how did they compare to being here as a tourist?

I didn't have much of a chance to form an impression as a tourist, as I hardly spend a full 72 hours in the country as an actual tourist.

What were the main challenges and what were the main pleasant surprises of living here?

Settling in in Thailand takes time, but eventually it'll work out if you dot your 'i's and cross your 't's. In terms of business and work it required a lot of diligence and persistence but I felt that was more about putting in the necessary legwork than overcoming massive obstacles that we had no idea how to tackle.

I did ask one question on a popular expat forum, but when the answer was 'that's something you should have researched before moving here', I pretty much gave up on that as a source of help. In the end my business partner and I had to mostly rely on ourselves as the professional service providers, lawyers and consultants we encountered seemed to have little experience dealing with tech companies back then. That has changed in the 12 years since I moved here.

Richard McCully & Stephen Saad

What have you learnt about Thailand life that you did not know in the first few months?

I came here when I was very young and professionally inexperienced, so I feel a lot of lessons I picked up were not necessarily 'Thailand lessons' but more 'life lessons'. If I'd sum it up:

If things get done well, I shouldn't worry about them getting done in my specific way.

I need to stop sweating the small stuff and accept little things will go wrong while I focus on the big ones.

Understand that how people perceive themselves doesn't necessarily correlate to how I perceive them.

Since Thailand and especially Bangkok have continued to grow and develop at a fast pace, I feel the place is more similar to other large cities and countries in the world than it ever was before. This makes life probably less exotic and more similar to other locations, but also less stressful.

What are your top tips for settling here successfully? Conversely, what are your top tips on what to not do?

Based on the reader e-mails I receive, the single best 'universal' advice I feel comfortable sharing is to assume positive intent on behalf of the people you encounter. Yes, you read about all the Thailand scams on the internet. It's a good thing you've been warned. But only use that awareness in a passive way. If you treat everyone like a potential scammer, only actual scammers will be willing to put up with you. This goes for both, business and personal interactions.

To what extent have you integrated into Thai society?

I speak and read Thai to a satisfactory level. Culturally though I feel there are some gaps that'll result in most of my friends usually being fellow expats. I used to have way more Thai friends in the first few years of living here. Over time I just felt at home in a different crowd which has also influenced my social circle. I'm definitely 'an expat', but it's something I enjoy being rather than resent. My fellow expat friends are integrated to different degrees and I see them happy at different degrees.

What have you learned about Thai culture, values and social practices that may be different to people back home?

Relationships and harmony are more treasured in Thailand than back home. If you can find value in that behaviour, it makes it easier to understand, accept and work with it. If you consider that to be dishonest or irrational, you'll have a much harder time to navigate that.

Have you found it difficult to relate to your partner's friends and social circle?

It's mixed. We have social circles where we 100% overlap – meaning on the occasions we meet those friends we meet them together. Then she has her own circle of friends which I rarely join and likewise I have my own friends who I usually meet on my own. I consider that a healthy setup. It's nice to have mutual friends, but also nice to have your own crew and not do everything all the time with your partner.

Tell us a little bit more about Thailand Starter Kit.

thailandstarterkit.com is a website that provides free in-depth guides for tourists, expats, entrepreneurs and investors who are interested in coming to Thailand. Meant to help with figuring out the practical stuff, it skips the coffee shops, tourist attractions and foodie recommendations and instead provides practical pointers on travel insurance, renting an apartment, starting a company and handling banking matters.

How did you find setting up a business here in Thailand? What were some of the challenges?

Thailand is a lot more bureaucratic than Germany. Back in Germany everyone was talking about how much paperwork things require and how bureaucratic it is. Going to another country means getting a lot more perspective, not only on the world but also on your own home. It certainly put things back home into perspective. I wish there was a digital and legal infrastructure that would allow for more automation.

What other resources would you recommend potential expats to look at?

I've set up a Q&A database that helps people find answers to a wide range of questions and issues faced by tourists, expats and foreign business owners in Thailand. It also allows you to ask your own questions and have them answered by experts. The entire thing is free of charge and available at: questions. thailandstarterkit.com

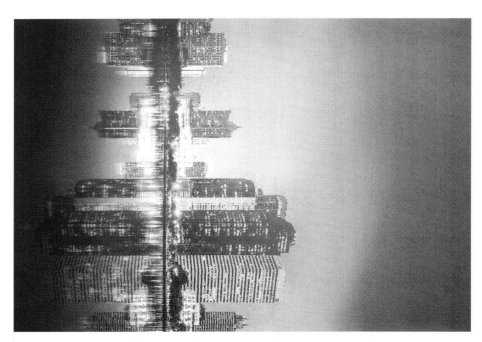

Lifestyle in Thailand

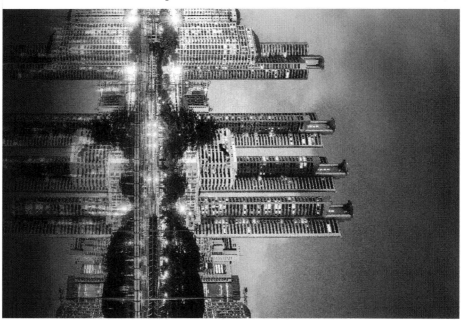

Before we begin

Now that we have covered the main practical aspects of setting up your life in Thailand, let's look at some of the subtler aspects of life here as well as cover some points not mentioned in the first few chapters. This section – consisting of several chapters – gives you more of a well-rounded flavour of day-to-day life in Thailand, focusing more on social interactions, cultural practices and suchlike. By definition, this section is more opinion-based than the first section of the book and, as mentioned in the Preface, where possible, descriptions of frustrations are balanced with explanations of why things are the way they are in order to provide a balanced view of life here. However, we will also not falsely try to downplay the bemusement expats may feel living here in an attempt to convince readers that everything is down to their lack of understanding of Thailand.

Some further notes before we begin – as we both live in Bangkok, our perspective is based more on life in the capital, although I have lived in Mûak Lèk, Saraburi for a few years so have a pretty good idea of small town life in Thailand. Neither of us, however, is retired and living in Phuket and neither of us has been a backpacker travelling through Thailand so if you are from one of these backgrounds, our comments may not be in line with your experiences in Thailand.

This section is mainly written by me (Steve) with input from Richard while, as mentioned previously, the first few chapters are the other way around.

Finally, it is worth mentioning what this section is not – it is not intended to be an essay on Thai cultural customs and a lesson on needing to respect Thai culture. Obviously, we hope you are already doing so but we do not intend to use this book as a vehicle to preach Thai culture and there are many books, including pretty much any decent guide to Thailand, that cover all the basics. Having said that though, the next chapter contains a list, which is by no means comprehensive, of some well-known cultural and social rules and etiquettes that you probably already know but worth covering before we get onto more interesting matters.

Richard McCully & Stephen Saad

Some cultural preliminaries

FEET

Don't point feet directly at people. Feet are not only the physically lowest part of your body but also in terms of respect or cleanliness (even if you have washed your feet!). In line with this, do not enter someone's house with your shoes on (even if you think they are clean), especially if you see shoes at the entrance taken off by other people. Obviously, you should also remove your shoes before going into the inner sections of a Thai temple and again, it will be obvious as you will see lots of shoes at the entrance. Some shops, hairdressers and Thai spas, for example, also prefer you to take your shoes off first, as is preferred sometimes when you want to view the showroom at a new condo sales office.

HEAD

Conversely, the head is not only the physically highest part of the body but also the most spiritually precious. Don't touch people's heads you don't know. And obviously don't touch people's heads with your feet! (Not sure how you would be in a position to do so).

TOUCHING

Thai people do not shake hands (they wâai) and they do not hug and they certainly do not kiss to say hello. Unless you are with very internationalised Thai people, the vast majority will not touch someone they do not know. Even when Thais know each other they rarely touch so for example, somewhat comically, when two friends (more so if they are from opposite sexes) have not seen each other for a long time, they will run up to each other and do all the things Western people would do apart from actually hug. Try to visualise it.

PDA

Public displays of affection are pretty much a no-no. Thai society is relaxing and becoming ever so slightly more influenced by Western concepts with every passing year but still, you will rarely see two lovers do more than hold hands in public and even that can be considered to be a little unnecessary by elders in society.

MONKS

Monks are on a higher social (and spiritual) status than ordinary citizens, which is why people sit on the floor when in front of monks, so that they are physically lower. Similarly, people will show respect to elders (parents and especially grandparents) by remaining humble in their body language and physically lower i.e. a woman going back home to see her parents would not sit on a sofa while her mum or grandmother is sitting on the floor. Women should not, under any circumstances, touch a monk, although, again, not sure how this situation would arise but anyway, ladies, you have been warned!

MONARCHY, RELIGION AND POLITICS

Thais love their monarch and the royal family and you should not, under any circumstances, comment on the royal family or anything to do with the King. In fact, it is best if you refrain from saying anything on this matter, even if positive. Just avoid it or it could be the worst mistake you will ever make in your life. If in doubt, do your research on past incidents. Note, this warning extends to religious and political matters too – do not defile (or do something that could be interpreted as defiling) religious monuments or artefacts of worship and steer clear of making comments on politics. Quite frankly, these are all common sense but somehow, some visitors seem to not have any, and throw around all kinds of opinions in public, having limited experience of Thailand and only as a tourist and so, unsurprisingly, this is not well-received. So, again, just restrain yourself and steer clear.

INDIRECTNESS

This is an extensive topic and beyond the scope of this book but in summary, Thai culture teaches people to respect others' opinions and so not be too strong or direct in order to be polite and save others' face. I will, however, discuss later in this chapter how this so-called indirectness manifests itself in social situations from the perspective of an expat. It is not that different to Brits, who use indirectness to be polite (or to be viciously sarcastic / contemptuous).

CALMNESS

Similarly, Thai culture is all about being calm. From a Western point of view, this might be all very well but many situations require a bit of direct talk and a bit of passion or even anger but that is not the Thai way.

ADDRESSING PEOPLE

Finally in this section, in Thailand, you address people formally by their first name prefixed by 'Koon' and this is the equivalent of saying "Mr…" or "Mrs…" in English. Surnames are used rarely, usually only, for example, when announcing people to a group but generally, even in meetings and so on, people refer to each other with their first names. So this would be the equivalent of "Mrs. Pam" or "Mr. David". The reason for this is probably the length of surnames in Thailand, which are often (but not always) longer than the often still quite long forenames but I have not researched the actual origin of the practice.

Almost everyone in Thailand also has a much shorter, almost always one syllable, nickname. Again, the reason is that forenames are quite long and when people have established a connection, they tell each other their nicknames and refer to each other using these nicknames from that point on in all situations apart from formal situations where they would revert to forenames. You can also go for a halfway house, as many do, when you want to add a touch of formality and politeness to a conversation that may be in an informal, social context or even a semi-formal context e.g. when addressing a tour guide or a condo salesperson or an acquaintance or neighbour who you have got to know. You can say "Koon Mŏo" or "Koon Ploy" or suchlike, which uses the nickname but also uses the formal prefix to make it more polite

As I said, I could carry on with this list but hopefully you have already done your research on Thailand and know all of these points so let's move onto some perspectives of expat life in Thailand. But before we do, let me quickly mention one point regarding what to be aware of when bringing your Western culture in an Eastern environment.

A CONSPICUOUS FOREIGNER

As a Westerner, which can be taken to mean in this case, a Caucasian foreigner, you are always being noticed. This is not because of some sinister plot by Thai people to spy on you, nothing of the kind; Westerners are generally physically bigger, white-skinned and often louder and (obviously) usually speak English in Thailand. When you put all these together, you begin to understand that Westerners' actions and words in Thailand attract attention without any particular effort by Thai people to do so. It is also true to say that many Thai people are 'curious' about foreigners and many are keen to understand alternative cultures, ways of speaking etc. So, given all of this, the poor Westerner attracts a lot of attention in Thailand…often without his knowledge. Why? Because Thai people are far subtler than Westerners and can observe Westerners without giving any physical indication of doing so.

Asian expats e.g. Japanese, Chinese, Indians and so on also do get noticed but not to the same extent. Japanese people are absolutely loved in Thailand because of obvious reasons – they are well-behaved, quiet, humble, clean, have high standards in everything they do, usually come to Thailand to take up high value jobs, always pay rent on time, often learn to speak Thai, are respectful and so on. The attitude toward Chinese and Indian incomers may not be quite so positive but both of these have an element of 'Asian-ness' that allows them to blend in better.

So what can you do to attract less attention? Well, in short, you could try picking up some of the characteristics of the Japanese. If that is too outrageous a suggestion, maybe try these for starters.

- Try to be more self-aware. It is always amazing to me how self-unaware many people from Western cultures are when they come to a country with an Eastern culture. This extends to how you talk, your body language, how loud you are, how considerate you are of others in the group etc. In short, you are in their country, so you need to adapt, not they.
- Do not – as I did in my early days – discuss your weekend activities in the office on a Monday if those activities might, in any way, be open to judgement…you know what I mean. To be honest, this includes going to Pattaya (even if it was for non-sexual purposes) or the Full Moon Party or simply getting drunk with your mates – try to refrain from revealing these things to your colleagues or any Thai people from whom you want respect. The moment you mention any of these things, you will automatically and subconsciously be thought of as "another typical farang".

Similarly, do not take phone calls or even check messages from girls in front of your colleagues or anyone from whom you want respect.

- Try to not dress inappropriately when in Thailand. If you look around, you will see that Thai people do not wear flip-flops, shorts and t-shirts all the time, especially badly fitting, cheap looking ones, especially not when going to more upmarket malls such as Paragon or Emporium. Nobody is suggesting you walk around Thailand in a three-piece suit but you cannot blame people for silently judging you if you turn up totally underdressed to a social gathering or whatever. Over a century ago, Thais went to the UK and other Western countries and brought back new standards of dress and social etiquette from the West. So, whether you like it or not, you are a representative of the West – countries that Thailand still respects to this day as advanced nations of the world.

- You may not care about all this but when you try to ask out the pretty girl in the office and she keeps rejecting you, the chances are it is because she and others have been gossiping about you for weeks and months already. While they bear no malice toward you whatsoever, they would rather have nothing to do with you because they assume you spend your time drinking and / or go with 'ladies of the night' on weekends, you are a player, you would embarrass them in front of their parents, you dress badly and they do not want to be seen with you in public (because other Thais may assume they are a call girl or just 'easy'). To top it all, you are an English teacher on a low salary. Yes, it might be unfair but it is in your power to not give these impressions in the first place. Try to differentiate between different social situations and be a little more self-aware, especially if you work in a respectable office and surroundings.

First Impressions

So, you have been to Thailand previously once or twice for holidays and now have been sent here for work or have chosen to relocate to Thailand, perhaps to take a career break or teach English maybe, or you may have come to start a business or run a bar, for example. What are your first impressions?

Well, if it is Bangkok or one of the other big cities, it is certainly not the image of Thailand that was maybe in your head or, more likely, in your friends' heads back home. Before you left, you probably had lots of conversations about how envious your friends were about you going off to Thailand while they have to carry on slogging away at their job and their boring life while you are off to an exotic country and so on and so on. Note, by the way, if you are a retiree and reasonably well-off and moving to Phuket, planning to stay in a luxury villa and spend most days chilling by the beach, then you probably are having exactly the kind of life that your friends back home would envy but this section is more about those less fortunate. Similarly, if you are in Thailand as a backpacker, you may well be living an amazing life seeing exotic cultures and so on but you are not really an expat, right?

So, for most of the 'average' working age expats, real life in Thailand is certainly not chilling on beaches and working on your tan. Bangkok (which I will mainly focus on but many of the comments apply to other big cities) is a busy, bustling metropolis and like any big city in any country, life is hectic and weekends are used to relax before you start another week of the daily grind. Provincial life i.e. outside Bangkok in the surrounding provinces or in the North East Isaan provinces, is a lot quieter and so, again, not too different to back home in terms of pace of life. If you have only been to Phuket or other Thai islands for holidays and now thinking of moving to Thailand for 'proper' work (i.e. not as a diving instructor or running a beach bar), at least come with your eyes wide open – the country might be a tropical paradise but five days of every week, you will be going in to the office in rush hour, in a busy, hot and humid, congested city.

Sights, sounds and smells

As you settle in to your first few days of real life in Thailand, you will notice sights, sounds and smells that will remind you that you are in Thailand and not back home. From the pavements lined with food vendors to the 'toot-toot' of mobile fruit carts to the incredibly loud wheeze of the older style buses when the driver pulls away, not to mention the clouds of exhaust fumes from the diesel engines, Bangkok can be a heady mixture of sensory experiences.

If you spend any time walking around you will pick up the scent of pine-apples and other fruit being freshly cut and sold in roadside stalls; the most exotic smell you will encounter is the durian, whether by the roadside or often in the promotion section right at the front entrance of Tesco and other super-markets. It is hard to describe but you will know it when you have walked past and gotten a whiff. Add in the smells of food being cooked in roadside restaurants, meat being barbecued by mobile Thai style kebab vendors and fish sauce scents wafting in the air from sôm-dtum (the famous Thai papaya salad) being prepared, the walk to the skytrain station and back home is a truly exotic sensation for Westerners.

And I have not yet talked about the 'Bangkok smell'. If you spend any time walking around you will undoubtedly get a whiff now and then of the drains underneath the streets. Of course, if you spend all your time flitting between your five-star condo and Siam Paragon in taxis, you will not know what I am talking about and if you are of a delicate persuasion, probably all for the best. But for the rest of you, this smell is a source of comfort and when you know you are back in the city you love.

While it might seem I am describing these first impressions in a negative way, that is certainly not the case. I hope most of you will see these new sights, sounds and smells as less of an assault on your senses and more as what makes life in Thailand interesting and colourful. When I came to Thailand for holidays, these are the things that stayed with me and made even the most mundane journeys interesting and exciting and exotic. Bear in mind though, expat life is not a holiday so a tricky walk back home along a narrow, broken pavement with power cables hanging off poles, motorbikes driving along the pavement to take a shortcut, barbecue smells going on your work shirt and so on may not be your idea of fun. But for most people who move here, it remains the best thing about everyday life in Thailand and life back home seems almost bland in comparison – if you're from the UK and used to trudging home from the Tube station in the rain in near darkness, you will love Bangkok's streets for their imperfections and seeming disorder and would not have it any other way.

So now you have a taster of what life in Thailand is like let's continue to explore what it feels like here day to day. While many books can describe this country, few do it in terms of what it feels like to live here from a Western expat's perspective. But before we get into that, I need to take a slight diversion into a breakdown of the types of expat who live here in order to place the comments on what it feels like to live here in sufficient context.

WHICH CATEGORY OF EXPAT ARE YOU?

By no means exhaustive, not in any order and definitely a generalisation, these are some of the more prominent types of expat that come to Thailand:

1. Retirees – as mentioned before, some of these are having a very relaxed time living out their retirement in luxury in Phuket and other Thai islands. Many, of course, are in Bangkok and Chiang Mai too while there are quite a few in the Isaan provinces, often married to a Thai girl they met in Bangkok.
2. Backpackers and students – not really expats but often long term or frequent visitors; gap – year students and post-graduation young people often earn money by tutoring and teaching English and spend weekends making short trips and then taking longer breaks when they have got enough money together.
3. CEOs and other professionals – these are often executives or senior teachers who have been transferred over to Thailand.
4. English teachers – a significant share of the expat scene, these are generally younger expats who want to spend a few years, at least, in Asia.
5. Entrepreneurs – a more recent category, these are the guys usually working out of cafes or co-working spaces, developing apps or other digital things that I barely understand.
6. The lovesick – these can be either those Westerners who have fallen in love with a girl from their last trip to Thailand or those who want to take things further with the girl who worked in the same company as the one which sent the foreigner to Thailand on a business trip. And to an extent, includes those foreigners who simply fell in love with Thailand full stop.

The reason for mentioning these categories of foreigners is that when we continue the discussion on what Thailand feels like to live in, it very much depends on which category of expat you are. So, if you are here for a couple of years to head up a department in an international company or school, you will probably have relocation assistance, help (either from HR or some other nominated individual in the company) with applying for visas and work permits etc. and getting a condo and so on. You may have transport arranged for you e.g. a van to pick up and take you to school or to your office or you may even get a driver. Or, alternatively, you may be placed in a very central condo, very close to the Skytrain or MRT station from where you can get to work fairly simply and you do not have to face the inconveniences most Thai people have to face in their daily lives.

You may well get some Thai lessons arranged by your company and although you started off keen, after a while you realised you would actually have to put in a lot of effort to speak Thai correctly and by the end of the lessons, you can basically mispronounce hello, thank you and sorry. You have no real need to speak Thai as everyone at your company or school speaks really good English and, on the weekends, you tend to hang out with your family and other expat friends or colleagues anyway. Most Thai people you deal with are in a customer / seller situation and again, in the big cities, they usually speak enough English for you to get by.

While the above characterisation is true of several of the categories of expats above, other categories have a very different entry into Thailand. For example, retirees who have found a Thai girlfriend or workers in companies who offer some initial relocation assistance but then expect the foreigner to manage his life by himself, often when the foreigner establishes a friendship or relationship with a Thai woman, which almost always is the case.

In summary, your perspective of Thailand and life in Thailand very much depends on to what extent you live your life as a Thai person of similar social standing would do. If you have to handle all your own affairs and have to manage your life yourself, you have a set of challenges that the expats in blissful ignorance never have to face.

When I first moved to Thailand, all my visas, work permits and other government dealings were handled by HR who went with me from Saraburi to Bangkok and spoke on my behalf and filled in the forms on my behalf and so on. My room was arranged for me and bills and cleaning expenses were debited from my salary and food was available at the office canteen and I could take a van to Bangkok on the weekend, party hard, barely need to speak Thai (unless I wanted to, which in my case I actually did) and get a van back to Saraburi on Sunday evening.

If I ever had any questions, I could ask my Thai colleagues who all spoke good English and were happy to advise. If I could not explain where I wanted to go to the taxi driver I could call up one of them and ask them to speak to the driver and explain.

Many expats and many expat couples remain in mostly this mode throughout their stay in Thailand and there is absolutely nothing wrong with this. Indeed, in some ways, this is the best of both worlds – you do not have to deal with real life, you do not learn the language to any meaningful level while you continue to live in Thailand as an expat in much the same way you did as a tourist and it feels like an extension of your holiday.

On the other hand, I and many other foreigners, quickly went from an initial few weeks of being hand-held and feeling like a customer in every single social interaction to wanting to live a normal life – getting to work myself, learning the language and speaking to people in Thai and not as a customer or enquirer only, sorting out where to live, getting the air conditioning fixed, buying property, walking to the Skytrain station in the heat and so on...basically, real life. And in my case, I can say for sure that if it was not for meeting my Thai wife and learning the language myself, I would have found it quite difficult and that is an understatement. Generally, foreigners go from being helped with relocation and settling in by their employer, to meeting a girl, who becomes a girlfriend and then takes over and manages those interactions where she can speak in Thai and make things easier.

So, having said all this, let's return to what it feels like to live in Thailand.

WEATHER

You obviously know it is hot over here and pretty humid but what does this actually mean in terms of your day to day life? When you come to Thailand for a holiday you probably love the hot weather. You spend time on the beach and at the bar by the beach and every day is a shorts and t-shirt day and life is good. When you are here for work or business and need to manage daily life in over 30°C heat every day with average humidity of well over 50%, you might just think differently!

Having said this, in my observation of Westerners (and in this particular context, I really mean Caucasian foreigners), they rarely seem to be bothered by the weather and indeed, many like it. So, if you like roasting in the sunshine in your shorts and singlet, well, Thailand's the place for you.

Generally, the weather cools down and becomes less humid in the 'winter' and may even drop below 25°C during the day and obviously, in Chiang Mai and other northern provinces, it is quite a bit cooler and is more like spring back in the UK. The humidity is pretty uncomfortable in the warmer months from March to October and again, more so in Bangkok where it adds to an already congested feeling, often with no breeze blowing in the daytime. The air is thick and heavy, which you notice immediately when you step from an air-conditioned room into a room where you have left the window open, or out of the mall to the taxi stand outside.

So, what this all means in practice is if you have to walk more than 10 minutes outdoors e.g. to the train station, you will sweat considerably, which can be a bit of a downer if you just had a shower before leaving. You will spend most of your time indoors and time your trips outdoors for the evening when things are marginally cooler and slightly less humid.

By the way, these are all the kinds of mitigating actions Thai people take, who find the heat and humidity just as much of a pain as you may do and, in some ways, even more so. It is easy to assume that Thai people are used to the heat and are therefore not that bothered. They are. A lot! As the anecdote below highlights, Thai people integrate coping with the weather into their daily lives because it is part of their life and there is no avoiding it.

So, if you notice, when standing by the road hailing a taxi, Thai people will always walk over to stand in the shade; some people (usually women who are fair skinned) will almost run to get under a tree or whatever because they do not want to get the sun's rays on their skin and get tanned. (Generally speaking, being fair-skinned is seen as desirable and even an indicator or social class, as compared to the darker southern and north-eastern Thais. Attitudes are slowly changing though). If you're walking along the road in daytime with your Thai girlfriend and she suddenly cuts right across you, now you know why!

I had just arrived in Bangkok at Don Mueang Airport (there was no Suvarnabhumi back then), having accepted the offer to transfer to the Thai office of my company and take up a role here. The (Thai) General Manager and her (British) boyfriend – also an employee in the same company – picked me up in their car to take me to my hotel. On a typically hot day, the sun was blazing through the windscreen and competing with the air-conditioning to determine the environment inside the car.

Given all this, when the manager, who was wearing a sleeveless top, exclaimed "Ooi...ráaawwn!", I wasn't surprised. I had learnt that word while studying Thai by going through my books at home in London and recognised the Thai word for 'hot'. What I was surprised about, to say the least, was what happened next.

The manager asked her boyfriend to pass her her jacket from the back seat next to me and she put it on...because it was so hot! As crazy as this sounds, this makes perfect sense from a Thai perspective as I would understand later on – sure they are hot but they certainly do not want to be any darker (or look older from having skin that looks aged from exposure to the sun) and so they need to cover up in the heat!

You probably have not noticed but if you pay attention you will see that, actually, many Thai people do not wear shorts and t-shirts. Women (who care more about their skin remaining young and fair) can sometimes be seen wearing sweatshirts or jackets! At least now you know the reason.

They also walk slowly...very slowly! Remember the saying "Mad dogs and Englishmen..." well, that's pretty much what you seem like when you sizzle in the lunchtime heat while your girlfriend is desperate to get inside and in air-conditioning. The heat and humidity are two of the main reasons why Thai people choose to go to work by car and sit in traffic for two hours rather than get public transport. I will discuss all these topics a bit later in this chapter but for now, let's get back to the weather and its impact on life in Thailand.

The pace of life is slower due to the heat, you get tired more easily and you will need to shower at least twice a day. If you need to get through some errands or odd-jobs e.g. sort out your visa and pick up your dry cleaning and get back in time for the plumber to take a look at your leaking tap or whatever, be realistic. Not only will these things take longer than you think, you will be utterly drained by the time you get back home. Better to take things slower and if possible, defer one of the three things to the next day. In other words, over time you will find yourself adjusting yourself to the Thai speed of doing things because that is the only sensible way in a hot country. Then you will begin to understand the concepts of jai yen and sa-baai sa-baai. Bottom line, you can either be the crazy foreigner, running around, going red in the face and sweating profusely or you can be the calm and collected foreigner who fits in better in Thai society, it's up to you.

Finally, apart from the heat and humidity, it is worth mentioning the rain. As you may be able to guess, it is a tropical climate so when it rains, it really rains! Often quite awesome to behold, the rain is heavy, almost lukewarm when there is no breeze and often over in a few hours. However, it does quite a bit of damage in those few hours and even Bangkok gets flash flooding from time to time. When that happens, it is not uncommon to see people sloshing through streets in rolled up jeans and barefoot if they are caught out in a shopping mall while a whole world of rain suddenly came down in a couple of hours and it is now time to make it home somehow!

After three years with the company I was with in Saraburi, back in 2006, I left and moved to Bangkok, initially to study for a CFA but also to explore if I could get a job on my own in Bangkok that was at the same level and salary that I was used to in my last company. While the studying did not go too well, mainly because my heart was not really in it, I did manage to get an interview at an internet-related international company...even though I knew nothing about technology. The office was on Wireless Road and I decided to wear my suit to the interview, which, in itself, was foolish.

To make matters worse, I got to Phloen Chit and looked down to the road and there was water sloshing about everywhere. With no choice and barely believing

I was standing in the centre of Bangkok and it was flooded, I soldiered on down the steps and sloshed my way halfway down Wireless Road before I gave up, realising I was in no state to appear for an interview. The water was up to my knees and the suit went to the dry cleaners and I learnt an important lesson – this is Thailand! That's it. These things will happen. even in central Bangkok, if the drains are blocked or whatever and you have to simply admit defeat and respect the elements in a tropical country.

When it rains, things tend to slow down even more. It becomes a little more difficult to get a taxi and people in malls who do not have an umbrella (which is not uncommon as it is not normal to carry one as it is in the UK, for example) will crowd around the entrance, facing the choice of stepping out to get a taxi and getting totally drenched or waiting out the rain or maybe calling someone to pick them up. Yet another reason why so many people drive rather than get public transport but we will come to that later on.

In summary, the weather in Thailand is great when you are a tourist but not really so great when you live here permanently. There is not much you can do about it apart from do what the Thais do – get a motorcycle taxi to the Skytrain station rather than walk, stay in the shade, slow your walking speed right down, shower often, generally slow down, take taxis even if it means you get there slower, buy a car as soon as you are able and defer outdoor activity to the evening if you can. Notice that I did not say wear shorts and sandals everywhere – I'll talk about this later too.

THE BANGKOK SHUFFLE

Since I have just mentioned walking speed, let me say a few more words on that here. One thing you will definitely notice when you live in Bangkok (or anywhere in Thailand I suppose) is how slowly some people walk. Even accounting for the hot weather, the speed at which some people move along is positively glacial. Whether on the pavement or in the mall or pretty much anywhere, you will see people shuffling along, barely moving and not necessarily because they are checking their mobile phone, indeed, in most cases, that is not the reason. It is simply that the pace of life here is slow and it is normal to just take things easy and stroll around.

Since moving here I have slowed my walking speed down considerably and I am still faster than most people around me. I would say I now walk at a speed equivalent to a purposeful stroll (if that is not an oxymoron) and I am often having to slow myself right down to avoid running into the people ahead or, as is more often the case, having to overtake them on a pavement that is uneven and full of obstacles along the way, forcing people to zigzag. A recipe for pavement rage for the uninitiated Westerner and sometimes, even my Thai wife who has spent many years in the UK. And to top it all, don't expect to get an apology for blocking your way or walking into your path or just dawdling along side by side with a friend, taking up most of the limited space on the pavement – this is Thailand and the culture is "chill out, relax, take it easy" and there is nothing to be sorry about because everyone is just trying to negotiate the tricky terrain of the pavement to get to their gŭay dtĭao (Thai noodle) place so just deal with it.

Bottom line, do as the locals do, or, gracefully overtake and move on. And if it is not easy to overtake and you are stuck behind some shufflers shuffling to the escalator in the mall or wherever, just count to 10, take a deep breath and mutter jai yen yen (keep calm / chill out) to yourself. And if all else fails, get a car and minimise your need to deal with the heat and the obstacle course pavements as well as the overcrowded skytrain and MRT during rush hour... there you go, now you're thinking like a Thai! Why do you think there are so many cars (which are taxed more than 100%, making them twice as expensive as back home in a country where salaries are not even half as much as in the West) on the road? Even though every single person knows the traffic is going to be horrendous.

LOCAL CUSTOMS OR BEHAVIOURS YOU MAY NOT BE USED TO

Living in Thailand you will come across some behaviours that you may either not understand or misinterpret so since we were talking about walking before, let's cover off some other everyday things you may notice. There are many of these and as I said earlier, this is not a culture comparison book so I am not planning to go through an exhaustive list. However, here are a couple of things that I have noticed that should illustrate the point and hopefully give you pause for thought when your first reaction may be to get annoyed or frustrated.

- People not looking at you – you are less likely to get eye contact from people around you as you walk down the road or in the mall or whatever. If you do not care, that is great but for some newcomers to Thailand, this might be a little off-putting. People avert their gaze as soon as you appear in their line of vision perhaps making you feel even more of a stranger in a strange country. This is quite an Asian thing and I have noticed this in Japan and Singapore too but not necessarily everywhere in Asia is like this e.g. Hong Kongers are more confident and make eye contact. Thais are more reserved and conservative and also want to give you respect but you could be forgiven for not recognising this when everyone you pass slides by you with their eyes on the ground.

- People not saying thank you when you hold a door open or let them pass ahead of you – is this rudeness or something else? Almost certainly the latter. All those little chivalrous acts that would elicit a smile and a thanks back home may not necessarily have the same effect here every time. Sometimes the Thai person, say in your condo or in the mall, will just slide through the door you are holding open with barely any acknowledgement and eyes on the floor. Sometimes you will get a little head bow or a barely perceptible nod and on other, hopefully, most, occasions, you may get a thank you in English.

- The reason is partly that some people are automatically more awkward around foreigners they do not yet know. This goes double for many Thai women who are taught to be 'ladylike' and so do not look men in the eye, especially Western men. So, you will sometimes see, for example, a Thai girl, standing in the same lift as you but either standing right at the front staring point blank at the doors or at the back facing the back / mirror. Somebody doing that in the UK or US would look a bit weird but here, it is quite common. Also, more to the point, people do not feel the need to physically say thanks all the time, as it is implied and these kinds of formal social graces are more a part of English culture than Thai, which is more easy-going – for some people, better to quickly walk through than waste time in the doorway thanking people.

- Another example of this is in the area of greetings – you will notice Thais often do not need to say hello to start a conversation with another Thai person, whereas in the UK, one of the most traditional cultures in the world, it is almost unthinkable to start talking to someone without first saying hello or good evening or whatever. For example, in a British radio phone-in, you might get "Our next caller is John………. (an explanation of the topic and then) …John, what do you think?" The caller will, without fail, start off with "Good morning Dan" or similar and maybe even a "How are you?" before he feels capable of getting to the answer to the question. Thai is simply not that formal in everyday life.

- Anyway, bottom line, don't take offence and just smile and over time people will get used to you and act more naturally around you. I have had several occasions when I have held the door for someone in my condo and not even received a glance in my direction, never mind a nod of thanks but hey, it could also be because they just don't like the look of me! Hey ho, that is all part of life in Thailand.

- Thai smile – you should really already know this but if not, just be aware that the Thai smile that is so famous can sometimes be used to cover up people's frustration or even anger at your behaviour. If you are generally self-aware and can read body language, you will know when this is the case and pick up on these subtleties. If you are not, I guess you will just carry on in blissful ignorance but after reading this, you may be able to read Thai people's reactions a bit better.

- Face – this is a big enough topic to write an entire chapter on (along with indirectness mentioned earlier) and cuts across every aspect of Thai society so is not easily explained in brief. In short, try not to make people lose face and look out for when people are trying to save your face...which is much more difficult to spot for the average Westerner. You just need to know how to manage face issues as an expat, even if sometimes the Thai person is clearly in the wrong, you are better off not ramming it home or being blunt or direct as you may do back home. Sure, it might be their fault but if you deal with it sensitively, you can come out of it well whereas if you make a scene and blame people in harsh terms, you may feel good about getting things off your chest but you will destroy goodwill and you may well need that if you have to deal with anyone associated with that person in the future.

- When Thai people try to save your face by being indirect and not pointing out your misunderstanding or mistake, it can be very difficult to handle because what they do say to be polite and considerate in good faith does not resolve the confusion in your mind and may end up escalating the issue. This problem is obviously exacerbated when there is a language barrier so you can imagine how bad misunderstandings and resentment can occur from something that could be resolved easily. As you stay in Thailand longer you will learn to handle this better so give it time.

- Face considerations can be extremely frustrating for foreigners because they force Thais to tip-toe around the real issue (at least from your perspective) and get you even more wound up because you are convinced that they are not addressing the central point and wasting time and so on. Criticism has to be delivered in an indirect way because people are very sensitive to being criticised and so in return, Thai people rarely point out your faults or mistakes directly. It's a cultural thing and the cause of many foreigner / Thai misunderstandings but over time hopefully you will learn to live with it. The best advice is to let Thai people deal with Thai people so if you have a Thai girlfriend or acquaintance who speaks good English, use their help as much as you can when you are new to Thailand.

- Not a place for analysis or 'complex' questions – Thai ideology is all about sa-nòok (fun), sa-baai (chilling out / relaxing / being comfortable) and yaa kíd mâak (not over-thinking) …in short, being easy going. And that is great in many aspects of life. However, if you are curious and want to understand your new home country, which is so different, weird and wonderful compared to where you are from, you may struggle to get extensive explanations.

- If you are a Brit and used to enjoying a bit of healthy cynicism, sarcasm and criticism of everyday occurrences as you might do in the pub with your mates, you are going to struggle over here as people want lightness and fun and positivity. Simple questions from your perspective can sometimes be difficult to get answers to and the more you delve deeper or just ask why this, why that, the more you frustrate your Thai friend who maybe doesn't spend much time analysing things.

- Over the years I have had many frustrated, angry retorts from my wife at my constant questions about the mechanics of the Thai language or whether a character in a Thai TV series truly represents real people or in short, why things are the way they are in Thailand. Perhaps if you were asked these types of questions back home, you would be only too happy to launch into your opinions as that is part of pub or bar culture back home where everybody is an expert on every topic and social and political discourse is much more analytical but here in Thailand, people don't spend too much time wondering why things are the way they are. They just make the best of things and get on with life and tend to talk at length about things that are sa-nòok to talk about. Life is too short.

- But things are changing and more and more TV programmes discuss controversial social topics in more detail in a Western style than would not have been done say 20 years ago. In any case, perhaps this is not a real issue as you will find it almost impossible to get into any discussion like this with someone unless their English is good or your Thai is excellent.

Getting around

SKYTRAIN

The most well-known and practical way to get around Bangkok. The service is good and getting better with each year that passes by. Nowadays you have integration with the LINE app, called Rabbit, which works much like an Oyster card in the UK. You also have other smaller improvements but on the other hand, the demand has gone up since the early 2000s when the Skytrain was first built and so, if anything, it is even busier than ten years ago, even though there is more automation. Ultimately it is a success story as it clearly shows that the skytrain is absolutely critical to Bangkok life.

The speed of the trains can be a little slow (think DLR in London) but overall, it is still quicker than going by road in rush hour (including a couple of hours either side of rush hour). Outside of peak times, a skytrain journey is not necessarily the fastest way to get to somewhere, nor is it necessarily the most convenient in certain situations and if there are more than two people travelling, not always the cheapest either, when compared to say a taxi ride. Yes, I know, this is totally not what you expected to read and you simply don't believe it...because the traditional wisdom is that the traffic in Bangkok is terrible and you should always travel by Skytrain.

The reality is, unless you live in an expensive condo right next to a Skytrain station, you will have to walk to it or get a motorcycle taxi. Then you climb the stairs, get to the barriers, go through, up the escalator to the platform, wait a few minutes for the train to arrive and by this time, you may have spent 20 minutes from the moment you stepped out of your condo. People never compare like for like when extolling the virtues of the skytrain and somehow seem to completely ignore the heat, inconvenience, time and hassle of the journey just to get to the skytrain in the first place. And the same things can be said from the point you leave the train until you get to your final destination. When compared properly, the taxi wins in many situations and over time, you will develop the judgement to know when the traffic is likely to not be so bad and despite slow progress initially, once you get on the tollway, you can make it across Bangkok quite quickly. You will realise that getting somewhere door to door in an air-conditioned car is a blessing, especially if you are going to the movies on a date and trying not to look like a Cheap Charlie and making your date walk with you to the skytrain station.

MRT

The underground system is much like the Skytrain i.e. clean, reliable and efficient and gets very busy in rush hour so not much more to add beyond all of the above.

MOTORCYCLE TAXIS

These are great for short distances (when it is not raining!), with the most common usage for Thai workers being the trip to the closest skytrain or MRT station in the morning and evening. Note that while these are practical and convenient if you are in a hurry or if it is too far to walk from the station back to your place, they (and every other form of public transport) are very much a 'lower' form of travel compared to having your own car. Most middle class and higher social classes would never be seen on a motorcycle taxi unless it was really necessary and many women from these backgrounds would expect their boyfriend or husband to drive them to work.

Of course, society is changing and the traffic in rush hour is bad and so practicality ends up winning over image and status but even then, the motorcycle taxi is really more the mode of transport of the younger or lower paid office workers or tourists. Most professionals would drive (unless they live in an area where the traffic is particularly bad and always gridlocked) as a matter of course, even if they have to get up early to beat the traffic and sit in traffic on the way back home. Obviously, part of the reason is also that most Thai people do not live near to train stations as these are normally expensive condos for rich Thais and foreigners.

Anyway, the point is, you may not care about all this because as an expat, you are in blissful ignorance of any silent judgement Thais pass on you and you care even less and that's fine. However, just be aware that if you turn up to the club (and I do not mean Soi Cowboy clubs but a 'normal' Thai bar) on a motorcycle taxi in your shorts, you better hope your good looks and charm are in order because the first impression a middle class, Thai office girl will get will be...well, to be blunt, that you're a Cheap Charlie and a loser foreigner. Right or wrong, fair or unfair, that is the reality so up to you if you care. If you do, at least turn up in a taxi if you don't have a car and put some damn trousers on!

BUSES AND OTHER 'CHEAP' MODES OF TRANSPORT

When on holiday, buses are ok to use but when you are here for good, you are unlikely to use these and expats are rarely seen on these, especially the non-AC buses. As with the motorcycle taxi comments, if you are queuing up for these at a bus stop, that's fine but the underlying impression you are giving off is that you're a foreigner in Thailand who has no money. Remember, Thais assume that the fact that you are a white foreigner means automatically that you are reasonably well-off, in Thai terms, and let's face it, in a country where a security guard earns less than 10,000 baht (less than £200) a month, in most cases they are correct.

So, to see a Western guy queuing up alongside a whole load of Thai office workers, most of whom probably earn no more than around 20,000 to 30,000 baht, implies he earns around the same. And that, quite frankly, is not the image of a Westerner that Thais have – why would a guy who comes from a first world country with a much, much stronger currency and potential to earn a decent Western salary be queuing up for a bus to get home in Thailand. Of course, if you could not care less and are just getting on a săwng-tăeo (or 'songthaew' if written in the official romanisation way without the tone marks) because it makes sense and is cheap and convenient and who cares what anyone thinks, great, that's fine.

Finally, note on an air-con bus, you will need to explain to the conductor where you are getting off so some knowledge of Thai (at least the clear pronunciation of a destination) will be necessary.

SCOOTERS AND MOTORCYCLES

These are really useful to get around and you will see a lot of expats zipping around on these, especially outside Bangkok e.g. Phuket and other seaside destinations as well as Chiang Mai.

TAXIS

In my opinion, one of the absolute best things about Thailand is the ease with which you can get taxis in Bangkok. I simply love it. You may have guessed already that I am more of a fan of the comfort of taxis than the supposed speed and convenience of other public transport options. In my opinion, sitting in traffic for an extra 15 minutes but getting to where I want to go door to door in an air-conditioned car is worth the delay. I just plan to leave a bit earlier. Sure, it is frustrating sitting in stop start traffic where it takes 20 minutes just to get to the top of your road. But often, once you have got past the traffic lights, progress is faster and for me it is worth the frustration if I am travelling in non-rush hour i.e. say between 10am and 4pm and after 8pm. Most of you will not agree and I am sure prefer the convenience of getting to where you want to go quickly but, for me, I am rarely in a hurry to get somewhere and even if I have an appointment, I plan to leave a bit earlier. As I said though, I think twice when it is rush hour and choose the skytrain or MRT instead and I rarely travel to central Bangkok i.e. Thong Lor, Chit Lom, Siam and so on. I certainly would not go from, say, Udom Suk to Siam Paragon by taxi as that would be a bit crazy.

Taxis are so easy to get in Bangkok that it is, in my opinion, one of the best things about Thailand. You can be standing pretty much anywhere, on almost any part of the roadside, in any part of Bangkok and there will probably be a taxi driving by within a few seconds or at the most, a few minutes. Compare this to the system back home and there is simply no comparison. For those who have been to Singapore, you will know perfectly well that the system is very well ordered and controlled (in perfect line with Singaporean ideology) and so you can only hail taxis from taxi stands. So, you can be walking along with empty taxi after empty taxi driving straight past you and not permitted to pick you up from the roadside and then, when you arrive at your taxi stand, there are ten people in front of you because making people queue creates a funnel effect where it is one taxi at a time, slowing everybody down. But hey, it is orderly and fair!

In contrast, the Thai system, just like Thai ideology, is liberal – you hail a taxi wherever you want and sure, when the driver sees you and veers over to pick you up, he cuts across some other car or motorcycle who then has to wait for you to get in and the taxi to get going before everyone is moving again but in practice, over 15 years that I have observed things in Thailand, I have never seen this to be a big problem. Long may this continue. The last thing we need is for Thailand to slip-slide toward so-called 'international standards' and in so doing, remove all the little freedoms and conveniences that make Thailand the easy-going, liberal, laissez-faire environment that people love about the country. Anyway, I said I would not get political so I digress.

Taxi issues faced by expats (and Thais)

Let's talk about some of the common issues and things to note when travelling by taxi that will be useful for you if you are a new expat and still seeing things at face value through tourist eyes:

- Refusing to go – one of the most common complaints of foreigners is taxi drivers refusing to go to your desired destination. Sometimes they drive straight past you, which in some ways is better than what usually happens, which is they stop, wait for you to get in, hear where you want to go and then say "No go" or a more verbose explanation if their English is up to it. You are then forced to get out and wait for the next car, which may well do the same. By this time, you have thoroughly had enough and end up being slightly aggressive with the next guy who, as it happens, is fine to go but noticed that you were a bit loud and immediately put you in the same category as all 'farang' (from his point of view, having experienced this many times in his career).

This, unfortunately is the kind of thing that happens due to a culture clash and a language barrier, ultimately leading to people forming firm, deep-set opinions about other people. And it could all be different...but the bad news is that it is you that will have to change but the taxi drivers will not. Why? Because you are in Thailand and it is incumbent on you to fit in, not they. This applies to every aspect of your social interactions in Thailand, not just when you try to get a taxi.

So what do you need to do and why do they refuse to go anyway? The simple answer to the latter is, often, they have to return the car – which they do not own – and if they do not do so by their shift end deadline, they will be fined. These drivers often earn very little and being docked a day's pay is a big deal to them. So they will only take a passenger if the passenger is going in the direction that they are heading to return the car. On top of this, if they are in a hurry and you say you do not want to go on the tollway because you want to save a bit of money, you can imagine their reaction, which is usually an understated and slow-burning, resentful, passive aggressive grumbling and tut-tuts at the heavy traffic. Also, in some cases, the driver maybe owns his car and so simply cannot be bothered to go to where you are going; undoubtedly, in some cases, the need to return the car is an excuse and the truth is the driver simply does not want to go that way.

The other day, while delivering an invoice, it started belting it down outside, making it impossible to step out of the building I was at without getting totally drenched. A taxi dropped someone off and I popped my head in and asked the driver "bpai dtàw mái krúp?" – "Are you ok to take me next (after your passenger gets out)?" When he asked where and I told him where my home was, unsurprisingly, he said no, almost certainly because he didn't want to get stuck in traffic, which is always a little worse when it rains. So I asked, "Tâa yàng nán paa pŏm bpai têe sà-tăa-nee rót-fai-fáa dâai mái krúp" – "In that case, could you take me to the (nearest) skytrain station?" And he did. It helps to speak Thai and it helped when he asked me where I wanted him to drop me off so as to not get too wet getting out and under cover.

As for what you can do, it is simple – be Thai. Be as courteous as you can muster and move on. Hail the next one, don't get in, open the front passenger door and ask politely again. Don't get stressed – practice your zen like patience and hide your anger. That's the Thai way. And learn Thai! Yep, you might think that you do not need to learn Thai, especially in Bangkok but this is one of many, many examples where being able to speak Thai (by which I mean speak credibly and pronounce accurately at least to beyond basic level) does make a difference.

The driver will never initially speak to you in Thai once he sees you are Caucasian and so will only give you the most rudimentary of explanations for not going. But if you make your request in Thai and give him the confidence you will understand his Thai response, he will engage in Thai. If your Thai was good enough, you could explain that you are just going up the road or you are happy to go on the tollway or that he can drop you off at the nearest skytrain or MRT station or, at the very least, understand what his reasons are for not going, genuine or not.

Finally, never, ever lose your temper with taxi drivers. You have no idea how vulnerable you are in Thailand, especially with taxi drivers so, trust me, just bottle it up and vent at the bar, not in his car.

- Not putting meter on – a very common complaint among Westerners, albeit less common now than it used to be in the old days when metering was not mandatory under the law. In this case, you are absolutely right to suspect that these guys just want to earn a few extra bucks off you, especially when it rains and it is harder to get a taxi or at the airport. Conventional advice is, as above, politely move on to the next car, although in some cases, you may have to move a bit further as there is often a collective agreement among the group of drivers hassling you to not turn their meter on. Bear in mind though that there is often at least half a reason to not turn on the meter e.g. they know the traffic is bad so they will 'lose money' by sitting in traffic compared to doing two or three shorter journeys in the same time.
- So, although your first instinct might be to bridle at being ripped off, in some situations if the difference between what you are quoted and your estimate of what the metered rate would be is about 50 to 100 baht, you

might be better off just going with it rather than getting worked up trying to find a meter driver. Again, if you can speak Thai, it helps a lot as you can have a bit of banter with the driver gang and nobody loses face and you settle on a win-win outcome. Life in Thailand is all about being a little flexible and not taking an absolutist position in your everyday dealings.

- Another source of contention between passengers and taxi drivers is when they ask you the way! Sometimes the drivers are new and unlike black cab drivers in the UK, they do not have to pass The Knowledge in order to start driving a taxi so they may not know all the routes. This can be quite frustrating but guess what, again, if helps if you can speak Thai. Admittedly though, a driver is unlikely to ask you for guidance in the first place if you cannot speak Thai so this problem usually would only occur when you do speak Thai!

- So maybe you're better off speaking in English in this case but then, not having been asked, you may notice that the driver is a little lost or the journey taking longer than normal. Of course, he will not admit to this because of lack of English and more so because of losing face reasons. Your best option is to politely grin and bear it or if not, politely ask the guy to stop and get another taxi from that point on.

- Finally, regarding paying the fare, I usually don't insist on getting every single baht back from the driver in change. If the fare is 52 baht, I may well give three 20s and say <u>mâi</u> <u>bpen</u> <u>rai</u> (don't worry about it (the change) / never mind) and thanks and get out or, at worst, maybe just ask for a five-baht coin back. These guys are really not well-off in any description so insisting on getting the equivalent of a few pence back in change is a little churlish when you could just consider it a tip. I have often refused change for, say, a 160-baht fare. having paid with two 100-baht notes. It's appreciated and will leave you feeling good too, especially if you managed to have a bit of a conversation or banter with the guy during the journey.

TRAFFIC

So, is the traffic as bad as it reputed to be? Well, the short answer is yes but it needs some qualification. Outside of rush hour, the traffic is slow and stop-start but not that bad. As I said, I tend to get taxis if I am not going into central Bangkok and in many cases, after one or two traffic lights, things free up and progress is much better so it ends up being a reasonable journey. Obviously, mornings and evenings, especially in areas such as Lard Prao, Sukhumvit and so on, tend to be gridlocked so if you can help it, avoid these times.

One point that may be up for debate is whether the system of u-turns (minimising right turns and requiring cars to drive on past where they wanted to turn right and then u-turn and turn left) makes traffic flow better or makes things worse. I am not knowledgeable enough on traffic flow science to know the answer but newcomers to Thailand will notice how long some traffic lights take to change and the ubiquity of the u-turns. Perhaps a point for readers to work out for themselves.

As I said earlier, you may wonder why Thais still love their car so much if the traffic is so bad and cars are so disproportionately expensive for Thai incomes and the answer is 1) they avoid the hassle of having to deal with the elements and the hassle of walking to and from public transport, 2) owning a car is a sign of status, elevating someone above 'the commoners who have no other choice but to take public transport' and 3) the availability of cheap finance.

Social Life

SOCIALISING IN THAILAND

I want to spend a section talking about what your social life will be like in Thailand...although, immediately, I have to qualify that statement with the point that my comments are only based on my own experiences and those of other expats who I know or know of in Thailand. I have had a reasonably broad exposure to life in Thailand so let me describe this as a way for you to get some insight.

I was lucky enough to have had the opportunity to work in an office with mainly Thai people, in the Thai headquarters of a British company with a British boss. Moreover, I was fortunate that the office was located outside Bangkok in a small town. These set of circumstances gave me the best of all worlds:

- Working for a company with British standards of work and work ethics and English language in written documents, British level holiday entitlement and so on.
- Working in a Thai environment with educated Thais that quickly accelerated my progress in learning Thai so that I was fluent in everyday conversation after 18 months to 2 years
- I saw 'real life' in Thailand and also, I mixed and was surrounded by people who were more genuine, salt-of-the-earth, non-judgmental and kind. Anyone who has lived in big cities and in small towns and villages knows what I mean and it probably applies to any country – life in a big, metropolitan city changes people so, for example, people on my floor in my condo walk straight past me in the corridor without saying hello or even glancing in my direction whereas in Mûak Lèk, people were much more accepting of a brown-skinned foreigner and just treated me like everyone else.
- I could go into Bangkok on the weekend and party hard or whatever and then return to sanity and calm for another week at work – the perfect balance of work and play.
- I integrated into Thai society and understood Thai people way, way better than I would have done had I been sent to work for a big multinational in Bangkok and spent my time in a luxury serviced apartment in a central part of Bangkok.

- I had Thai friends, which is extremely unusual for a Westerner; in all of my years here, I do not remember seeing or knowing of any male foreigner with a male Thai friend. Of course, the main reasons I formed friendships with colleagues at work was because I spent so much time with them day to day and after work and also the fact that I learnt the language, without which there can never be any real connection. Also, it is worth pointing out that I was able to form friendships because my colleagues were educated, middle class Thais and therefore, of a similar background to me and so we had things in common.

Making male Thai friends

Before I move off the topic of Thai friends, let me say a few more words here. The reality is that the majority of Western expats, especially the ones that come for work, come to Bangkok and stay in condos in Silom and Sathorn or, if they are teachers in one of the many international schools in Bangkok, will probably settle close to the school in a condo where other foreign teachers are already living. So, the chances of experiencing what I have described above and integrating as easily and quickly as I did are extremely remote. Indeed, many of the people who come over and settle here have no desire to make as much effort as I did to get into Thai life and feel more comfortable amongst the expat community when outside work. And that is just fine. It is not the job of this book to preach or dictate how foreigners should live their life in Thailand, merely to give you some flavour of what to expect when you are here and explain things that may be difficult to understand when living in a foreign country with different social dynamics.

The reality, therefore, for the majority of foreigners who will not be coming to Thailand in a similar set of circumstances as I had in my life here, is that you will probably never have a Thai friend, by which I mean a male friend. The reasons for this are first, that your life is so different to theirs that you really do not have much in common.

Also, unless you can speak Thai fluently, you are basically a burden to have around in a social context (sorry, it's harsh but more or less true) because everything has to be translated or explained to you and everyone has to consider whether you would be comfortable doing what they want to do so your very presence would end up dictating everyone's day i.e. in short, they would have to play host to you. (Note – there may be an exception if you happen to meet male Thais who have studied or worked abroad, experienced Western culture and speak good English).

Then there is the issue of cultural differences and also the fact that it is very likely that they all earn much less than you and they have to put money aside to send back home to their parents so they will not want to do things that they think are a waste of money or expensive.

Cultural differences are difficult to overcome in a big city where people do not spend time with each other at work, unlike my situation where I would play tennis or football at the back of the office or have dinner with my colleagues in town and then give them a lift back in my car.

So, for example, you might want to try and make an effort and, say, invite a colleague to watch the football with you in a sports bar or even at your home with a few beers but you will see that this suggestion will probably be met with some uneasiness and even if the guy did meet you, he was not really comfortable and could not really fit in with you and your expat mates at the bar. Generally speaking, the types of conversation and banter that Thais and Westerners find entertaining are quite different, not to mention your cultural references (TV programmes, metaphors, insults etc) and language.

All of this may lead you to despair at why it is so difficult but before you jump to the attractive conclusion that you have made an effort but it is not going to work, stop and think whether that is really true. It is possible to make friends in Thailand but the onus is very much on you understanding Thai people and what they like to do and how to fit in with them rather than the other way around. And, as I have said many times already, language is the first and most important step to integration so if you do not want to learn Thai beyond a few basic words, that is fine and is your choice but then, you cannot expect to have Thai friends and a social life amongst Thai people and so on.

Making female Thai friends

Finally, while I have spent a long time talking about the fact that it will probably be difficult for male foreigners to find male Thai friends, the same is not true for finding female Thai friends. You may jump to the conclusion that this is because Thai girls want a foreign husband but this is not necessarily the reason at all in many cases. You will realise that relationships between male (and even female) Westerners and Thais are usually with female Thais and the nature of these relationships is diverse.

In many cases, the Thai girl who hangs out with you is the colleague who has offered or been asked to do so in order to help you out with something e.g. to get your mobile contract sorted or some other admin matter. The girl may fancy you deep down or she may just want to have an opportunity to speak English or she may just want to be seen with a foreigner in society or she may have absolutely no interest in you sexually but she, like most Thais, is proud of her country and wants to help you in any way she can to see the good aspects of Thailand and feel comfortable living here.

Whereas foreigners who go to settle in the UK or US, for example, are often left to their own devices because people do not want to intrude or be over-bearing, over here, leaving a new expat or tourist to struggle to work things out for themselves would be seen as shameful for Thais and they could not live with themselves if they did not help you out and spend time with you. So, in many cases, as you can see when you go to the Chaeng Wattana Immigration office, the foreigners who are with Thais are always with female Thais – either paid agents or the office HR or admin person or Thai girlfriends or wives.

For most people who come over who are not already in a relationship, a route to entry and understanding of Thai life comes from meeting a Thai girl. This is when you start to see Thailand in a different way to how you saw Thailand in your previous expat bubble or, sadly for some people, in your previous lonely existence as a single foreigner in a foreign country, trying to resist some of the so-called vices of nightlife here but with no idea what to do with your time outside work.

This is a sad truth for many expats and I have experienced this to some extent myself – when you are single, do not really know any Thai people and do not want to hang out with other foreigners, you are pretty much left twiddling your thumbs and end up going to Western male-oriented bars just to relieve your boredom and have a bit of human contact and some conversation, ahead of any sexual reasons.

For me, as with many foreigners, my slow exit from that lifestyle to a life similar to what I had back in the UK, came from meeting my wife at work and also, learning Thai, which also became easier because I had someone I could practice with every day.

Unsurprisingly, in many, many cases, initially platonic or semi-platonic relationships with Thai women turn into something more. Do not assume that the only Thai girls that are interested in foreigners are bargirls – this is a common misconception and things are changing with each year that passes by. Many perfectly 'normal' Thai girls, even middle class and possibly upper middle class (albeit less in this latter category) women have a preference for Western men and have no interest in Thai men who they may see as lazy or too physically short or not earning enough to earn their respect or simply not worldly enough in their eyes. A foreigner is a very attractive proposition for these women. Also, there is general agreement that Thai-Caucasian children are beautiful because they are whiter-skinned than local people.

Whatever the underlying reasons, many Thai women are happy to spend time with foreigners in shopping malls or whatever, perhaps initially, for totally non-sexual reasons. So, if you are interested in understanding Thailand better, you will have a much better chance of doing this if you find someone female who you like (not necessarily romantically) and who can speak reasonable English and arrange to meet on the weekend to maybe check out some tourist places or to get some aspect of your settling in process sorted; in both cases, having a Thai speaker will help immensely.

FITTING IN

Let's spend a bit more time talking about integration into Thai society and life in Thailand. Before we get any further though, I need to repeat the point I have made several times already, which is that there will be many expats who have no real interest in fitting in or understanding Thai people's ways or learning the language to any significant extent at all. Every person has their own level of desire and drive to fit in and invest in a life in Thailand – some people spend ten, twenty or more years here and can barely speak more than a few words of Thai and pretty much never speak to a Thai person apart from when as a customer or tenant or some other role receiving a service.

If you are one of these people and you are perfectly happy with this state of affairs, that is absolutely fine. Many expats have a strong expat friend network and if they live in Bangkok or Chiang Mai or Phuket, pretty much do not need to integrate with Thai life to any description and spend their time working in a foreigner environment e.g. an international school, travelling on the weekend and have a lot of help to negotiate the more challenging aspects of everyday life. To put it simply, this section is not for these people.

This section is for those people who maybe have found a Thai girlfriend or who work in a company which is majority Thai or who simply have a desire and curiosity about their new surroundings even if they have no immediate connection to Thai people. As I mentioned, in this group, the level of desire to understand and fit in will vary on a spectrum and I assume this group represents the majority of expats in Thailand.

Finally, this group also excludes those people at the other end of the spectrum i.e. those people who are so obsessed with Thai culture and Thai social etiquette and so on that they are more Thai than Thai people! These people probably would not be reading a book like this anyway and are probably in a temple somewhere teaching Buddhism or writing a blog on the subtleties of the Thai language to an excruciating level of detail so let's leave them there and focus on the people in the middle who are the 'normal' expats who want to fit in a bit more.

If you are interested in seeing 'real' Thailand beyond Bangkok and want to leave Thailand at the end of your tenure having learnt more about Thai life than what is new on Sukhumvit Road, I would strongly urge you to find some outlet to allow you to do that. That could mean you join a school or some other organisation that is a mainly Thai place and arranges trips to other provinces in Thailand in a Thai environment, not amongst a busload of Western tourists.

Or, if you are coming to Thailand with skills that Thailand needs e.g. technology skills, and you are in the lucky position of being able to choose where you want to work rather than just having to take the first job that is offered, you may want to consider a job that is not in Bangkok. Or, if in Bangkok, based in the outskirts of Bangkok. Sure, you will face more inconveniences than if you are in Silom or Sukhumvit and you will earn a lot less but if you wanted to have world class transport links, a high salary and so on, why would you come to Thailand to achieve those things?

If you choose to live here, as opposed to visit for a while, one assumes it is because you want to be part of real life in Thailand. It does not mean you have to slum it in a wooden shack and eat 20-baht gŭay dtĭao but if you are young and single and want to have local friends and live here almost as well-integrated as you are in your own country, you may want to consider working in an international company with mainly Thai staff as that is often the perfect combination.

Capital city life, in any country is more detached and driven by the needs of the workforce than the slower paced, gentler life in towns and villages so these comments are not really specific to Thailand. If you come to Bangkok and work in a big company and live in an expensive, centrally located condo, your life will probably have similarities to your daily commute into work in London where you speak to nobody and trudge back home in the evening before you do it all over again the next day. The difference is, in Thailand, you...

- do not speak the language,
- do not understand any of the conversations around you,
- cannot read any of the Thai around you,
- do not understand the culture and why people behave the way they do,
- do not watch local TV or keep up with Thai musical trends,
- do not keep up with Thai current affairs (apart from what you read in the Bangkok Post),
- do not get Thai sense of humour,
- do not know how to order Thai food apart from a few dishes you have already had a hundred times...
- so, in short, what is the point of you living in Thailand?

If you were transferred here with your wife and kids to take up a role, you may have no desire or need to integrate in any way and that is fine because you have your own family and you are probably here for a limited number of years and you may well then move on to another Asian country, as many Western professionals do. If that is not you and you are, as I was, a young guy who was excited to have the opportunity to live and work in Thailand, you may want to consider what you can do to fit in better.

As I said before, while Thais are very welcoming and understanding of you as a foreigner in their country, this is where they play the role of host or explainer of things to you, as opposed to just being your friend and speaking to you no differently to their other Thai friends. So, to even come close to Thai people seeing you as one of them, assuming you do want to make the effort to integrate, the onus is on you to find outlets and circumstances that allow you to mix with Thai people as an equal, not as a customer or receiver of service or information.

When I first got here, my colleagues offered to speak English with me and in meetings, they suggested they speak in English for my benefit. I insisted that they do no such thing and within a few weeks, I was able to pick up a lot of what was being said because my ears got used to hearing Thai, in a context I already knew i.e. I knew what the meeting was about so could guess the meaning of many words even if I did not know exactly.

You will have to find your own ways to fit in...which, for example, may involve having a chat with male colleagues about how to flirt with a girl who you fancy in the office or ask them whether she has a boyfriend already to avoid making a fool of yourself. Of course, the drawback of doing this is that you will have opened the door to people gossiping about you in the office so use your judgement as to whether you mind that much or are not that bothered.

THE FIVE STAGES OF INTEGRATION

Let's try and create some imaginary stages of fitting in and describe what it feels like in each of these stages to give you more of an idea:

Stage 1

As mentioned above, this is where your role in life is to speak when you are spoken to by the one or two brave Thai people who have been introduced to

173

you by your Thai girlfriend and apart from that, you pretty much do not feature in any conversation. This is probably due to either the fact that the friends of your girlfriend having limited English ability or limited knowledge of how to do small talk or a combination of both. So, you will get one or two questions about where you are from and maybe how old you are and then the conversation will switch back to your girlfriend.

Alternatively, if you are working in a Thai company, the nominated Thai person who hangs out with you at lunchtime (and yes, I do mean nominated because you probably do not realise but there have been multiple conversations about how to handle you and manage your wellbeing long before you actually joined the company) will play the host role and introduce you to food available near the office and explain Thai snacks and fruits that you are not familiar with and answer all your other questions. Sooner or later, the Thai person will grow weary of this role – just as you would if you had to do it for a foreigner coming to work with you in the UK) – and will want to hand you over to another Thai person or wean you off them into independence.

So this is stage 1, where you are a foreigner who cannot speak more than a few words in Thai and do not really understand even the basics of Thai life and you are there to be looked after or to stand politely while your girlfriend has a chat with her friends. Quite frankly, this is all you are really good for because you cannot really join in your girlfriend's conversation in Thai and if you do join in in English, you will break the rhythm of their conversation while they have to explain all the background and context to bring you up to speed. Note, stage 1 is not necessarily a newly arrived expat because as I said earlier, some people spend several years here without really wanting or needing to fit in and so they progress to stage 1 over a number of months or years.

Stage 2

This is where you start to venture out by yourself in Thai – you might try saying a few words in Thai to the boy at the cashier in 7-Eleven or you might attempt a bit of banter in Thai mixed with English with the front desk girl in your condo. You can now pick up little strands of conversation between your Thai girlfriend and her friends or when she is on the phone or maybe you start to understand a few words spoken between people on the MRT platform.

You have spent a few months or maybe even years observing how Thai people behave so you are a slightly more restrained version of yourself when having dinner in a Thai group. You are maybe aware that you are physically bigger than most people around you so you try to control your body language and you are also slightly more careful about butting into conversations and dominating with your opinions about everything.

You have noticed over the duration that you were in stage 1 that while Thai people would politely listen whenever you would blurt your thoughts and opinions in a social situation, they were just being polite and you were not really in sync with them at all. One sign that you are making progress (from stage 1 to stage 2) is when you are in a social situation and do offer your opinions, you actually get some responses, not just "ummm"s and "aaah"s and polite "oooh"s. In fact, just the fact that you are even invited to a dinner or some other social interaction is probably a sign that Thai people around you do not see you as so detached and in your expat world that you would not be able to fit in so they do invite you to things.

Stage 3

This is where you have got married to a Thai woman or recognised as a long-term boyfriend of her or, if not in a relationship with a Thai person, you are seen as one of the boys in your office or, maybe you are finally (secretly) being mentally accepted by the Thai ladies in the office as a genuine boyfriend prospect i.e. who can fit in and live in Thailand and will possibly be able to accept her family and the complexities of Thai society.

You can, by now, speak Thai well enough to join in conversations in Thai albeit having to resort to English quite often. You know that you are in stage 3 because every conversation you have in Thailand is not either a request or a question as a customer, or a conversation about you. Admittedly though, you do struggle when the topic is not about you and is a neutral topic but you can sometimes still keep up with what is being said and nod in the right places and maybe even offer an intelligent comment.

At this stage you can manage most of your interactions in Thai and people will, sometimes – but not always – respond to you in Thai. You may have been invited to a dinner party or two with an almost total Thai invitee list and you do not feel totally out of place and can manage to get through it ok. You have watched Thai TV series, possibly with your girlfriend or wife and you recognise some Thai songs and you can pick up a few words here and there. You also are starting to understand office dynamics, office politics, 'typical' Thai characteristics, why people react the way they do, how to approach people, what not to say and so on. In short, you are finally starting to get Thailand.

Stage 4

This is the holy grail stage that you want to get to and the stage that you never thought you could reach in a million years when you first came to Thailand. You are fluent in everyday spoken Thai, you can order your food in Thai, you can explain if it wasn't what you ordered in Thai and with the appropriate tone of voice and choice of words to not make the waitress lose face. You speak Thai in over 90% of your daily dealings with Thai people, you understand most of the Thai spoken around you or being announced around the mall. You understand what the Thai people sitting behind you on the plane are saying. When you go to the hospital or to buy a condo or a car with your Thai partner and the receptionist or seller realises you can speak Thai, they speak to both you and your partner, not just her. In short, you are now an active part of society as opposed to the foreigner who needs to be handheld.

Most important, you get a massive sense of satisfaction at being able to engage with Thai people and be accepted by them as a person no different to a Thai person i.e. you are no longer a 'fa-rang' for whom they have to consult their fa-rang playbook, handed down through generations of Thais, on how to deal with you. You can have conversations not just about who you are and where you are from but you can almost talk about all the same things you would talk about back in the UK or US in Thai e.g. football, the weather, your family background, your last holiday etc.

You can participate in meetings at work in Thai and you can blend in Thai to your presentations or when you are explaining things to a colleague. You also know Thai sensitivities so you know how to and how not to speak in order to get your team to work for you and you understand that team dynamics and Thai office culture is quite different to back home and you can restrain your natural urge to be brief, direct and blunt as you might do back in the US or UK.

Stage 5

I imagine one in a million expats reach this stage so it is easier to say that you will almost certainly never reach this stage, which is basically being able to live in Thailand as if you were Thai. No matter how good your Thai language skills are, you are unlikely to ever be seen as if you are a native speaker and have people open up to you in the way they would with a Thai person. Your girlfriend's friends or her parents or any other Thai people in your life will appreciate your fantastic Thai but, ultimately, they will still see you as a foreigner and will not speak to you as extensively, as openly, as casually or as emotionally as they would with a Thai person. And here's the good news...you really do not need to reach stage 5.

While your wife or girlfriend appreciates that you can fit in to Thai life and you can speak great Thai and you are independent and you understand Thai culture and so on, she still wants to feel there is a part of her that is a level of Thai-ness that is between her and her family and friends that you cannot fully intervene in. In short, she needs her space. Just like, if you were to live with her in the UK, for example, no matter how good she becomes in speaking English, she will never be able to banter with your mates the way you do, at the same speed of thought or with the same sense of humour etc. So, stage 5 is for the very, very few who are that keen on and that socially aware and that able to transform themselves and that good at Thai that they are as confident in any social interaction as they would be back in their home country.

For mere mortals, stage 4 is a good target and is the stage at which, you are likely to reach your natural point of final resistance i.e. the point at which you are not willing to try much harder to fit in because you are pretty comfortable in your everyday dealings with Thai people. You realise that when dealing with civil service officials or in other specific situations, you are better off relying on your Thai wife to speak on your behalf because things will just go smoother that way. Similarly, while you understand most Thai TV to a decent extent, you don't want to learn Thai to an advanced level so that you can fully understand these programmes because, again, you feel you are comfortable at stage 4.

Quite frankly, given that people are constantly impressed with how clearly you speak Thai and how naturally everybody responds to you, you see little need in going out of your way to go much further to fit in. At the end of the day, you are a foreigner in a foreign country so if you have gone 80% of the way to integrating into society, you should expect that the locals you deal with can meet you 20% of the way – sometimes accept your views and opinions, which may not be the way they would think.

Or, for example, while you have made a lot of effort to explore Thai food, understand the range of tastes, dishes, spices etc, it is not too much to expect that your Thai friends be able to accept foods you like from back home now and then and not react with horror that it is far too oily or far too bland and nothing is tasty unless it is super spicy and sour.

I would rate myself as a stage 4 member who is passively on the way to stage 5 but certainly not actively i.e. while I still pick up subtle social dynamics when I watch Thai TV series or interact with Thai people, I have reached the point where I do not really want to change myself too much more. In fact, actively, I may even be moving slightly back toward stage 3, by which I mean, for example,

I am not as keen on having sôm-dtam as I was when I first moved here and wanted to learn and try everything. I now recoil at the smell of fish sauce more than I used to when I first got here and I tend to have more Japanese food when I am out.

Also, while I used to be fine sitting in a non-air-conditioned little restaurant having my gŭay dtĭao drenched in sweat and loving it, these days I am more high maintenance and spend a higher proportion of my time in AC places, if possible. In spite of the fact that I can speak Thai pretty well, I tend to let my wife lead in interactions where there is potential for confusion or where it is something important such as passport and visa matters. The reason I do this is simply that I have lived here long enough to be wise enough to know when I should be independent and use my Thai skills and when I should know better to get a smoother outcome. So, while I am passively moving toward stage 5 because I am learning more and more about Thai life with each day that passes, my natural resistance has kicked in and I am more able to find a middle ground that works for me and allows me to understand my environment but not be totally dictated by it.

Stage 4 also suggests that I doubt I would enjoy hanging out with an all Thai group of guys but if it was in the context of sport, say a golf game, I could do it and still feel reasonably comfortable speaking Thai and hanging out with them. The reality, as I said before, is that most male foreigners never form any friendships with male Thais but have several relationships of different descriptions with Thai females. So, I, like so many Westerners, only really have meaningful interactions with Thai people when I go out to dinner with my wife and her (mostly female) friends in a group and even then, even though they know I can speak Thai, they rarely ask me anything particularly interesting or challenging. Anyway, that is me; if you are happy when you reach stage 3 or even stage 2 and that is enough Thai-ness for you, no problem, that is totally understandable and your efforts will still be appreciated by Thai people.

GETTING YOUR 'WESTERN FIX'

Continuing on from the previous section, on the assumption that you are being a good little expat and are willing to integrate into Thai life to some extent, how should you manage your life so that you neither feel totally alienated in a foreign country nor do you start to crack under the strain of having to fit in and watch yourself in every social interaction and end up leaving Thailand because you are so homesick and dying for some familiar conversations and a bit of banter with mates.

While this book cannot seek to dictate how you live your life in Thailand, I can offer my opinion based on my 15 years travelling to, working and living here. The best way to live here long term if you are single is to try to find some way to interact with Thais socially as without that, you won't understand Thailand in any meaningful way; you will just be an observer floating at the shallow end. For many, this means a Thai girlfriend, which clearly, you would not acquire just because of having a Thai touchpoint!

Secondly, possibly just as important, you need to get your Western fix now and then by hanging out with your Western friends (a reminder that I am using Western as a convenient adjective to mean foreigners from the US, UK, Europe, Canada, Australia, NZ, South Africa etc) every so often (but certainly not every day!). For example, if some friends come to visit Thailand, it is the perfect opportunity to release a bit of tension, let your hair down, so to speak and have a laugh in your own language. Go out and have Western food (a curry!) and a few beers and talk about all the things you can't talk about with anyone else in Thailand. Being able to do this every now and then will give you something to look forward to when you start to feel homesick, which you are likely to feel even though Thailand is such a fantastic country.

On the other hand, though, to have a successful stay in Thailand, you may well need to progress through a few of the stages described previously so your Western fix should be more of a fix rather than your permanent state of affairs because if your whole life is spent with other expats, speaking in English, what is the point of you living in Thailand and how can you possibly integrate, even to a minor extent? Whether you belong to a sports club, get into Thai songs and love karaoke, meet a nice girl at work, whatever it is, you need a Thai touchpoint to feel some connection to the country so that you want to stay a while.

If you are a Western couple, I would assume you have each other to support you through the challenges of negotiating life in Thailand so you may well not bother mixing too much with locals (apart from at work) and if that works for you, fine. You may well have Thai colleagues, say at an international school, who speak excellent English and the school may support you in visa and other admin matters so, in short, you may not feel much pressure to understand 'real life' in Thailand. However, having lived and worked in Singapore myself, I can say with some confidence that, even with help from colleagues and so on, Thailand is not as easy to settle into as Singapore. Obviously, the main reason for this is that Singapore speaks English as a first language whereas English is a second language in Thailand.

So, if you are a Western couple and looking to stay for a reasonable length of time, I can only see one realistic way to feel comfortable in Thailand and that

179

is to learn the language to basic level, at the very least. That way, even if you do not hang out with any Thai people and you both speak English exclusively at work, you still can negotiate everyday social situations in Thailand in Thai thus minimising your frustration and feeling of alienation.

Thailand is a wonderful destination for a holiday but settling down, working and managing your everyday life in Thailand can be quite challenging. The culture is different, the pace of life is different, values may be different, the way to get things done is different and so on, so, your best way to cope with all of this is to make a little effort to integrate, learn the language to some level and still retain your links to your Western friends so that you get the best of both worlds. The exception to this may be the expats who are in the lucky position of working in an English-speaking environment, living in a big city in a central area in a luxury condo, having help from HR at work or agents to deal with visas and other Thai speaking situations. For the rest, a balanced approach to life in Thailand is probably the best bet.

Leisure and Relaxation

SHOPPING

One of the very best things about life in Thailand is the shopping! This is one of the few areas of life where it is probably even better when you live here as compared to when you were here for a holiday. So, if you loved coming over to Thailand and spent time in one of the many shopping malls in Bangkok on your last trip here, believe me you will love it even more when you spend time shopping here as part of your weekend or evening relaxation routine. The reason for this is simply that you will discover more and more stores and activities the longer you stay here and so you will happily spend half a day or even a whole day here...

- browsing shops,
- having a coffee,
- buying everything from luxury brand name goods to a pair of shoes for 199 baht from a market stall,
- watching a movie,
- getting a massage,
- having amazing food,
- getting your admin and errands done,
- getting a facial,
- ordering your furniture for your new condo,
- reserving a new condo (!),
- ordering a car (!),
- doing your banking,
- getting your weekly groceries
- and lots more, all under one roof!

But what makes shopping in Thailand so special and so fulfilling are a set of intangible factors that are actually quite hard to explain; taken together, they form the feeling you feel when you spend a day at the mall and that feeling is simply far better than back home:

- Somehow or other, goods simply seem more attractive and 'buyable' over here than back home. This may be to do with the fact that they are often on sale most times of the year (or, at least, that is what it seems like) or it

181

may be that, as an expat, you have more relative wealth in your pocket than you did in the US or UK so you can simply afford more. Whatever it is, there is something about how irresistible shopping is in Thailand.

- Second, there is probably a feeling of being welcomed and served with humility and grace that Westerners simply love to bits. Year after year, decade after decade, Thailand welcomes millions of tourists who, almost to a man / woman, agree that Thai people are so lovely and polite and kind and this mainly stems from their interaction with Thai people as a customer or receiver of a service. Thais do hosting and service better than most, leaving foreigners enchanted with their softly spoken ways, their humble body language, the beautiful sounding language, their attention to detail when it comes to customers' comfort and so on.

- Finally, there is probably also a factor related to how relaxed and pleasant an atmosphere it is walking around in a shopping mall in Thailand. Compared to shopping centres and malls back in London, I can say, with no hesitation, that I would choose Thai malls every single time. There is something about the way people walk, their loudness, teenagers and so on that makes shopping back home an ordeal rather than relaxation...at least for me. If you have been to Thailand before and spent time shopping here, you will know what I mean.

As ever though, nothing in life is perfect and there are aspects of shopping in Thailand that are somewhat frustrating or annoying or just slightly disappointing but given my comments above, obviously, these slightly negative points barely have any meaningful adverse impact on your enjoyment of this national pastime in Thailand.

- People walk slow! As I mentioned earlier, people walk very, very slowly sometimes and not necessarily because they are on their phone while walking. The pace of life is simply more relaxed over here. So, get used to it and learn to stroll...by which I mean shuffle and you will probably not run into the heels of the person in front.

- While on holiday you loved your shopping over here, you probably did not have to exchange or return something in a store. As an expat, there is every likelihood that you will do so at some point, either because the item is faulty or damaged or because you just changed your mind. While exchanges due to faults are still ok, albeit with quite a lot of activity and papers being shuffled before you get your replacement, a refund is a trickier affair.

- The big stores will process your refund but you may well see the famous Thai smile vanish and rather more serious faces in front of you. This is when you realise that holidays and real life are two different things – Thai people do not go around smiling all the time any more than any other nationality; they simply host and serve you with a warm smile because you are a treasured customer (or, at least, made to feel like one).

- Although I have no factual basis, I expect that consumer rights are not quite as strong here as they are back home so things like refunds are not that common and certainly not expected at all in smaller, independent stores outside shopping malls. So, if you are used to 'abusing' your rights back home and getting a dress for a night out and then returning it the next day, well, good luck.

- As with the walking speed point, those people from the US or UK, say, who are used to going in, choosing, purchasing and leaving in an organised, quick and direct way may well struggle in Thailand. As I said, the pace of life is slower and suited to those who are more relaxed and happy to receive a more well-rounded service. Let me illustrate with an example.

- Say you are at a mall and are browsing some shoes. You will be served by a very attentive assistant who is only too happy to go and fetch each pair you want to try on. Then, when you have chosen, you may be invited to carry on sitting on the stool while the assistant takes your card to the cash desk herself and comes back with the slip for you to sign and then goes back over to the desk to complete the transaction and then returns to give you the bag with your shoes in.

- Overall this process may have taken a few minutes longer than back home and so, if you are the kind of person who likes to get on with things and would rather forego your comfort and just walk to the desk and pay and leave, you may get a bit frustrated. So, either indicate that you are happy to go and pay at the desk or, chill out and sit back and relax!

- Finally, you may notice that while the service is great here, sometimes the product knowledge or ability to answer questions can be limited. Partly this is to do with language so you may end up in the familiar situation where you ask a question about a product and suddenly there is a look of suppressed panic on the assistant's face while he / she tells you to wait there and runs off without any further explanation. You then stand there, wonder what is going on and if you are impatient or short-tempered, you may even just wander off and out.

- In fact, the assistant probably ran off to get a colleague who can speak better English or, at the very least, knows more about the product. So, while his / her intentions were good, due to lack of language skills, there is every chance of a misunderstanding arising. This happens a lot in dealings between Thais and foreigners.

- As far as product knowledge and explanation, I am not convinced that it is just language issues because my wife and I often have the same disappointment and frustration. You indicate interest in a large flatscreen TV and the assistant confidently tells you that it is on promotion and then you ask what it particularly good about that TV over others and he can barely come out with more than one feature but says it in a way that is rather smug as if just mentioning that one feature is all the customer needs to know. If you try to probe further, you get nowhere fast.
- So, my advice would be to do your research online beforehand for things like electronic goods and if it is clothes or something where you cannot really research first, try to ask yourself first whether your question is really necessary and whether the answer to your question will be critical to your decision to purchase. If not, save yourself the hassle and just buy it without asking too many questions in English.

I will end this section on shopping with two anecdotes from my own experiences that illustrate the best and worst (although by 'worst' I mean a softer, more bemused feeling, not any harsh criticism) aspects of shopping in Thailand.

My first three years living here in Thailand were spent in Mûak Lèk, Saraburi, a province about 90 minutes north of Bangkok just before you get to Khao Yai National Park. I was working in a banking software company and on Friday evenings I would head into Bangkok (as did many of the employees). Usually, both on the way there and on the way back on Sunday evening, my wife and I would stop at a petrol station for some food and a bit of shopping at 7-Eleven or whatever. I can tell you without any hesitation that I simply loved these little stops and something so basic as picking up a few bits at a motorway service station was a pleasure because of all the points I have discussed previously. So, the point here is if I could enjoy shopping in a service station that much, it just shows how much you will love Thailand shops, markets, stalls, malls and yes, even service stations.

On the other hand, sometimes shopping in Thailand can be a little bemusing and trying on your patience. My wife and I recently went to buy a printer and were immediately recommended a particular model without much of an explanation as to why it was recommended (bear in mind, this is all in Thai). Anyway, we then explained what features we wanted and were then directed to another model which the assistant assured us was the right one. After answering our very basic questions and being convinced it was the right one and it was at a reduced price, we agreed to go ahead...only to be told "Oh sorry, it's out of stock" literally as soon as we had agreed to buy.

It was so ridiculous it was almost farcical. Both of us exclaimed in frustration and I could not help asking him (in Thai) why he had spent ten minutes selling us the printer if it was out of stock. Cue...loss of face and indignant silence and no apology. Then when I slightly forcefully asked for him to point out which printer fulfilled our three key criteria and was also in stock and in our specified price range, awkward silence. Luckily a more knowledgeable sales assistant came over and found us the perfect printer we were looking for but this highlights the points I mentioned before – sales of electronic goods without much explanation of features and benefits and comparison between models; my regrettable loss of patience in a very un-Thai way and the inevitable loss of face reaction from the sales assistant. Now that you know, I am sure you will exercise more patience than I did and just go with the flow as best as you can.

COMEDY

One of the most difficult things to get to grips with in a foreign country, especially one that is so culturally different to the Western world, is local sense of humour. The reason is that it is a double whammy – 1) the language of jokes and comedy (in any language) is the language of wordplay and obscure references to things. In most cases, you cannot break down the language in a joke and work out what was funny – you simply have to know what the comedian is referring to. And 2) the cultural difference is at its most acute in comedy. So, you can think of the sense of humour of a nation as the ultimate challenge to understand and will likely be the last hurdle you will need to overcome if you want to fully integrate into any culture, especially Thai.

In spite of being fluent in Thai, I am often left cold and confused by some of the comedy on Thai TV but over the years, have picked up the feel of the jokes more and more, the longer I have been here. The Thai is quite difficult to understand in the first place and when you throw in references to showbiz gossip as a lead in to a joke, it can be challenging to say the least. Then, to top it all, sometimes, you just simply do not find the joke funny – you might understand the joke but you just do not think it is funny. For example, a lot of Thai comedy is slapstick and some of it is wordplay involving English words being mispronounced by Thai people or Thai being mispronounced by Myanmar immigrant workers or suchlike. Or sometimes it can be, as a lot of Thai comedy is, just quickfire slapstick. Unsurprisingly, to a Western ear, it can all be a bit hit and miss, even if he / she speaks good Thai.

For those who are interested in such matters, I can promise you one thing – if you start to watch Thai TV and Thai comedy – perhaps with your Thai wife or girlfriend – over time, your Thai language will improve massively and you will appreciate the feel of the language and the culture better than you ever did before. You might not find much of it that funny but if you understand why they find it funny, you will be able to function better in society. You will become familiar with the sound effects that accompany slapstick comedy – the boom, boom drum roll, for example – not to mention all the other sound effects in popular Thai TV programmes e.g. the "wow!" sound or the "oh nooo" sound and over time, you will become so used to these that when you have been away for a while and come back to Thai TV, it will be like meeting an old friend.

TV

I assume the majority of expats do not watch much of Thai TV, which is unsurprising really. The first thing to do if you do want to give it a go is to stop comparing Thai TV to HBO or BBC or any other Western, well known TV channels. It is very tempting to scoff and make condescending comments about the quality of the TV programmes here, especially compared to what you are used to back home but this is neither fair nor with any resolution... ever. After all, Thai TV will not change to please your tastes and standards so what is the point of complaining?

I freely admit I have made many observations of a critical or condescending nature when watching a particular scene in a soap opera or a gameshow that seems ridiculous to me – and in some cases, with justification – but the longer I stay here, the more I try to overlook these and accept local TV for what it is – a representation of life in Thailand. If you have a Thai girlfriend or wife, you should probably consider trying to watch a bit more Thai TV with her because, without doing so, you have one less thing that the two of you can share and if the two of you went back to live in your own country, you would probably expect her to get into your TV programmes rather than sitting on the sofa next to you bored out of her skull.

Thai soap operas

Lakhorn Thai are a national favourite type of TV programme – often people translate these as 'Thai soap opera' but we are not talking Eastenders or whatever. Some are more like Dynasty or Dallas and some are like comedy dramas while some others remind Thai people of their heritage and history and so are like Downton Abbey. This latter category often features old fashioned Thai language for which even Thai people need (Thai) subtitles – you can relate it to Shakespearian language in British culture.

The majority of the famous (or perhaps infamous) lakhorn are the ones that are more like Dallas; one recent example that has just finished, at the time of writing, is Pleung Boon, featuring Janie, Louis Scott (who is half Thai, half 'farang' and speaks very good but not native speaker level Thai) and other Thai stars. Janie plays a spoilt, selfish brat type of character who has an affair with a married guy and with each episode, her character does increasingly selfish and outrageous things but seems to get away with it every time. By the end, everybody in the country was desperate for her character to get her comeuppance; in a chat show featuring the show's stars, Janie admitted that people had become so obsessed with her character and had so much hate for her character, she could barely step out in public herself...in real life! For British readers, think Dirty Den from Eastenders or other small screen characters that become so much part of people's lives, we forget they are only characters.

Anyway, the point of me relating all this is that if you do invest some effort into learning Thai and watching these lakhorn with your girlfriend, you will feel more part of society and understand the buzz around the country when a new, hotly anticipated series comes out. Not only that, the very fact that you know the characters in a lakhorn and watch lakhorn Thai will be amusing to Thais as they do not expect any 'farang' to be into their local TV shows so this can be a way to break the ice and cross the culture barrier when in a foreign country.

Other TV programmes expats may like

Apart from lakhorn Thai, for those who are interested in learning the language, it is worth watching programmes like Club Friday, Saam Zap and other chat shows. They are the equivalent of Graham Norton or Loose Women so the format is familiar and more importantly, because of the format, easier to pick up the language from. If you can just about guess the subject of the question, you can guess parts of the answer and so, over time, pick up more and more words. In general, chat show style of programmes will help you to learn Thai and there are a lot of these apart from the two mentioned previously; for example, there is a well-known show where a group of presenters go to visit a celebrity at his / her home and check out the home and have a chat and maybe even have a meal together. This type of programme will not only help attune your ears to Thai sounds, – the most important first step to learning Thai – it will also allow you to observe how Thais interact in a social situation, which again is key.

Richard McCully & Stephen Saad

Watching TV from back home

Finally, no matter how much you try to get into Thai TV, you will miss your own favourite programmes terribly. For many people, the easy solution to this is to subscribe to Netflix through their SMART TV. Some others, like my wife and I, use YouTube but this can often be a bit unsatisfactory as you are dependent on whether your programme is uploaded and in full or not. Obviously, you can just go for the top Platinum package that the satellite providers offer but bear in mind, this is, unsurprisingly, not a cheap option (in Thai terms).

If you are fortunate enough to earn around the same in Thailand as you did back home, you probably do not care and are happy to spend several thousand baht per month to ensure you get all your movies, sport and documentaries from back home. Even the top satellite packages will not, however, have BBC One and Two, for example and BBC iPlayer will not work outside the UK. If, like me, you really miss these channels, there seem to be alternative ways available to access these channels but that is as far as this book will go – you need to do your own research and decide whether any of these methods suit you and your circumstances.

MUSIC

One of the very best ways of learning Thai is to listen to Thai music. I am not talking about lôok tôong (traditional Thai country / folk music) or some weird cultural music and I certainly do not mean anything to do with Thai dance, I mean Thai pop and rock. Many of the songs are absolutely great, in my opinion of course, and are ideal for learning Thai in a format that is enjoyable and crucially, give you an indication of how Thai is actually spoken i.e. you can pick up many expressions from listening to Thai songs. Not only this, Thai people love karaoke and so, if you manage to learn a song or two, you will be the 'talk of the town' (in a good way) and will be held in higher esteem than previously. There are sites that have the full lyrics to Thai songs, where each song's lyrics is written out in triplicate i.e. Thai, transliterated or 'karaoke' Thai and English. Sometimes these sites will also have the Youtube video of the song alongside the lyrics.

I have listed below some of the most well-known artists and some my favourite Thai songs over the years, not because I think you should all like all the songs that I like but you have to start somewhere and so I am just giving you an entry point from where you can explore other songs if you want. In most cases, you can simply tap in the name of the band in Youtube and where this

188

does not immediately yield the result, you can add on 'Thai song' to the name of the band e.g. entering 'Micro' does not yield the band's songs as Micro is a common English word and there are other videos that are related to that word but if you add 'Thai', it will come up straightaway. In most cases, the most well-known / popular songs of the artists below will be listed first anyway so I have not listed all the songs you should listen to but what I have done is indicate songs worthy of note for one reason or another.

- Micro – one of the all-time greatest bands in Thailand! Everyone in Thailand will know Micro songs even though they are from twenty to thirty years ago and pretty much all of their songs are awesome; my favourite band. Think Oasis or even Bon Jovi as a comparison in terms of their fame (in Thailand) and maybe Air Supply in terms of their style / genre.
- For those readers who think they are good at Thai and well beyond basic level, a good test for yourselves is to listen to <u>jum</u> <u>fŭng</u> <u>jai</u> จำฝังใจ and see if you understand every word and every line of the song and can follow the Thai subtitles. The song uses simple Thai and hardly any metaphors or indirect expressions found in most songs so it is a good test of your Thai skills.
- If you want to show off your Thai singing skills, learn bàwk maa <u>kum</u> diao บอกมาคำเดียว, even if you only manage the chorus. The words are simple and it is a song that is perfect for singing along to and probably everyone in Thailand knows the song so you can be a superstar the next time you go to karaoke with your Thai friends if you manage to sing even just the chorus of this song.
- Pong Pat – Another absolute icon of the late 80s, his two most famous songs are so well-known that if you hear them in a Thai club or bar, every single Thai person will sing along with all the energy they have. If you understood the words, you would know why Thais sing these songs so passionately. The songs are: <u>fûn</u> feuan ฟื้นเฟือน and <u>jai</u> <u>núk</u> <u>leng</u> ใจนักเลง.
- Big Ass – another massive band whose songs are seemingly known by everyone. Their album Seven from 2004 has many songs that are still absolutely guaranteed to get a bar singing, with the song <u>lên</u> kǎwng sǒong เล่นของสูง possibly the most famous.
- For a song that is easy to follow and easy to learn Thai from, listen to náam dtaa น้ำตา. Or <u>kon</u> <u>mâi</u> <u>ao</u> tàan คนไม่เอาถ่าน. Both are excellent.
- For two slow songs that stir the emotions, check out <u>fòon</u> ฝุ่น and gèuhd maa kâeh <u>rúk</u> <u>gun</u> เกิดมาแค่รักกัน.

Let me take a break at this point to highlight something that is a very common misconception about Thai songs, namely that they are all love songs. Assuming this is meant to mean that songs that are all romantic and essentially convey the message "I love you", nothing could be further from the truth!

Many Thai songs talk about missing someone who has left after a break-up, the hurt of breaking up, the bitterness that follows a break-up and many are bittersweet where the singer wishes the girl who has left him well and sometimes even offers to take her back whenever she chooses. Many describe the philosophical position people take once they have come to terms with the other person cheating or running off with someone else. Some say the singer is grateful for having loved the girl even if it did not work out while others ask how many times should I put up with your cheating and look the other way? In the West we would probably call the majority of these sentiments over the top corniness but not so much here, at least among the younger generation.

So, most Thai songs are sad or bittersweet songs and that is why they evoke so much emotion in Thai people because every Thai person can empathise with the words and probably has some experience themselves. Many songs evoke a sense of a male singer either singing that he can take it that the girl does not love him anymore and other similar romantic martyr sentiments. To understand Thai people, how they think, how Thai relationships between men and women work, it helps a lot to listen to Thai songs, as these songs are just a reflection of romantic culture. So, for example, there is a lot of infidelity in Thailand so, as I said earlier, many Thai songs are not so much "I love you" as more like "I always knew I was not good enough for you but at least I got to love you for a while..." and so on. So, when you go to a Thai bar or club and everyone is singing along with so much passion, it is probably some heroic sentiment or some bittersweet emotion that is perfect to sing along to with a few drinks already down you.

You cannot really appreciate Thai songs without understanding the words so if you are going to listen to the songs I have listed here, it is really necessary to have the translation (from one of many sites online) open alongside. The translation is often not great and the lyrics sound corny or stilted when translated but you get an indication of the feeling behind the song. As a foreigner, you may not necessarily be into the songs below because many of them are sung by young twenty somethings and not in line with your musical tastes. But it is worth learning a few words of some of these songs in the same way a foreigner to the UK would benefit from learning 'famous' English songs such as by Westlife or Spice Girls, as they are fairly recent songs and known by everyone.

- Labanoon – one of my (and Thailand's) favourite bands.

190

- Listen to the song <u>kon</u> dtua <u>dum</u> คนตัวดำ – as a brown-skinned guy in Thailand, it is almost as if this song was written for me as I can identify with the words completely. The song is a response to the social bias against darker skinned people.
- Check out the video to páe taang แพ้ทาง – if you have ever wondered what it is that makes so many foreigners fall in love with Thai women, year after year, just watch this video.
- Listen to the song faen <u>gào</u> แฟนเก่า – it is as good a test of your Thai as there is, as the song is slow so you have enough time to keep up with the words sung and the subtitles on the karaoke version on Youtube. If you manage to understand more than 90% of the words, you are probably legitimately beyond basic and nearing intermediate level.
- Loso – possibly the most famous Thai band outside Thailand (and within Thailand too), their style travels well and therefore, they have had success in the UK, playing at festivals etc. After many years of success, the band broke up and the lead singer – Sek Loso – continued solo. Pretty much all of their songs are great and many are good for learning Thai too.
- Bird – if Loso is huge in Thailand, Bird may be even bigger. He is like the godfather of Thai pop and dance and has had simply massive success, again mainly because his style – more pop in the early days and dance more recently – translates well outside Thailand. The closest comparison is Cliff Richard – just like Cliff, Bird is not just known for his success but also his unbelievably youthful looks (at the time of writing, he is 59) and his clean-cut image. There is every chance you have already heard a Bird song without knowing it as his songs are often played in places where there are foreigners because they blend in well with Western dance songs.
- Two of Bird's more recent big songs are maa <u>tam</u>-<u>mai</u> มาทำไม and faen jăa แฟนจ๋า.
- D2B / Dan & Beam – possibly the biggest boyband of their time, which was 15 years ago, their songs are incredibly catchy – think Take That. One of the three original members died ten years ago and the band disbanded soon after. The 'kids' obviously no longer listen to D2B but they are so well-known that if boyband style pop songs are your thing, you could not do better than learn a D2B song or two.
- Clash – the band that got me loving Thai songs in the first place. Absolutely huge band from the early 2000s with a very distinctive style – as well as the lead singer's voice, their lyrics are also very emotionally evocative and describe the bittersweet nature of relationships perfectly. Many of their songs talk about saying to the girl "It's ok, I know you want to leave and go with that other guy but I'll always be here waiting; if you

want someone's shoulder to cry on one day, let me be the one to comfort you" and so on. In the West, we might find all this to be overblown cheese but for many, this is just the kind of old-fashioned ballad that they miss and cannot get back home since the 70s and so love Thai music to relive those days. Four of the more noteworthy songs are:

- kăw <u>chét</u> náam dtaa ขอเช็ดน้ำตา – their first big hit
- <u>rúp</u> dâai <u>tóok</u> yàang รับได้ทุกอย่าง – an easy song to understand if you learn a bit of Thai so a good song to test yourself against
- pleng pĕe sêʉa เพลงผีเสื้อ – one of the most beautiful and emotional songs you will hear anywhere
- teuh kɤʉ naang fáa <u>nai</u> <u>jai</u> เธอคือนางฟ้าในใจ – an incredibly (or sickeningly, depending on your point of view) romantic song; if you like it and happen to have plans to marry a Thai girl, consider using it as your wedding song.
- Other notable bands you may like (and Thai people like) are:
- Blackhead
- Bodyslam – check out săeng <u>sòot</u> táai แสงสุดท้าย (for fanclub version) on Youtube and you'll understand how big they were and how much Thai rock is loved by Thais.
- Silly Fools
- Potato
- Hyper
- I-Zax
- Peacemaker
- Thaitanium – Thai hip-hop
- Palapol – gentle, easy listening Thai music
- Some really catchy one-off songs are:
- Neo-X – <u>jai</u> teuh gàwd <u>krai</u> ใจเธอกอดใคร. This is another song to test your Thai.
- Ster – 100 hèd-<u>pŏn</u> 100 เหตุผล. I talk about the chorus of this song in my intermediate level Thai language book – it is simple Thai and easy to understand.
- Gear Knight – <u>dtòk</u>-<u>long</u> <u>rao</u> <u>bpen</u> <u>a</u>-<u>rai</u> <u>gun</u> ตกลงเราเป็นอะไรกัน. I think this song got to number one in the charts and it is not difficult to see why. It is quite different in style to most Thai songs and is more like a Western style ballad.
- Syam – geuhn <u>jai</u> <u>jà</u> <u>òt</u>-<u>ton</u> เกินใจจะอดทน. This is another song that you will appreciate once your Thai reaches intermediate level.
- Bie Sukrit – <u>jang</u> <u>wà</u> hŭa <u>jai</u> จังหวะหัวใจ. This is a crazily catchy song that was played everywhere in Thailand, especially around Song-kran time, a few years ago.

- Taxi – kíd-tĕung mái we-laa têe teuh... คิดถึงฉันไหมเวลาที่เธอ... This is one of the most well-known one-off Thai songs by expats and it is often played during Song-kran street parties. A total feel-good song.
- Ying Li – kăw jai teuh lâek beuh toh ขอใจเธอแลกเบอร์โทร. It is hard to over-state how good this song is – it is possibly the catchiest song I have ever heard in Thailand. The Thais go absolutely crazy for this song and with good reason; imagine a song as catchy as Gangnam Style and you will get it. Not only is it catchy, the words are really flirty and romantic and the video is simply impossible to tear your eyes away from. On top of all this, Ying Lee is the very definition of Thai (Isaan) beauty. With all this and the fact that it is the traditional lôok tôong country music style, it is quite simply one of the greatest songs in Thailand. Period.
- Even if you have ignored this whole section and have no interest in Thai songs, you will probably still like this song and have probably heard it played, as it is only a few years old at the time of writing. For those who want to learn a Thai song, unfortunately, this is a difficult song to learn and sing because it is quite fast but if there is one song you should, at least, learn the meaning of, this is it.

SPORT, HEALTH AND FITNESS

Sport plays a big part in the life of a lot of people in Thailand. Sport is a major part of school life with Sport Day being the highlight of the academic calendar for many students. This tradition continues on in many companies throughout Thailand and acts as a form of teambuilding.

Whilst Thailand isn't well known for sports stars it has given the world Muay Thai which has become more popular thanks to the rise of MMA. Outside of the ring Thailand has a number of high profile female athletes in badminton and golf. The women's volleyball team also performs well globally. The country usually wins a couple of medals in the Olympics in weightlifting and boxing.

When it comes to playing sport the number one choice for many is bad-minton. With a low cost and high volume of courts it is easy to get into. It is also a sport that men and women can play together. Football is also popular with many men playing every week. There are good artificial football pitches throughout the country. Thailand also boasts a large number of golf courses which attract many local and international players. The cost is very high for the average Thai so it is considered a sport for the wealthy here.

Yoga has remained popular in Thailand over the past 5 years. An increasing number of people take part in sessions both at home and at gyms. Gym membership itself is quite popular with middle class Thais. Monthly subscriptions can be as low as 500 baht for a place with decent facilities.

The government also promotes health and fitness through local community sports clubs. These places usually consist of swimming pools, fitness and badminton courts. They are heavily subsidized with membership only costing around 100 baht per year. Foreigners can use these facilities too.

It is a good thing that sport is being promoted as it is undeniable that the average Thai person today is less healthy than ten years ago. Younger people today do less exercise and have a worse diet. The increase in fast food joints and snacks may well have a large impact on this.

When it comes to living a healthy life, there are a number of obstacles in Thailand. As we have already discussed there is a lot of pollution in many areas. Even places like Chiang Mai are now experiencing rapid development and all the negatives that come along with that. The sight of people walking around wearing surgical masks to protect themselves from pollution is pretty common. My doctor advised me not to take buses or songthaews due to the negative effect it will have on my lungs.

The sun also plays a factor in leading to an unhealthy life. A lot of Thai people will do pretty much anything to avoid the sun's rays. They will walk around with umbrellas and run into shaded areas. A lot of people will also avoid going out which means they are not getting even basic exercise. Many people head to shopping malls in their free time just to enjoy some free air conditioning which isn't good in the long run.

Mental health awareness is quite low in Thailand and there doesn't seem to be a lot of help for sufferers. In terms of the expat community there are a surprisingly high number of suicides. Being away from friends and family can cause a lot of stress. Most expats here will go through a stage of wondering why they are in Thailand and have days where just about everything goes wrong.

Nightlife

Whilst you are probably aware of the rather raucous reputation Thailand has for nightlife our aim here is to show you some of the more positive, less well-known nightlife options in Thailand as well as a brief overview of the touristy side too.

During your time in Thailand you will probably hit the well-known party areas at some point so we will have a quick overview of them too.

For a comprehensive explanation of nightlife, you can visit Bangkok.com, which offers extensive explanation of what each area offers and reviews of all the major clubs and bars.

BANGKOK

Bangkok has several different areas for nightlife. These range from good places for a drink through to red light districts and backpacker hotspots.

Khao San Road has a worldwide reputation as a spot for backpackers and travelers to hit. It's also a popular place for younger expats to hang out. You can expect cheap drinks, a mix of western and Asian food and a late night here!

Nana (Sukhumvit Soi 4) is home to the famous Nana plaza, a 3-story red light district full of go-go bars and pickup joints. Nana, and nearby Soi Cowboy, have become somewhat of a tourist sight with many people just going to look rather than partake in the activities there. The Patpong area in Silom is the most famous, or perhaps infamous (!) and certainly the oldest red-light district for foreigners, with a lot of its infamy gained during the Vietnam War when US troops were stationed nearby. Many veterans of the go-go bar scene say the whole scene has become more mercenary these days and the girls are less willing to just have a chat and were more like companions to Westerners, not as explicitly out for money as they seem to be these days. Maybe times are tougher these days, who knows.

Silom Soi 4 is the main gay friendly street in Bangkok. Soi 2 – the previous soi – is smaller and is much more 'full-on'; Soi 2 is actually good fun even for straight people and worth a look. There are a variety of bars, restaurants and clubs with an infamous reputation throughout Asia and beyond.

In terms of a more chilled out place to socialize at night you should look at the train markets dotted around Bangkok. Although more tourists are becoming aware of the train markets you should be able to enjoy a more Thai atmosphere. These train markets are made up of numerous stalls and bars. You get loads of food joints too where you can bring food to a bar. Live music is pretty common.

The areas between BTS stations Thong Lor and Udom Suk are becoming more popular for nightlife, especially with younger expats. There are a large number of craft beer bars and trendy restaurants. Prices can be expensive.

Even in the unknown suburbs of Bangkok you will find areas with fantastic restaurants and bars. A street that looks pretty shabby might have a few great bars or famous restaurants to hit. Take a look at Kaset-Nawamin road for a load of great restaurants and bars away from tourists.

Noise Pollution

Something which is an issue in a lot of Thai restaurants and bars is noise pollution. For some reason the music is always turned up to 11. It can be really difficult to just sit and have a chat with your friends.

Asking a bar to turn down the music will result in a confused look so just try to sit as far away from the speaker as possible.

PATTAYA

Pattaya supposedly rivals Las Vegas when it comes to nightlife. If there is a place on earth where you can do and see whatever you want, it is probably Pattaya. However, there are still decent areas where you can head out at night and avoid the red-light activities. Also, as with the adult areas of Bangkok a lot of people just come to look and things aren't as crazy as in the past.

Jomtien is around 5 minutes' drive from the main part of Pattaya and is where many expats prefer to stay and hang out. There are a wide range of bars and restaurants here. Also, in the housing complexes there are restaurants and bars which have none of the adult entertainment found downtown.

Many families and expat couples live here and find lots to do without the need to resort to strip clubs and ping pong shows.

Walking Street is obviously the most famous part of Pattaya nightlife. It makes the red-light districts of Bangkok look tame. There are also many other connecting streets offering more of the same in the area.

CHIANG MAI

There is a famous walking street market on a Sunday evening. It is a good place to chill with friends. The central area of Chiang Mai has a rather backpacker vibe to it and is home to many cheap places to get a beer.

Nimmanhaemin is home to nightlife similar to Thong Lor in Bangkok. Trendy bars, craft beer and good restaurants are easy to find in this area.

The riverfront also hosts some good restaurants with live bands. The Riverside is a particularly good place if you like rock music.

PHUKET

Parts of Phuket are becoming a mini Pattaya. Patong in particular is now full of bars catering for hookups.

There are still areas where you can find good restaurants and bars to chill. Most of the better restaurants in Phuket are more expensive than other areas in Thailand. Bars will normally cater towards tourists but you can find English style pubs and burger joints too.

In the 5* resorts you will find elegant bars and beach front joints with amazing views to admire the sunset.

ISLANDS

The most famous nightlife on the islands is the Full Moon Party on Koh Phangan. If you feel the need to party on a beach until the break of dawn whilst thousands of people around you dance and make a mess of the area then head there.

The government has cracked down on island nightlife and things are more subdued than the past. Curfews are enforced in many places and most places close down at around 1am.

Koh Samed, around an hour south of Pattaya is famous as a travel destination for gay nightlife.

THAI STYLE NIGHTS OUT

Although Thai people do like to drink it is almost always linked to eating as well. You will quickly see that most Thai people don't just pop out for a few drinks. They go for meals and drink at the same time. Having said that, there are still plenty of clubbers, especially from middle-class and upper-class backgrounds who like to party like Westerners and are aware of Western culture and so on.

Most Thai bargoers and clubbers still party a bit differently to Westerners. For example, while Westerners might stand around a bar and drink and mingle, Thais will, almost without exception, book a table or get there early enough to get a table and a bottle of whisky to share. They do dance but only once the evening has moved on and they have had a few rounds of whisky coke and generally loosed up. Although people make a big deal of this difference, really, the only real difference is Thais like to sit while Westerners like to stand and small talk.

Nightclubs are not easy to find outside tourist areas. The most famous are probably Route 66 in Bangkok and Insomnia in Pattaya. Around universities you won't find the drinking culture which is seen in western countries so there aren't many nightclubs.

Karaoke is popular in Thailand but be aware there are two very different types of karaoke joints. The first type is the legitimate kind, they have private rooms for groups where you can sing away all night. Staff will be waiting to bring food and drink to you. There will be a selection of Thai and western songs to choose from. Thais love karaoke and there is a chance you might be invited out to join, especially work-related groups.

The second type is usually in a dark back alley and has ten or so girls sat outside in revealing attire. Actually, although it is a karaoke joint there won't be much singing going on. Frequented almost solely by men this kind of place is little more than a strip club / brothel. A lot of the patrons go to drink with their friends and have a few girls come and join them to chat before deciding whether to take them elsewhere after.

Another new feature to hit most non-tourist areas in Thailand is craft beer. The idea of microbreweries is quite popular here especially among the middle and upper classes. People are prepared to spend 200-300 Baht for a small bottle of craft beer. Due to legal restraints none of these are actually brewed in Thailand and many actually come from Cambodia. Some of these are actually pretty decent beers but you will need to decide if they are worth three times the price of a local beer.

As mentioned in the food chapter night markets are a fun way to spend a night out. They have a huge range of snacks and finger food and mini bars to check out. Most places have live music and sport on the big screen. You normally get special deals on drinks and the food is pretty cheap. For around 300 Baht you can get a couple of beers and two or three small dishes.

Live Music

Major artists don't really tour here very often and when they do tickets are very expensive. You will have to pay at least 4,000 Baht for a decent seat.

To make up for this a lot of bars and bigger restaurants have live music played by cover bands. It is great to sit outside eating and drinking with good music in the background. The later into the night the more likely the place will turn into a mini music venue with everyone dancing and singing along.

NIGHTCLUBS

You will find nightclubs in Thailand but they are mainly in tourist areas. A lot of nightclubs have international DJs and play western music. Most places charge an entrance fee but you will usually get at least one free drink.

ADULT ENTERTAINMENT

Strip clubs, "massage parlours", ping pong shows and brothels can be found all around the country. Bangkok and Pattaya are probably the two areas that tourists and expats know of but in most towns you can find somewhere offering these services. Prostitution is illegal in Thailand but you will quickly see that police do not stop it.

GoGo bars are bars where you can watch scantily clad dancers perform on stage and negotiate with them to leave the premises with you. In the past you would see groups of naked women performing but these days it is rare to see nudity as it is something the police are cracking down on. These bars are strip clubs but are much more out in the open. They normally are themed and have girls outside waiting to drag customers in.

The bars are not necessarily as seedy as made out to be by judgemental Westerners and indeed, in recent times, have made attempts to go a bit more upmarket in order to satisfy the more 'sophisticated' Westerner client coming to Bangkok these days. Some bars have an additional class of bargirl who are 'models'. They are taller and wear more 'classy but sexy' outfits and are supposedly not available for hire for the night. The more cynical expat may, possibly correctly, say that they are the same girls and the difference is purely superficial.

Ultimately, what makes the bars seedy is not the bars themselves but the

199

Western tourists and their behaviour when in these establishments so passing judgement on the girls, who are often from poor backgrounds, is a bit pointless. What is, unfortunately, true is that these red-light districts have gone from places where Westerners socialised with local girls in a 'fun' environment to being more and more commercially orientated. If you have ever thought that the celebration of Christmas in the West is becoming more about shopping and sales year by year, you will know what I mean about the bar scene.

Ping pong shows have long been associated with Thailand. You can find them in the tourist hotspots but beware these are places where your bill could be a lot higher than expected.

There are many massage complexes in Thailand. These places are usually aimed at Thai customers but foreigners can visit too. They have bars with performers and you can choose your favourite and negotiate for a massage or something else. Note that 'soapy massage' and Thai massage are not the same thing! The former is the racier version where there isn't a lot of actual (non-sexual) massaging involved while the latter is the world famous and limb-bending, sinew-stretching massage technique of Thailand. Do not confuse the two to save embarrassment; most legit Thai massage places will be shut down by police if they are caught offering any extra services so don't ask and don't put your masseur in the awkward position of having to decline your request while trying not to make you lose face. Having said all this, there are hybrid traditional massage places, often near to red light districts or sometimes in quiet parts of streets where the ladies will offer you a 'happy ending' or even more, subject to your negotiation skills and ability to be discreet. This is Thailand!

PUBS AND BARS

There are many bars and pubs around Thailand. These are similar to the places you find in your home country. They are a good place to meet friends, watch sport or play a game of pool. Note that Thais usually refer to what we would call bars as pubs so if you are talking to a Thai person and want to go to a traditional English pub, you will probably need to state this in full to differentiate.

As previously mentioned the idea of going out for a drink is not usually for most Thai people so these bars are usually located in tourist or expat hotspots. Most are well decorated and are family friendly unlike the gogo bars. They usually have some form of western management and a mix of local and international food. The international food at bars and pubs is normally better than most other restaurants in Thailand.

LGBT NIGHTLIFE

In general Thailand is pretty LGBT friendly, especially when it comes to for-eigners. Thai people are quite accepting of everyone and in reality, the majority of troubles you might face here would come from other tourists or expats.

As mentioned above there are specific areas famous for LGBT nightlife such as Silom in Bangkok. In Chiang Mai check out Chang Phueak for gay friendly clubs, bars and hotels. However, wherever you go in Thailand you should feel safe. Problems have been mentioned involving tourists however as Thailand attracts many people from conservative countries.

MEETING OTHER EXPATS

Whilst living overseas you will want to experience a little Thai culture but you will probably want to retain some links to your own. Many people build up social networks of people from their own country or others from similar backgrounds.

In the past, bars would be the social center for many expats here and that still rings true for some. However, there are now more options for expats look-ing to extend their social circle. A quick Google will show you there are plenty of clubs and societies to join. From sport to art there are many special interest groups always looking for new members.

WATCHING SPORTS

You might be used to watching the big game at home but a great part of being in Thailand is that you can watch it on the big screen at a bar or restaurant.

Thai providers carry most sports from around the world and you will be able to find somewhere showing the big match if you are in one of the tourist hot spots.

Everywhere in Thailand shows English Premier League games on a Saturday and Sunday night and you can even get commentary in English. Thais love English football so even in the middle of nowhere you can usually find a restaurant or bar which will stick the game on. The other benefit is they show all the games live, even those 3pm matches you couldn't see in the UK.

If you're looking for games from other countries you can usually find somewhere which will show them. The big sports bars usually have multiple screens and Thai providers show Italian, Spanish, French and German leagues.

Richard McCully & Stephen Saad

However, depending on the match they might be reluctant to change over from what is currently on. Champions League and Europa League matches are on at around 2am Thai time which means it is unlikely many bars will stay open late to show them.

NFL, NHL and NBA games are also easy to find with many expat bars opening up early to show matches or even putting on replays later in the day. Just ask in most sports bars and they should be able to put it on a screen for you.

Rugby League, Rugby Union, Aussie Rules and Cricket are also shown in many sports bars. Most Thai style places will only show football but find a specialist sports bar and they will be able to screen the game.

Special events such as Boxing matches or MMA fights will also attract many people to the local sports bars and expat hangouts.

INTERNATIONAL DRINKS

Something you might miss from home is your favorite drink. Whilst you can get a lot of good local lagers you don't have as much choice as back home when it comes to ales, wines and spirits.

Bars and supermarkets in tourist areas do carry a wider selection of international drinks but they charge a high premium.

DATE NIGHT

If you are going on a date then there are a range of options. Cinemas are found in malls and show movies in Thai and English. If you are with a Thai partner then the English version will have Thai subtitles which makes it ideal. Expect to pay between 100-220 Baht a ticket depending on the day you go. Wednesday is the best day as tickets are 100-150 Baht all day.

There are also local fairs that travel around the country which make for a nice date. There are normally games, snacks and shows to watch.

There is a growing arts scene in Bangkok and there are even cinemas showing independent films. Live Lounge on Sukhumvit 13 is one example of an arts venue and there are other comedy clubs and so on.

BEING SAFE AT NIGHT

Like everywhere in the world there is the chance of something happening to ruin your night out in Thailand. Also, some people tend to "go big" on a night out here which could lead to more problems.

Drunk and disorderly conduct may well result in being kicked out of a venue. If you harm a Thai person then there is the chance more could happen. Tourist locations are quite used to drunk behavior but Thais will think very badly of you if they see you in a bad state.

Theft is a problem, especially in the red-light districts. Pretty much every story of theft from Pattaya is linked to people walking along beach road (a notorious street full of prostitutes) at 2am. Foreigners normally have their phones out or wear expensive jewelry which is irresistible to the pickpockets and grab thieves. In a similar vein don't let anyone you don't know hug you as the chances are they are feeling you up to take your wallet and phone.

Sometimes people complain that their bill is much higher than expected in some bars and restaurants. Again, these tend to be tourist trap places or in the red-light districts. As an expat you will have a greater knowledge and will be able to avoid these type of places (if you want!).

Some Final Random Practicalities

GETTING CLEAN WATER

Pretty much all the practicalities of life in Thailand have been covered by Richard in the first section of this book so I will just mention one further point – getting drinkable water – as, after all, it is probably the most important aspect of anybody's life. In Thailand, nobody really drinks tap water. It may be technically safe to drink but it just does not taste that great and in everyday life, I do not remember seeing anyone drink tap water. Having said that, the water is perfectly fine for when brushing your teeth or whatever and if you have ice in your coffee (or beer!), you are maybe having frozen tap water and there is no issue at all. So you really do not need to panic if you swallowed a bit of water while gargling or whatever, you are perfectly safe.

But when it comes to drinking water, everyone, including Thais, tends to stick with bottled water. This is fine for when eating at restaurants and suchlike but for home consumption, you are going to get sick and tired of having to get bottled water every day, especially when you have run out and you really do not feel like stepping out at that particular time. You can mitigate the situation to an extent by getting larger bottles or fill up at water vending machines, which you may have in your condo somewhere or even on your road. It is usually a few baht, using 1-baht coins, for enough water for at least one day, if not two. If you do not mind carrying your empty bottles to the vending machine every day or two and filing up and then carrying it back to your place, this is the way forward for you.

If you end up also getting sick and tired of this too, you may end up going for the solution that you should probably have gone for in the first place to save you a lot of trouble – get a water filter and separate drinking water tap fitted to your kitchen sink / water pipe. Obviously, if you are not staying long term, this solution will not make sense as the filter, which you can get from homeware stores, has a cost associated with it. Over the long term, however, getting this sorted will make a big difference because you will need water every day!

GETTING YOUR THAI VISA

Applying for a Thai visa is possibly the most common topic related to Thailand on the Internet – at least, it seems that way. There are tons of sites on the process and the requirements for each type of visa and there are also many forums with expats discussing their experiences of the application process and things to be aware of. With this in mind, I propose that this book will not go through all the visa types and the requirements for each but make some generic comments based on my own experiences. Every foreigner's experience is likely to be different and indeed, this is one of the key conclusions I reach at the end of this section – one person's experience is not necessarily the same as the next person's.

The place for all visa matters is the Immigration Division at Chaeng Wattana, which is in Nonthaburi, a small province in the north-west of Bangkok. The division is located in a massive building that contains multiple government departments and along with the other surrounding buildings, is part of a government complex – think of Westminster or Washington D.C. (albeit on a smaller scale) and you have got the idea. Compared to where it used to be in Sathorn, in cramped surroundings, the new building is a huge improvement and everything is open and spacious, clean and well-ordered. In the old building, which I turned up to recently not realising everything had moved to Chaeng Wattana, there was barely enough space to move and the queue would sometimes extend outside the room into the lobby and beyond. Old skool readers like me will remember the old building with a bit of perverse fondness in the same way many people have a real fondness for Don Mueang Airport – while the new airport is big and shiny and clean, there was (and still is) something more real and more Thai about the old airport.

Having said all this, the new building is a little trickier to get to than the old place. While the old building was in central Bangkok, in Sathorn in the heart of the banking and business district and therefore, a short trip for high-powered executives and their HR person, the new building is to the north of Chatuchak with no skytrain or MRT station nearby. For Sukhumvit expats, you have the choice of taking the skytrain all the way to Mo Chit and then taking a taxi (or a bus if you are watching the pennies…although not sure why you would save a few baht on a taxi fare if you live in Thonglor or Ekkamai in a luxury condo, paying tens of thousands each month in rent). For expats not in Bangkok, there are local offices in other provinces around the country.

In my case, as you might guess from my previous comments, I always get a taxi and get on the tollway and get there in relative comfort. For me, it simply is not worth it to save a hundred baht if I have to walk 15 mins to the skytrain station (or get a motorcycle taxi), carrying my documents in a folder (possibly in the rain), get to Mo Chit and then jump in a taxi, especially if it is both me and my wife going (which it has to be if you are applying for a marriage visa). I try to leave after 9am or even 10am to avoid the worst of the traffic but anyway, all this is up to your preference and priorities.

Once there, you go through airport style security and then go to the Immigration Department entrance and get your queue ticket and sit and wait to be called. If you have missed the morning shift, you will see the queue for the afternoon shift starting to form outside the door from before 12.45pm on very busy days such as Mondays. Note, by the way, that there are photocopying facilities downstairs as well as cafes and restaurants and bank branches...every bank is there apart from UOB so be aware of this! The chances are you will need both the photocopying shop and possibly even the bank branch if you have not followed the requirements for your visa exactly as listed so best to familiarise yourself to save getting in a panic if you are running out of time at the end of the department's working day (which comes early, as it probably does for any civil service around the world).

Let me now give you a few suggestions you may want to keep in mind when you go to Immigration to get your visa – there are lots of people offering advice via expat forums and suchlike on the Internet and like them, my suggestions are based on my experiences over the years I have been here and everyone's experience is different, which is, in itself, one of the main lessons to learn.

- You may want to avoid Mondays as it is usually very busy. On the other hand, if you have turned up and there are 30 odd people ahead of you, do not despair – there is every chance that about half of these people will take less than two minutes each. This is because they are either making an enquiry or, more likely, they have turned up and been told they are missing one or more documents that they need to produce and so cannot register their application on that day.
- I have no experience of going to Immigration by myself and speaking in English so cannot comment on how foreigners who do so, get on. From my observation, the officials do speak in English with these foreigners but I would suggest going with a Thai person; obviously, if you are marrying a Thai person, you will both need to go anyway. As with other aspects of Thai life, while you will be served even if you only speak English, things will go smoother and you will get more explanation if the official has someone Thai to speak to...but as I said, this is just my assumption, I have no personal experience of applying by myself in English.
- Dealing with the Thai civil service is one aspect of Thai life where you

really do need to be on your best behaviour. By this I mean, you really should not be turning up to the Immigration Division to apply for a marriage visa in your shorts and t-shirt – there is no dress code and obviously your application cannot be refused based on your appearance but really, if you want to be taken seriously and with respect and you turn up in shorts, well, let's just say you are not making things easy on yourself.

- Secondly, if you are accompanied by a Thai person, let he / she speak on your behalf and only speak when you are spoken to. Believe me, if your companion or girlfriend or wife is a reasonably educated Thai, she will know how to address the official and what level of respect to show and so on while you do not.

- Third and possibly most importantly, do not, under any circumstances, show any emotion – frustration, anger or even bemused confusion – as even the slightest flicker of reaction will register with the official and I do not mean in a good way. This is not that different from back home, say in the UK, where civil servants have to deal with members of the public complaining about the process to apply for a government service day in, day out. So, stay totally neutral no matter what feedback you get about what you need to do for your application to succeed, even if it means you have wasted your trip and need to go back and get a couple more documents, which is a fairly likely scenario.

- Do as much research as you can and as much in advance as you can so that you are as prepared as you can be and have all the documents you need. For a marriage visa, for example, there is a whole raft of requirements and even many of the legal and expat sites you will come across that list the requirements are not comprehensive and detailed enough. Check out the Immigration Division site, preferably the Thai language version and follow the instructions on there as this is supposed to be the best and original source. I have to admit the English version of the site is not that great or easy to use so not sure the Thai version will be any different. Be aware and prepare yourself mentally for the fact that in spite of all your preparations, you may still be missing a particular document or may not have followed the requirements exactly as required. If it is something that can be resolved by running to the bank (e.g. to get your bank book updated), great but if it cannot, you will just need to come back another day.

- If you want to avoid the hassle and uncertainty of the above (and assuming you do not have an HR person from your employer who will handle this for you), you could go via an agent. There are many of these in Bangkok, many on the other side of the intersection from the British Embassy on

Wireless Road. They offer translation services (which you will almost certainly need for your English language Affirmation of Freedom to Marry and, if applicable, your English language marriage certificate or other relevant documents) as well as broader agent services to do all the running around on your behalf in relation to the visa application. For what you will come to realise is a reasonable fee, they will tell you exactly what is required and make sure you have exactly what you need and go with you to Immigration and do all the talking on your behalf. Many expats choose this option as the cost is simply worth it to them.

- In my case, and I can only assume in other types of visa applications too, you will need to produce original copies of ALL documents AND photocopies of ALL documents, which even includes the other side of your Thai marriage certificate, for example, or, for your passport, not just the photo page but also the page with your latest entry stamp and your departure card. There may be exceptions to this that professional visa agents are aware of but if you are not going via an agent, just assume that turning up with only a photocopy of a document and not the original will result in rejection.

- Also, English language documents will NOT be accepted. Either get it translated or get a Thai language document in the first place e.g. the bank letter confirming your bank balance I refer to later on can be produced in Thai or English. You need the Thai version!

- When we went, we separated all our documents into one folder of originals that the official will want to inspect and then return to you and one folder of photocopies that he / she will keep as part of your application. You do not want to be sitting in front of her struggling to sort through your huge stack of papers each time she asks to see a document on the list.

- In our case, – a marriage visa application – one of the requirements was to have at least a 400,00-baht balance in a Thai bank account in my name for at least two months. To get your bank to produce the letter to verify your balance can be a bit challenging even though it is supposed to be a standard process. The reason is, some staff at your local branch may simply not be aware of this letter and how to get it done. You may get a couple of 'oh's and a few 'mm's and you might get the impression the poor girl at the bank has never heard of this letter and what is required and after a few more of these sound effects, your patience might be wearing thin! Count to ten in your mind and say nothing and let your girlfriend talk.

- Secondly, since this letter has to be produced on the day of the application (because otherwise Immigration does not know if you still have 400,00 in your account on the day that you apply i.e. you could have borrowed, got the letter and then returned the money), you will probably need to go to your bank before you turn up at Immigration. Or, at least...this is what I thought!

- It turns out the letter does NOT have to be produced on the day as it is valid for 7 days so the two times I set out to apply for my visa (first unsuccessful attempt at Immigration because I did not have all the required documents and then the second one that went through) and had to rush to the bank first thing in the morning were unnecessary and I could have made it to the morning shift at Immigration if I had not wasted time getting the letter in the morning. I only found out when I had to go back a third time (because even though we had gone through the entire marriage visa process, including interviews etc, I had only got the initial Non-Immigrant 90-day visa previously and not yet the 1-year marriage visa) and the official told us that we should come as early as possible and recommended getting the letter sorted out in advance.

- As I mentioned earlier, every bank is represented on the ground floor of the building in Chaeng Wattana apart from UOB, which happens to be one of the easier banks for foreigners to open a bank account with in Thailand. If you are getting the letter at your local branch, you may get told that they need to fax it to their head office to approve and it will take several hours. This is one of the many occasions when, if you have an educated Thai girlfriend (who will be taken seriously by bank staff), she can politely but firmly ask for them to ask their head office to prioritise this approval.

- Having said that, as with many things in Thailand, if you get lucky and get an experienced member of staff who has done this type of letter before, there is no issue whatsoever and everything goes smoothly and the service is great. Your impression of Thailand constantly changes based on your experiences which can, in turn, often depend on your luck in terms of who you deal with and that person's competence, English language ability and so on.

- Third, note that as well as the letter, you need to get your bank book updated to show your balance <u>on the day</u> and so make sure, as I foolishly did not, that you make a small transaction e.g. withdraw 100 baht from the ATM, before updating your book. Obviously, the reason for this is that if your balance is as of any previous day, it does not fulfil the criteria that you need to have the required balance when you are actually sitting in front of the immigration official.

- For marriage visa applications, make sure you get your story straight about where and how you met etc! Even legitimate couples can feel nervous or somehow come out with slightly different versions of events when interviewed separately and you do not want to be like the Gerard Depardieu, Andie Macdowell film Green Card!

- Having said this, you were probably already interviewed separately when you registered the marriage in Thailand at the local government office so you should be used to it and you will probably only get a couple of questions at most at Immigration to satisfy the official that you are in a real relationship. In my case, I was asked if I could speak Thai, which I can and so I was asked these questions in Thai while my wife was asked to sit in the waiting area. If you say no, I would imagine they will still go ahead and ask you in English but I cannot say for sure as I have no experience of dealing in English with government officials, as I mentioned before.

- For anybody wondering, it is possible to enter Thailand on a tourist visa and then 'get it converted' to a marriage visa or a retirement visa (obviously, it is not actually converted, I just mean you can go from one visa to the other without having to go back to your home country). You need the 'Change of visa' form at the ticket desk.

- It takes about 15 days to process the visa, or at least it did for me, so do not leave it too late to apply. If you do not have enough days of valid stay left on your visa, you may be told that you have to go out of the country and come back in and then apply.

- You cannot travel while you are waiting for your application to be processed so if you are going to go on a holiday to any other countries, get it all out the way before you apply for your non-immigrant visa.

- If your Thai girlfriend is a bargirl (and I am not making any judgements whatsoever here but the chances are she will be judged by your official), you are probably better off doing the talking, even if in English. You should also probably speak to your girlfriend in advance to warn her of what to expect and ensure she dresses appropriately and tones down the make-up and basically gives the official as little excuse as possible to form any opinion about you two. In general, as I have said before but it is worth repeating, be as respectful, non-reactive and softly spoken / humble as you possibly can, as things will go easier for you if you do.

- Finally, it is worth clarifying a point that most people say with regard to the process of applying for a visa…or even a bank account. The most common comment amongst foreigners is that the rules are always changing so it is a nightmare process. In reality, this is half-true because the rules do change from time to time but the real thrust of foreigners' complaints is that there is no consistency to the rules. Again, this is half-true.

As with my own experience described above, in spite of researching and preparing well, it turned out I was missing some documents and each of the three times I have been, there has been some problem with my application...albeit, easily resolvable problems. Similarly, when I tried to apply to get a bank account, I was refused by a couple of banks before being accepted by a third bank without changing the nature of my application in any way. So, naturally, I, like most foreigners, got disillusioned and frustrated with the system, which seemed to have no consistency and was more or less pot luck.

- The reality is while the above has an element of truth to it, the real issue with visa applications is that you never really know where you stand and what exactly you need to do in enough detail. So, you get a bullet point list of documents you need to produce but not necessarily the detailed instructions of the fact that you have to photocopy everything, which pages you need to photocopy, what types of photo you need to take with your wife for a marriage visa, the fact that everything has to be in Thai, what alternatives there are to certain requirements, what to do if you have lost a document and so on. As I said above, I read that the bank letter confirming my income had to be done on the day of the visa application but it turns out it is valid for 7 days. So, you end up interpreting the rules and document requirements and hope for the best.

- As for my bank account situation, I was trying to open a bank account without a work permit or even a permanent address in Thailand. I later realised, or maybe rationalised, that it probably was not the case that the two banks that rejected my application should have accepted it and they were just being difficult. They were probably applying the rule to the letter whereas the bank that did go ahead with my request maybe had a way to get around it. Who knows?

- So, in conclusion, yes, the process of applying for a visa or a bank account or dealing with any authority or official process might well be a nightmare and you will, almost certainly, feel that things are not in your control and the rules are being made up as you go along. While this may well be true in some cases, especially in a country where people in authority such as the civil service are very powerful indeed, sometimes it is just that there is not enough detail on what the process is and what is required and / or the member of staff you deal with is not experienced and / or does not speak English well etc. And sometimes it is just that one place applies the rule to the letter of the rule while another, perhaps in a part of Thailand with more foreigners, takes a more relaxed approach to the interpretation of the rule and overlooks one or two things that make no real difference in the grand scheme of things.

- If you look at it this way, you may take a more philosophical view of things in Thailand and when you compare to life back home where there is no getting around the rule whatsoever, which sometimes can be a real pain, you may be thankful for Thailand's more relaxed approach. As for visas, the bottom line, if you do decide to do it yourself rather than spend money on an agent, just mentally prepare to go twice – the first time to fail and write down all the things you are missing and then the second time to get it right.

BUYING PROPERTY IN THAILAND

There is a lot of information on buying property in Thailand out there on international property solicitors' websites and suchlike so I will not try and replicate this here. Instead, here are some points to note based on my own experiences.

- I have no experience of trying to buy a property on my own and / or speaking in English so cannot offer any insight to those readers who are in this position. All of the condos I have bought over the years have been with my wife. However, Richard has shared his thoughts in the first part of the book.
- As most people already know, foreigners are allowed to buy condos but not landed property because no Thai land can belong to a non-Thai. Apparently there are ways to get around this based on my cursory browsing of property related websites so if you are that desperate to own a house in Thailand but do not have a Thai spouse, feel free to do your research,
- -If you do want to buy a condo, one of the main conditions for you to be recognised as the rightful legal owner of the condo is that the money used to pay for the condo has to be directly transferred from your bank back home to the seller's Thai bank account. In other words, you cannot use local money to pay for the condo. This applies even if you are buying an off-plan condo, as I found out recently. I was always under the assumption that the down payment instalments, paid over a number of months or years until the condo is built and ready to move into, can be paid locally and then when it comes to the date of completion and transfer, only then does the balance have to transferred in from abroad. But it seems this is not the case.

- I believe there is an alternative where you can transfer the money in from abroad to your own Thai bank account (assuming you already have one, that is) but you then have to get a letter from your Thai bank to confirm that the money was indeed transferred in from abroad. Then you can use that money from your local Thai account to pay for the condo. Do your research on this point as it can be a bit tricky to manage.

- Generally, condos do not go up in value that much year to year unless they are in a prime area of Bangkok or other big city, or next to a Skytrain or MRT station, or they are in a beachfront location in Phuket or whatever. Obviously, these condos will be more expensive to start with, compared to condos that are within a 10-minute walk of a station, which in turn, are more expensive than condos that are in more residential areas where you need to get a motorcycle or van to get to public transport. So, unless you can afford to buy a prime area condo very near to public transport, with lots of demand from foreigners, do not expect to get rich by investing in condos just because they are cheaper than property back home.

- Condos tend to hold their value better if they are managed by a good management company that has a reputation for high standards. Obviously, the big developers will work with the best management so you should not have too much to worry about. If the property you are considering to buy is already built, you can easily assess for yourself how good the running of the place is by taking a stroll around and observing how clean and orderly everything is, how many lifts there are to people living there, how well the communal area is looked after, how well staffed and secure the place seems to be and so on.

- Just as with other aspects of life in Thailand, if you approach a condo salesperson in a shopping mall and ask questions in English, your chance of getting satisfactory answers is low (but not zero). If the booth is in a foreigner area such as Thong Lor in Bangkok, you may just be fine but it is more likely you will struggle and may just be given a brochure and have to go to the sales office to find staff who are more used to dealing with foreigners. The same comments go for contacting property agents via property websites. If you get lucky, you will get a well-written email back and he / she will arrange the viewing but it is probably more likely you will get very little back, especially if it involves having to write back in English. Often when Thai people are not confident in their English skills, they simply do the minimum i.e. you may just get a brochure or something as an attachment or the briefest of brief responses. Your best course of action is to pick up the phone and try to arrange a meeting because you have more chance of a meaningful conversation face to face.

- When at a property showroom, do not assume the unit that you end up buying will look anything like the showroom. In most, if not all cases, the showroom has all kinds of decoration and design artefacts that you will not get so it is always good to confirm what you do get (e.g. built-in furniture, light fittings etc) and what you do not.
- The higher up the unit, the more expensive it will be and in theory, the more prestigious. Living higher up also means less road noise and less insects and so on. But, of course, you will pay a significant premium for this. And it will take you longer to get in and get out in the lifts than floors lower down.
- If buying to invest, it is worth considering if you will be able to charge a higher rent for a unit higher up; if not, – maybe because of there being a plentiful supply of condo units in the building and neighbouring areas – it may not be worth paying several million more for a higher floor unit only to have to reduce your asking rent to the same as others in order to compete for prospective tenants. For this reason, condo launches often hold back the lowest floors of the building to an event in a shopping mall where people queue up to have the chance to grab one of these units.
- As you would expect, there is quite a lot of paperwork and process involved in buying a property and if you do not read Thai, you will probably need to get a Thai solicitor – I am not sure if every document in the process is available in English, I doubt it very much. If you are buying from or selling directly to another person, you will need to go to the Land Department to sort out the sale and deeds etc. Again, I doubt you will be able to deal in English as I have never seen anybody there speak in English in my time in Thailand. Be prepared for a long day!
- As with other administration type activities in Thailand, you may want to get an agent to do all the running around and talking for you. If you do get your Thai girlfriend to handle matters, first, be aware that buying a property is a stressful experience in any country so make sure you are in a secure enough relationship in the first place. If not, you may find the stress and frustration that comes with the bureaucracy and administration of buying a property puts a major strain on your relationship. I have bought many properties with my wife over the years and have learnt to just let her handle it and not butt in too much.
- Second, if you do delegate to your Thai girlfriend, make sure she is of the educational background and has the worldly wisdom to be able to handle a property purchase i.e. if she is a waitress in a bar who rents a flatshare and has never owned a property, is she really going to be able to

ask the right questions on your behalf or even understand the terms of the contract?

- When you do finally get your condo and move in, one of the best things you can do is to get to know your management company staff. In Thailand, they use the term 'Juristic Office' to refer to these people, which I always find a bit strange but basically, these are the people who manage the condo day to day and to whom you pay the water bill etc. These people can help you out with useful information and tips that may not be obvious to you as a foreigner and generally be at your service. So best to be at your most polite and humble with them.

- Finally, to return to the point about being the legal owner of the condo, I should note that in almost every case that I have bought a condo with my wife, I have let her be the owner, even if the money was mostly from my account, which was the case for one or two of the condos we have bought together. If you have a Thai spouse, the easiest way in terms of minimising paperwork and process hassle, is for her to own the property. The second easiest option is for you to jointly own it where she is the lead (and therefore the money does not need to be transferred in from abroad) but you can still get your name on the deed. The most difficult or process-rich method is for you to insist on being the owner.

- Which option you choose depends on how bothered you are about having to arrange for international transfers of money, extra paperwork and most importantly, how much you trust your Thai wife!! If you have any doubts, you probably should not invest in a condo with your money and allow the deed to be in her name! I have read horror stories of idiotic foreigners doing things like this, often because they are head over heels in love with a girl and maybe with Thailand in general and, unfortunately, they only have themselves to blame. Possibly the best advice I can give, if indeed it is my place to give advice, is to just rent and not invest in a condo until you are sure you want to live here long term or you have a Thai wife, can speak Thai yourself, get along well with her family and a whole host of other common-sense precautions and conditions to protect yourself from being taken advantage of in a foreign country where you do not speak the language and are at the mercy of those who do.

Richard McCully & Stephen Saad

LEARNING THE LANGUAGE

Should you learn Thai?

I have mentioned learning Thai many times already in this section so let me spend the next few paragraphs summarising the main points. Whether or not you choose to learn Thai very much depends on the purpose of your stay in Thailand, the length of stay, the location of your stay (and workplace) and also how interested you are in understanding your new environment.

For many who are sent to work here from abroad or maybe are here to teach for a few years in an international school, there is no real need to learn Thai because Thais who they work with speak good English and they live in a big city where it is possible to get by without speaking Thai, especially if it is Bangkok. Furthermore, many expats simply do not really want to integrate that much and this book passes no judgement on this stance – it is perfectly understandable that some, possibly many, expats simply want to come here to work and enjoy the great beaches, the ability to fly to other Asian countries and Australia easily and basically have a great time living the good life for a few years in the sunshine. They may learn ten to twenty basic words and responses and pick up a word or two every now and then along the way and that is enough for them. No problem!

However, I and many others like me, as demonstrated in many of the interview responses in this book, always wanted to learn Thai from the start and be able to live a 'normal' life alongside Thai people but still retain my British values and preferences – in short, my British identity. Having spoken to other expats and using common sense and intuition, not to mention the wisdom of experience of life in Thailand, I can be confident in saying that being able to speak Thai (by which I mean fluently in everyday interactions) makes all the difference in the world in terms of your experience of life in Thailand.

This goes from something basic such as walking up to the reception counter in a hospital or shop or whatever and the ensuing interaction going smoothly and your questions answered fully and with helpful context and advice, to a wider point that speaking (and reading) the language sets you free. What do I mean? You do not need help to read a menu without English, you do not hesitate to ask someone for help, you do not get into confusion / arguments with taxi drivers due to misunderstandings, you can understand local TV and so know what is going on in showbiz / current affairs / gossip etc and so on. But mostly, speaking the language simply makes your stay more rewarding i.e. you are part of society and part of life in Thailand, not an outsider.

When you speak Thai, you can have real conversations with Thai people.

Sure, many Thai people speak English but there is a difference between speaking enough English to be understood and having a large enough vocabulary to be able to have a fluent conversation, with all the subtleties of feelings and opinions requiring the correct choice of word. Few Thais will speak English to a level where you feel it is like speaking to someone from back home so being able to speak Thai (well) helps. And the onus is on you to learn Thai, not the local person to speak great English – remember, in case you have forgotten, you are in Thailand after all!

On the other hand, it is also somewhat true that many Thai ladies prefer a Westerner who <u>cannot</u> speak Thai. Yes, it is true! For many Thai people, foreigners are interesting because they are different and speak English; once a foreigner has become localised, he is no longer as interesting and sometimes held in some disdain. You may notice that you, as a 'farang' who speaks a couple of words here and there in Thai send Thai women into appreciative giggles and they love to teach you a new word and maybe even flirt with you whereas a foreign guy who speaks perfect Thai gets much less enthusiastic service to the point of even surliness. This is indeed a paradox but it makes perfect sense if you think about it.

Having said that, this contrast in reaction is possibly mainly from less educated Thais you may meet in bars and service roles, as opposed to educated Thais who will only, very slowly start to accept you the more you show you are keen to accept the culture, speak the language and fit in. Anyway, if one of your aims while in Thailand is to score with lots of women (and let's face it, that is the case for many foreign men), you are probably better off not speaking Thai, as bizarre as that sounds. Conversely though, for those who want to find a 'proper' girlfriend, if you do not speak Thai and she does not speak good English, you will struggle to create any real bond between the two of you because you simply do not have the most basic thing to create an understanding: a common language.

Another point is speaking Thai badly and / or at barely beyond basic level can sometimes cause more problems than help matters. This is for the obvious reason that not only will the Thai person struggle to understand you (and may get frustrated if they can actually speak English and would have been happy to do so with you) but also, if they do go ahead and treat you as if you can speak Thai, they may well respond in Thai that you do not understand (either because you cannot translate their words quick enough in your head or you simply have a very limited Thai vocabulary). So, you end up making an effort only to make things more confused and having to, embarrassingly, switch back to English.

For these above reasons, it is perfectly understandable if foreigners do not bother to learn Thai while they are here in Thailand. As I said before, I do not intend to preach to readers to learn Thai or to tell people how to live their lives while in Thailand. However, as I said, for those that do bother, the rewards are huge if they manage to get to a level where they can hold simple conversations in everyday situations. The next question is how one goes about learning Thai.

How to learn Thai

Just as with the question of whether you should learn Thai, the question of how to learn Thai depends on who you are and why you want to learn. Many readers will decide to learn because they intend to be here for the foreseeable future (e.g. to retire in Thailand) while some only intend to be in Thailand for a few years but realise that their day to day lifestyle will be made easier by being able to speak Thai. Then there are other people who simply want to get to a very basic level and not much more because that is enough to get by and they do not want to put too much effort into learning much beyond that level (perhaps because they have a Thai wife who speaks good English and wants to speak English). And finally, there are foreigners who really, really want to learn properly, meaning to speak, read and write, either because they will actually need to do all these things in their job in Thailand or more likely, because they have so fallen in love with Thailand that they have taken an all or nothing approach and decided the only way to live in Thailand successfully is to learn Thai and the only way to learn Thai is to learn it completely.

When I came to work in Thailand in 2003, I had no particular plans to return to the UK and indeed, I had no plans to stay in Thailand forever either. So, in short, I was here for the foreseeable future. My method of learning Thai, which I believe is the best way, was self-study, followed by real-life practice with Thai people to test out what I had learnt. Incidentally, I have read many expats' accounts of how they have learnt Thai and many of the successful ones, including Adam Bradshaw, the well-known American English teacher and celebrity who speaks perfect Thai, used my method. But why is self-study such a great way of learning Thai? The simple answer is that with self-study, you do not delegate responsibility to learn to someone else, as you probably do when you sign up for a class. Especially when you are in beginner stages, you are not mentally invested enough in having to learn Thai so the easiest thing in the world is to just turn up at a class and expect you will retain whatever the teacher tells you. In reality, you forget the majority of the lesson within a week. Then you go for another lesson and the teacher has to first go over what you learnt last time because you have forgotten most of it.

To make matters worse, your ears are not attuned to hearing Thai so you struggle with the lessons and make hardly any progress and if you are unlucky enough to have a bad teacher and / or a Thai nationality Thai teacher who struggles to explain things from an English perspective, you will get even more discouraged. You may complete your course but your heart is not in it and six months later, you have retained less than half of what you were taught. By the way, the exceptions to this characterisation are students who are naturally good at languages, hearing tones etc and also, students who are taught by either Thai teachers who speak excellent English and have spent time amongst Westerners or, Western Thai teachers who can explain concepts from a foreigner learning Thai perspective (as they have been through it themselves).

Self-study puts the onus on you to be responsible for your own learning. I spent hour after hour, day after day over a few months in London, reading my two Thai language books – Essential Thai by James Higbie and Teach Yourself Thai by David Smyth – which, I can promise you are two of the very best books on Thai you will ever find anywhere. I have some natural talent for pronunciation and learning languages and also have a slight advantage that I can speak a little Bengali – my ethnic background language – which shares some sounds with Thai such as a dt sound, for example. Both languages have origins in Sanskrit so I guess it is not surprising that there are a few similarities. But in spite of these advantages, I am not a linguist and cannot pick up a language in a few days in the way linguists can. I need the practice and the study. So, my method was very much brute force learning – read over and over again, cross reference the same topic across the two books to validate what I had learnt and memorise.

I read the chapter on transliteration multiple times to ensure I had understood exactly how the Thai was being represented in English characters in each book and went back to the chapter each time I was unsure of how to pronounce a word. People will tell you it is not possible to learn Thai from transliteration. I can tell you this is total rubbish. It is absolutely possible if 1) the method of transliteration is good and accurately represents the Thai sounds (which it is possible to do if the chapter has enough explanation) and 2) the learner pays enough attention to that chapter and lets go of their own accent and commits to following the instructions and pronouncing Thai, as instructed in that chapter.

Because of all my time spent reading my books in London, by the time I got to Thailand a few months later and started work, I could pick up a few words here and there from other people's conversations. And I then went into the second part of my method – practise with local people. I had had very little opportunity to practise back in London so while I knew quite a few words and phrases, I had no experience of real life interaction.

My method was all-consuming – I planned what I wanted to practise the next day in advance and then deliberately tried to start a conversation (maybe in English, to start with) that would lead to that word being used by my Thai colleague so that I could hear it being used. I also jotted down (in transliterated Thai) any words that I managed to catch in meetings and looked them up in my Thai-English dictionary in the evening to check what they meant. Then I went back to my books and worked out how to use that word and then resolved to practise it the next day. If I made a mistake or got a blank look, having spent all evening preparing what I was going to attempt the next day, I would ask where I went wrong and then jot that down and go back and re-read my books.

Using this 'self-study followed by testing myself in real life and validation of what I had learnt' method, I made rapid progress because as time went on, I went from learning the one word I was trying to learn to inadvertently picking up a couple of extra words, which went to picking up short sentences to then picking up short strings of sentences and so on. My progress was exponential and I soon made sense of both of my books. From that point it was just a case of picking up more and more words by listening to songs, watching Thai TV, listening to people's conversations on the Skytrain (not in a creepy way, honest!), watching Thai movies, hanging out with Thai friends playing sport or whatever and so on.

And, as I mentioned earlier, my ears got more and more attuned to hearing Thai – my ex-boss gave me that piece of advice, which I consider to be the best advice in terms of learning Thai i.e. you have to let your ears get used to hearing Thai and little by little, it will not seem like noise and you will be able to distinguish the separate words in a sentence.

I also learnt to read but here again, I take a view that goes against the purists who insist that the only way to learn Thai properly is to learn to read and write from the start. This is totally wrong and I have read many other expats' accounts of their own learning process that agrees with mine. Ideally, you should NOT learn to read from the very beginning and you certainly should not learn to write...unless, you are fully committed to Thailand and want to learn Thai 100%.

As I mentioned earlier, it is possible to learn from transliterated Thai and I would argue, it is preferable to learn this way in the initial stages. You are familiar with English characters so it puts less pressure on you to bridge the gap between what you know and an entirely different, exotic language that uses completely different characters. In spite of what some purists who have learnt Thai well will tell you, learning the Thai alphabet, including the tone rules, is not easy and you really do not want to give yourself any more excuses to just give up because it is too difficult or not worth the effort.

The purists' argument is all very well for those who are good at learning languages but for the majority who are not so good, should we put them off even more by condemning them to an all or nothing approach? – unless you learn properly, you might as well not bother! Although I can read Thai, I still read rather slowly and struggle with difficult Thai such as in newspapers and I still read transliterated Thai faster and if available alongside Thai, I tend to read the transliteration first and then my eyes go to the Thai to confirm things (if I am unfamiliar with the transliteration system).

The best way to learn is to get up to speed using transliterated Thai to build up your confidence in the basics of the Thai language, test out what you have learnt with real people, ask lots of questions (assuming you have kind and patient Thai friends who are happy to explain Thai to you), take what you learnt in your real-life interactions and go back and look it up in your books, study and then repeat the whole process.

You will have Thai script alongside the transliteration in any Thai learning book anyway and there will be a chapter on reading Thai. In James Higbie's book – Essential Thai, possibly the best basic Thai coursebook out there, the chapter on reading comes right at the end of the book. That, to me, says it all and is exactly as it should be – you should learn to read as you are nearing proficiency at a basic level of speaking. At that point, you understand enough simple Thai and are invested enough in learning Thai that you can take on the learning of the alphabet and the grammar rules and the tone rules and run with it. Finally, do I think that you should learn to read? Absolutely! Nothing I have said previously should, in any way, be interpreted as seeking to discourage readers from learning to read Thai. Being able to read helps you speak better Thai and obviously helps you in your day-to-day life. It is merely a question of timing your efforts to match your increasing competence and investment in learning to speak Thai.

At the start of this section, I talked about the fact that some readers may not want to learn Thai per se but pick up a few words and phrases and maybe a few basics on forming sentences etc. For these people, I can see the attraction of signing up for a class or registering with a meetup group or whatever. It can be fun, interactive and learning Thai is almost a by-product. Some executives or teachers are sent on courses through their employer and I assume these are helpful to an extent. In summary, if you are not necessarily intent on being able to speak Thai fluently in everyday life but just want to, or have been sent to, learn a few basics, a teacher is ok as an option. Of course, nowadays, there are lots of other media such as online, podcasts, Youtube and so on. All these are fine for the learner who is not really a learner but just wants to get a few basics and indeed, for the more serious learner who wants to check their understanding quickly or test themselves.

The final category of learners are the ones who really want to or need to learn Thai properly, by which I mean being able to speak Thai in any situation, not just everyday life but in professional life and also speaking in situation-specific contexts e.g. politics or religion or climate change etc. I also mean when speaking in everyday situations, going from being able to speak reasonably well to speaking as if you were almost a native speaker, choosing the words and responses that a native speaker would choose.

For people who do want to learn Thai inside out and operate in Thailand using Thai as confidently as a local person, you should, in contrast to my view for beginners, engage a good teacher or go to a recognised school or university. Indeed, as I believe Adam Bradshaw did himself, the right time to do this is when you have reached a decent level of Thai but before you are so set in your ways and have developed bad habits, not to mention reached a plateau and lost your enthusiasm for learning any further.

Recently, I have been watching a programme called DaVinci on Thai TV, which is a gameshow for kids of five years old who are shown pictures and have to guess the word that the pictures make up when put together. I claim to be fluent in Thai but I can tell you, in all honesty, after watching ten or fifteen episodes, the kids wiped the floor with me completely. I did not know the word for dragon, remote controlled car, meteor, thorn or even the word, syllable! Learning Thai properly will fill in the gaps that self-study leaves behind.

For all readers, no matter whether you really are not bothered about learning Thai or are really keen to learn, if and when you do attempt to speak Thai, speak it without using your own accent. Yes, I know this sounds impossible but it is not – you need to copy the sounds of Thai exactly, not get to the closest approximation that you can say using your own accent. Open your ears, pay attention to what you hear and copy accurately. Even if you only know a few words, at least make the effort to speak them exactly as they should be pronounced and you will receive appreciative comments from local people.

Ultimately, as I said right at the start of this section, it is not necessary to speak Thai to be able to live successfully in Thailand and this book does not take a morally superior position that if you do not learn Thai, you are somehow wrong and need to be shown the error of your ways. There are perfectly legitimate reasons to not spend your time learning Thai while in Thailand and if your life is just fine without speaking Thai (apart from a few words here and there), that is fine. For those that do make the effort however, you will be rewarded massively, as learning the language is like the key that opens the door to an entirely new, broader, deeper, more meaningful and more rewarding life that can only be achieved once you can communicate with local people confidently in their language and can understand all the language being spoken around you and on TV or radio day to day. In short, you will, for the first time, feel part of the country and like you belong. Good luck.

Interviews with Expats
in Thailand 7–13

Interview 7: The Hotel Owner

Dave McNeil is an American hostel owner and general manager. Dave had some very interesting views on Thailand as well as some funny stories. We also left out some of his wilder escapades!

Tell us a bit about your background and why you came to Thailand.

I had been working for a while in restaurants and going through summer tourism season, saving for six months so that I could go travelling the other six months of the year. I had done a scuba dive master programme and so when I was considering my next venture the following year, scuba diving was high on the list. I had known a few people living in Thailand doing that so I put Thailand on the list of about five places I was going to be visiting. The first was India and Thailand was the second place; it was supposed to be for one month but I ended up cancelling all other plans and staying. During that one month I had a buddy of mine travel around with me. As we were travelling, I met a girl from Thailand. After one month it came to the time to decide whether I was going to move along or not and my decision linked back to my time in India...

When I went to India I went to this celestial tourist location where they had lots of grand sculptures and things from a long time ago that were basically focused on the stars and moon. My tuk tuk driver asked me "are you interested in all that stuff?" and I said yes and he asked if I would like to meet a guru and I said "sure". The Guru told me three things about my future. One was that I would live in this region – he felt Malaysia. He also said that I am going to create a business that is international, not like a huge multinational corporation but a business that has locations in different countries. Finally, he said that I would meet an Australian girl who would be a very important factor in my life but she wouldn't be my last relationship.

I was with 2 friends in a hostel in Phuket and on the second day, the hostel keeper said "oh, your girlfriends are upstairs". We said we didn't have girlfriends and he replied that he was only joking but there are three girls from Australia in your room. I turned to my buddy and said knowingly "Ok!" That night we headed out with these Australian girls and went out dancing. While I was dancing with two of the girls, a Thai girl came up to me and asked if she could dance with me. It really took me back as it was pretty obvious I was with these two Australian girls and so I said, "I don't pay for sex" and she said "Well, I don't pay for sex either". We ended up going home together and she travelled with me and my buddy to Koh Phi Phi for about a week.

Towards the end of my holiday in Thailand I decided I was going to give in to the sense of what the guru had talked about, which was "stop planning everything, your plans are holding you back from achieving what you really want in life. Stop being afraid and go all in and commit to something, whether it is a relationship or business." I said to myself "I'll explore a relationship with this girl and also business opportunities here in Thailand". I travelled extensively with the girl and after about six weeks, I moved to Bangkok. There was a period of about four months of researching business opportunities here and then, again, the moment of "do I go home or stay here with the girl and find a way to survive here while I find a way to start a business". I decided on getting my teacher's certificate – I did the CELTA, which took a month. As soon as I was finished, I had nine job interviews and nine job offers so it was really easy to transition into a life of working. In the end though things didn't work out with the girl.

What were your first impressions after a couple of months here?

Before I came to Thailand I had no idea what it was – I was working in a bar and I had told a couple of people that I was going to Thailand to go scuba diving and they were like "come on, scuba diving...seriously? You're going for the whores!" That was the first time I understood the world view of what Thailand is and so when I came here I tried to make my way without being lumped in with those men who were here for those reasons.

My first impression of Thailand was really, this is a place to explore and get lost and see new things and try new things. I would go up to the street food guys and they would ask what I want and I would just shrug and say I don't know and ask them to suggest something. I would usually go to this guy and get pork and make a slicing motion but one time I decided to make a chopping motion and got home and looked in the bag and it was not the usual sliced pork – there were pieces with pig's hair on it! I had a limited budget so decided I was going to have it anyway and it turned out, it was really delicious. I went back to that guy every week and made the chopping motion and got this really great pork dish. It was really a sense of "I'm in a new place and they eat different things and I need to go out of my comfort zone to be able to live here".

I stayed in my first apartment for about a month and then one day, I saw a couple of white people come out of a school and they looked like teachers so I decided to follow them to their building (as a shady person would do) and ended up renting a room in their building. It was a great little spot, about 7,000 baht, with a full kitchen and a bedroom with a door! It was in a great location where there were lots of little sois where you could get great street food.

So, were you on more of an exploration high as opposed to loving Thailand for the girls?

There was exploration of not just the city but the lifestyles of the people around me. Being in Bangkok and living where I was living put me in close proximity to Bangkok's seedier side and so I saw a lot of things about how life is in those areas. I lived close to this club which was basically full of working girls and drunk foreigners and I took a few girls home from that place. I realised that these girls were just like ordinary girls and just wanted to have fun and so I never had to pay for sex with them. They also had the same vulnerabilities as normal girls so, for example, if you did not call them the next day, they would get hurt.

After you broke up with the girl you met in Phuket you met a lot of other women. What do you think about your life then and do you feel your life is different now?

I am a much better human being now. I think most people, when they come out of a long-term relationship are going to want to explore new things and not jump into another relationship. I needed that time to be able to do whatever I felt like. As I went into this life of 'a different girl every night', I realised the loneliness that comes with that. It wasn't just my own loneliness but I realised that I was treating the girls as objects and that they were with me for different reasons than what I had them come for. They were sincerely dating and look- ing for a relationship and it changed my perspective on things and I thought "I need to treat women and people, in general, better.".

I made a decision to try for a serious relationship. I met a few women over a few months and ended up choosing one who it was just supposed to happen with. I would chat to her every single night on video for ages and when she would smile, I would smile and it made me happy. She didn't have the same jealousy as other Thai women so when I would go out to do something, she would just say "Ok, have fun, see you later." She came to stay with me and about two months later, she moved in. I rented the building for the hostel, started to do the renovations and once I got it ready to open, she was here, ready and willing to help in any way that I needed. As we were the getting the business going, I saw the commitment she had to me so I made a commitment to her – I asked her to marry me.

In the beginning, as we were running the hostel, I started smoking again. Running a hostel can be quite boring and being the owner was also stressful so a lot of people were smoking cigarettes. I was also drinking, maybe having five or six beers a night. It got to a point where, one night, I got drunk and the next morning, I was too hung over to manage the hostel and she took over. I had a go at her for dealing with this contractor but not asking the questions I would have asked him and afterwards, I self-reflected and realised that if I was going to continue to drink, I was going to put a lot more pressure on my relationship with my wife and I wouldn't be able to handle all the responsibilities of owning a business, maintaining a relationship and working Saturday and Sunday as an English teacher. On the same day, I quit smoking and drinking.

What were the main challenges in setting up your life here and were there any pleasant surprises?

In terms of things that were more difficult than expected, one thing was the negative reactions you would get from Thai people based on how you look. I've had many experiences where you are standing in a noodle shop and there are two Thai men in front of you ordering the exact same thing as you and they are charged 30 baht and you are charged 40. When you ask why, they say "White". That was really difficult to process. It extends to national parks too where you pay a higher price. You could say that foreigners do not pay tax but even if you show them your work permit, tax receipts and that you live here, they still tell you "No, you're white, you're a foreigner, you pay more."

In terms of relationships, it is also difficult, not necessarily sexual relationships but even just friendly relationships. Thai men are extraordinarily different to Western men in every way, in terms of interests, hobbies and the way they socialise with each other. It is really difficult to ever get to a point where you can make friends with a Thai man.

Then there is also the language barrier – a student of mine once asked me out and I could just imagine the struggle we would have to have a real conversation. The Thais that do speak excellent English and are 'internationalised' are typically the 'hi-so' Thais and they are in a completely different place compared to you. When an internationalized Thai was in the UK or US or whatever, they seemed down-to-earth, but their viewpoint was that "I'm slumming it right now so that I can participate in this new culture whereas when I'm home…".

In terms of things that were better than I expected…one…the food. When I was about 12 or 13, a Thai restaurant opened up near where we lived so we tried it, as a family. My older brother told me that a small green chilli was not very spicy so I ate it and then had a horrible experience of trying to get the spice taste out and it completely turned me off Thai food. I was not expecting to like Thai food, when I moved here, as much as I do. In Thailand, they have so many ingredients, you get a huge variety of Thai food. And also, the availability of food was a pleasant surprise – anytime, anywhere, if you are hungry, you can spot somebody selling some food somewhere. And finally, the relatively inexpensive cost of food here. Some of my friends would know how much I was making here as a teacher and they would compare it to salaries in the US. I would tell them that I might be making only $1,500 a month but I may spend only about $200 a month on food whereas, back home, if I were to eat out every day, it would be a much greater percentage of my income.

How difficult was the transition from being a tourist to having your hostel business now?

It was a long transition – it's not something that happens overnight. Anybody that expects to have overnight success, anywhere in the world, has the wrong mindset. For me, it was done in stages and a lot of it had to do with my progression as a teacher. I started out on 400 baht an hour and I did that for two years but the school were not providing enough hours and so I looked elsewhere and found a job making 600 baht an hour. Then I moved on again to the British Council, which probably pays the most of any language centre and it gave me some freedom, as I only work there Saturday and Sunday and make more than enough money to survive. I probably make enough money working on the weekend to survive three months so it gives me the freedom to explore my hobbies, which in my case, is building this business. And so, all of this happened over the course of four years – it took that long.

Have you experienced any problems here?

There are several key issues foreigners will face here and most link to the respect (or lack of) that Thai people have for life and people in general. A lot of these things seem to be ingrained into the culture itself, based off the fact that it is a hierarchical society and you only respect wealth and power and age. There is this false sense of respect that is just on the surface that people see through the wâai, which is not a show of respect...it's basically a hello. Real respect could be as simple as 'I'm going to hold the door open for you' or 'instead of driving my motorbike in front of you as you are crossing the street, I will go around the back or I will simply stop and allow you to walk in front of me'

I was hit by a motorbike once because I had already crossed halfway so my attention was on the cars coming toward me from the far side...and this person, instead of going behind me where there is an entire lane open, they want to go in front of me. It seems to me, everything is 'me, me, me' and there is some sort of loss of face if they let you go in front of them. You see these negative implications of a hierarchical society in the way they treat each other on the roads. When you are a pedestrian, it is automatically assumed you are not wealthy enough to own a vehicle so I do not need to respect you. Those are the things that have changed over the years and overall, I would say I have developed a negative view of Thai people and it really bothers me because there are times when I think "is it me? Am I this negative person? Is there something wrong with the way I view the world?". Deep down, I want to say, there are exceptions, not everyone is like this and still see the good but when every day, you have these interactions, it becomes difficult. And it traverses all walks of life, all industries, everything.

Another example of where I have developed a negative view is in education where the ability to have free thought or an ability to be competent at a job is lacking. We've had numerous situations where someone has come in through applications and job interviews and they have accepted the job and they are going to starting in a week...the day before they are starting, they say "ok, see you tomorrow at this time" and then they do not show up. If they are the type of person who even feels the slightest obligation to explain to you why they did not show up, it's always the same thing – "oh I got this other job so I am going with them". You can understand if the other job is paying more but why not call me or message me and just let me know you are not showing up. And similarly, with dating, I've stopped making dates to meet them somewhere in the city because I am not going to travel 40 minutes and wait 2 hours only for them to not show up. So, that sort of lack of respect for someone's feelings or time are because of the way they are trained through education where there is no accountability...they do not ever really get failed, they get passed up to the next level.

The West has its own problems too but here, you have a lot of students who are a different society because they have that family to rely on who can just hand them the family business. You have a lot of guys who don't bother because they don't need to. Also, the way that they educate them – often it is...here's a homework sheet, memorise some stuff and when I come back in, I'll tell you the answers and if you get them wrong, I won't explain. I've heard so many students of mine or students of friends of mine whose teachers will them they are stupid or yell at them and get angry at the fact that they got stuff wrong because they did not pay attention to the lesson. So, there are so many problems that are associated with the education system that it translates into ill-equipped adults.

Do you think that Thailand is a more libertarian society where you have much less government control?

There's a condo being built next door and it has been in construction the entire time we have had this hostel. We've had four-inch PVC pipes that are three metres long drop from 30 stories high onto our roof. My wife and I were sitting right here and if we were a little over that way, it would have killed us. We've had wrenches drop from 30 stories up, slamming through the roof and denting the concrete. When their representatives come over I ask them "why do you not have the proper safety nets up as you should, or at the very least, fencing around your building so that when things fall, they do not fall on my roof? What if this tool had killed somebody, what then?" He replied, "Oh, well, we will deal with it then. We will pay you maybe 300,00 baht for the loss of a life but we're not going to pay, say, 100,000 baht to put up the proper safety equipment that we should by law." The reason they won't do that is it is cheaper for them to pay someone off so when we go to the district office to deal with the government officials, when we make a complaint that they have destroyed something and they have not fixed it, they do not automatically lodge a complaint and send somebody to check and fine them and enforce regulations, they pick up the phone and call them and tell them "these people want to complain, do you want to go and fix something now instead of us filing a complaint?"

I definitely think a lot of Westerners come here with the idea that they will be freer here but in reality, you are not any freer here than in the West. In the West, I can talk openly and freely about my government; here you don't have those freedoms and liberties to do so. Also, in terms of traffic laws, for example, you have the same laws as in the West – seatbelts, not talking on mobile phone etc. – it's just that here, they do not enforce the rules. And so, if you get caught here, would you feel free? No, you are just as restricted.

What does your wife think about your views of Thai people and life in Thailand?

She's gone through a big change since we opened the hostel and she has had to deal with Thai people herself. When we first opened the hostel and were dealing with staffing issues (not showing up, quitting with one day's notice), she would just say I was wrong to assume it was something to do with Thai people and to tell me to not say that. Now, when I ask her, she tells me, you know what Thai people are going to be like and she has accepted it.

Anybody that comes to live here from the West needs to accept that you are going to get frustrated and furious with Thai people at times. However, reacting to it the way you would back home and expressing that anger and frustration gets you absolutely nowhere. You just have to suppress that anger and accept things will go wrong...basically, Murphy's Law – if it can go wrong, it probably will.

What do you think of other expats in Thailand?

I don't tend to hang out with other expats that much, partly because it usually ends up being a bitching and moaning session and that gets tiresome. When I am out with buddies and they start with all that, I try to steer the conversation away. It's better to hang out with those foreigners who have integrated here well and understand those differences and have accepted them and can process them. You can't change Thailand so, for example, if your wife's family is asking for money and you can't accept it, then leave it.

To what extent have you integrated into Thai society?

I haven't learned the language. My brain doesn't function well with language. At six years old in America, I had to go to speech therapy because nobody could understand me. And so here, with the tonal language, I can't get into the tones and the pronunciation. Even though I can learn and remember the words, I could never really communicate. So that has been a real barrier for me and probably will always be to really fully integrate into society. So, for example, I don't really communicate with my in-laws, which is really quite upsetting for me.

However, although I have not learned about the culture through learning the language, I have met numerous people who speak English well enough that when I ask a question about the culture, they understand and can explain it to me. I do understand the culture and the effects different aspects have on the culture e.g. Buddhism, the government, the monarchy

What about your top tips for settling in Thailand? And conversely, what are your top things to not do?

I'll start with 'not to do' – don't marry a prostitute! You would not marry or date a prostitute in the West so don't do it here. It's just common sense. But for some reason, a lot of men come over here and take a bargirl home, she treats them much more caringly than a normal prostitute would do back home and the guy is just dumbfounded…she's doing it for money! She doesn't actually care about you. If you really want to settle here and marry a Thai woman, there are plenty of good women who are not prostitutes; it might be harder to really get a relationship started but you might need to lower your standards…if you are a fat, old, unattractive man, don't expect to get a beautiful young woman who actually cares for you because back home, that kind of girl would have been with you for your money.

Secondly, don't come here expecting life is going to be easier than it was back home. Don't come here thinking that people are going to respect you just because you are from the West. Don't come here and think you are above people here for any reason. Just because you are from a developed country, it does not make you classier or better than anybody else.

As for what things to do, when you come here, be open to having new experiences, meaning do as the locals do, just try new things. Try to embrace the culture as much as possible. The people that seem the unhappiest are the ones who think the culture here is wrong. Maintain your own sense of dignity and respect for others. The one thing that drives me crazy about Thai people is they don't say thank you, they don't hold the door open and those other polite etiquette things. I still say thank you to the motorbike drivers every time I get off and to the store clerk at 7-Eleven. Another thing, don't flash the money around. You see a lot of people who come here and start businesses and don't shop around and assume what they get quoted is normal and they get taken advantage of. For example, I didn't get a lawyer because I realised that they are just filling in a form and submitting it to the government and so I did it myself with the help of my wife.

Are you fully invested into Thailand or will you and your wife move back to the US at some point?

My hopes are that from this hostel, we will be able to expand to other locations. Currently, my thought is to stay in Thailand and look at a second location down south on one of the islands. After we have the second location, I want to build hostels in four other countries in South East Asia then Central or South America. In terms of staying here education is a big thing. Many of my family have done the best they can to get the best education for their kids so I want to follow that. I won't be able to afford that here in Thailand so once we have kids and they are at an age where they will be going to school, I'll be moving back to the US. We'll definitely maintain the businesses here and we'll probably end up buying a home near my wife's family so that, in the summertime, the kids can come out with their mom and be involved with their history and people.

How easy was it to setup your business?

As Americans, we have an exclusive right to be 100% business owners; no other foreigner from any other nation has that right in Thailand. That is a route that a lot of people take, however I didn't. I went with the traditional 51% ownership by a Thai, 49% ownership by a foreigner. However, I didn't even do that because of the monetary situation. When you do that, the Thai partner needs to show cash in the bank that is equal to their percentage of the capital that is declared for the business. And for a foreigner who gets a work permit through the company, it has to be at least 2m baht registered capital, which would have meant I would have had to put 1m baht in cash in my wife's bank account, which I didn't have.

I spoke to people at the business department and they said when a Thai person opens a business it doesn't matter what capital they put in as the main thing that they are worried about with partnerships is money laundering. So, if the company is 100% owned by a Thai, no capital in the bank needs to be shown and I also asked whether I could buy the shares back in the future and they said "sure". So the business is 100% in my wife's name and although many people have an opinion of "you're such an idiot…", I say "she's my wife, if I can't trust my wife, who can I trust?" So, on the paperwork, I am not legally the owner but I can buy back the shares in the future.

There are two types of stock: common stock, which has one vote and preferred stock that has two. I can buy 49% of the company with all preferred stock, which means I have more voting rights. I can also put myself on as a second director so everything needs my signature as well as my wife's. There are various ways in which you can own a business and feel comfortable in how rules are set or people not being able to steal it from you or whatever.

What budget would you recommend for someone looking to live in Bangkok?

Around here in Asok you can get a condo for about 20,000 baht and you can find a similar condo about five train stations away for about 10,000 baht. You can live on around 30,000 baht if you live in a small condo, go out once a week and use mainly public transport. I spend about 6,000 baht a month on food, 2,000 baht on transport, around 10,000 baht on entertainment. If you want to get a massage every week and eat at decent restaurants you might need closer to 70,000 baht and if you want more luxuries, you will need closer to 100,000 baht.

Interview 8: The Tech Boss

Dwight Willis is an Australian banking technology executive. Dwight first came to Thailand as a student and learnt Thai as a student. After a successful career in Singapore, he has returned to Thailand and established Dollarsmart Global – an emerging giant in online payments transfers.

Tell us a bit about your background and why you came to Thailand.

I came to university here in 1988 and then went back into banking in a real job in Australia. I married the first Thai girl I met at university and ended up having two daughters together and living in Sydney, London and Singapore but I always wanted to come back to Thailand.

I moved here in 2012 and I was doing around 4 days in Thailand and 3 days in Singapore. I had divorced and got remarried to a Thai girl from Chiang Mai and gradually I was spending more and more time up in Chiang Mai because the majority of my teams were in KL or London or New York and so I was on the telephone all the time.

I thought I've got a beautiful house in Chiang Mai overlooking the rice paddies and a nice 'sala' office and I can just get on the speakerphone and Skype into anybody around the world. After about 18 months I left Standard Chartered and started my company – Dollarsmart, which is what I do to this day based out of here in Chiang Mai.

Why did you come to Thailand?

I came here originally because the Australian government gave me money and said go to Thailand! The Australian government has a huge plan to bring Asian kids into Australia for education and Australian kids into Asia and I was one of the original recipients from that programme. The benefit of the programme is the creation of a network between Asian countries and Australia so, for example, I have been to lunch at the Australian ambassador's house and some top Thai government ministers were there, some of whom had studied in Australia.

When I moved here to live in 2012, it was mainly because I had such a deep association with Thailand in terms of family and kids and so on.

Was your wife with you in Singapore and did she travel with you back and forth? If so, what was it about Thailand that made you feel you needed to be based here?

Intellectually, by which I mean understanding the culture, the way Thailand works, I had only scratched the surface in my previous visits and I wanted to learn more. I also had a pretty good network and lots of business contacts and wanted to see if I could get a business going here.

What were you apprehensive about in moving here?

I knew quite a lot about Thai history with other countries so I was quite apprehensive about moving assets here, who was controlling the assets and whether I could sell them and move them back out one day if I wanted to.

Had you developed friendships or contacts in Thailand when you were here before? If so, how did you do that?

I had quite a network here lot of professional contacts through the bank (Standard Chartered), both Western expats and Thais in senior roles in SCB. My Thai friends were all borne out of business relationships.

Had you started learning the language from when you were here at university?

Yes, from when I was at Silpakorn University in Nakhorn Pathom and we actually learned Thai formally at the university. We were told "don't speak, don't write, don't read – don't eat", which basically meant, given that it was mainly countryside in Nakhorn Pathom back then, if we did not learn how to ask for food in Thai, you weren't going to eat basically! The local students were told not to help us so we were forced to learn. By the end of it, we were writing journals in Thai as part of various projects.

My Thai is pretty great so, for example, I can have a commercial discussion with the bankers we are working with but at some point, we drop back into English. So, in my office, when my staff don't want me to know what they are talking about, they will, very plainly go into the Northern Thai dialect. I am gradually picking it up so I can understand about 1% of what they are saying so I am wondering what they are going to do next to stop me from understanding them in the office.

What were your first impressions after, say, a couple of months here? Was it different to your experiences as a tourist?

The difference between living here and coming here as a tourist is, as you start to integrate more, the hassles of everyday life hits you. So, having to take my son to school and then going to the office, which is about a 9km trip can be a 1-hour commute through three traffic lights. Then there is having to deal with government bureaucracy, like when you have to do your 'tá-bian bâan' (house registration document) and so on. You have got to have somebody who can

237

help navigate that part of life here, otherwise it's extremely difficult. I have one goal in life, which is never to go again to an Immigration Office. I have been once to go through the One Stop Service for a BOI company but other than that, never – I usually fly out for business before the 90-day report is due so I usually do not need to go to the Immigration Office.

Apart from that, other differences are, for example, getting certain things that are important to your life. So, say for food, while I love Thai food, ever since university, I've never eaten rice for breakfast…the thought of having cold rice in the morning…it's like a Thai person having bubble and squeak for breakfast. I need bread. Also, when I first came here, I was watching Thai TV dramas to keep myself amused at my in-laws' place and then wait for the world news at 8 o'clock and then the normal news but now you can watch any TV from anywhere around the world so it is not an issue.

What were the main challenges (beyond any mentioned already) in setting up your life here and were there any pleasant surprises i.e. where things were actually better than expected? How hard was it to set up your life here? Did you have help or was it you on your own?

Setting up my life here was not hard but setting up the company was hard. I needed a Thai COO to do the BOI registration and so on without the need for a third-party lawyer who speaks English to do it. In terms of setting up my own life, I remember I had to get ID cards sorted for my two adult daughters – from my first wife – and it was my second wife who helped get that done. Ultimately what helped get it done was my first wife's brother was a general in the army and when he turned up at the district office, they all stood up to attention and no questions were asked and they got their cards immediately. Up till that point, there were all kinds of hurdles put in our way but soon as he turned up, things got done. My daughters had never lived in Thailand but they were over 21 by then and it was useful for me because once I pass away, they could inherit the land on which the company is built or they could own property that I cannot own because I am not Thai.

In terms of pleasant surprises, the subtle differences between central Thailand and northern Thailand e.g. the food, the culture differences. Up north, it is more pork and less fish and there are differences in the way food is cooked so even curries are different. We have sticky rice everywhere in the north. Scenery wise – it is mountains versus flat land and this time of year (October), the rains have stopped and it is nice and cool and perfect for hiking or whatever. In terms of people, there are also differences, so, for example, the kids wear the traditional lanna dress to school in this region. Even though it is not as strong these days, still hearing the Northern language being spoken e.g. 'jâo' at the end of sentences instead of 'kà' really resonates that you are in Northern Thailand.

Also, when you say you are from Chiang Mai, you have different conversations with people about different things, compared to if you are from Bangkok. So, for example, if you are talking with an Isaan taxi driver, he will have a conversation with you comparing Isaan with the North and they somehow look on you more favourably, possibly because Chiang Mai evokes that romantic notion of the perfect life in Thailand in a pretty, ambient, quiet part of Chiang Mai.

What have you learnt about Thailand life that you did not know in the first few months?

The first thing is every day is not a holiday here! Real life does happen here and you need to deal with it day to day, where, for example, you go to the shopping centre and you cannot find a parking space and a trip to the shopping centre can turn into an all-day event.

Another thing is that it is extremely difficult to find workmen that you can trust. They are here one week, gone the next and suddenly uncontactable, which puts a lot of pressure on the wife to leverage her network to find someone. It is probably less of a problem in Bangkok but up north, it can be difficult. And the other thing is it does become really annoying that everybody has their hand out to you and you are seen as the source of wealth and for them to ask isn't a loss of face but to not give is a loss of face.

What has changed over the years in terms of your life in Thailand? Has it got better or have you become more jaded and homesick?

I understand a lot more but there are certain things I will never understand. Also, if you can't be accepting of other people and other ways of life, you're going to find it very hard to live here. I am not really homesick and am pretty settled here...if I moved back to Singapore for work, I'd probably be pretty upset!

What are your top tips to successfully settle here? And conversely, what are the top things to not do?

Anger in the right direction can be a very useful tool to get things done here – being direct without making it personal. People say don't get angry with Thai people but I see Thai people get very angry with other people. Just being forceful at the right time and not letting a bureaucrat walk all over you because the rules can be different from office to office in the government departments you deal with. Next, constantly showing respect to the monarchy and religion is crucial here. Never, ever, ever, do anything that shows disrespect to those institutions. But at the same time, realise that you do not need to participate in those things e.g. going to the temple.

In terms of what not to do, if you are in Bangkok, don't drive – don't buy a car, you don't need it if you don't have a need to go outside Bangkok. Get to know the place before you buy anything of value like a house or condo – do you have the things you want in your life close by around you. You can live here completely outside of Thai culture but it is worth spending some time to get to know the things that are important if you want to get the most out of your time here.

Do you feel Thailand is a cheap place to live?

If you're going to have non-sweet bread, it' going to cost more; if you want any Western stuff, it's going to be more expensive – even McDonalds is not really fast food here, it's quite expensive. Also, if things go wrong, how are you going to be able to look after yourself? The expectations are different in the Thai system compared to a Western system. My son had a breathing problem and we had to go to ICU at a hospital in Chiang Mai and the bill came to 120,000 baht for four days stay. I thought we had full insurance through my company but it turned out the insurance capped out at 25,000 baht so I had to cough up a 100,000 baht. And it was supposed to be the top AIA package in Thailand.

By the way, a quick thing – if health is important to you, live near a major city. A mate was in a motorcycle accident upcountry; I was behind him. It was a very slow, innocuous accident where a scooter knocked him off and he ended up breaking six ribs. I remember arguing with the doctor who kept saying "ah, it's only bruising". They stuck him in a van on a hard hospital bed all the way back to Bangkok for seven hours over bumpy Thai roads. He was screaming with pain all the way.

Going back to the 'anger in the right direction' thing, do you think the reason you can show anger is because you are quite senior and own a company and have a certain status here whereas your average expat may not be able to be as assertive?

Assertive is a better word. No, I don't think that is the case. I remember my son was building a Lego helicopter and one of his Lego pieces fell down the back of a table. The waiter was saying "no, I can't find it, I can't do it" and so on but I just kept pushing, pushing and pushing him to try and eventually he said, "Yes, we can move the table and find the Lego piece". You can often get that fob-off answer which is basically "I can't be arsed".

Do you think you are accepted in Thai society? And is it only because you can speak Thai?

Yes. Part of the reason is definitely because I can speak Thai. I went to the wife's grandma's family funeral and I was part of the pallbearers who had to put the body into the cremation chamber and I was the only Westerner there. At the funeral, I could go sit and talk and relate, it may be about why they think they have a particular cancer cluster in that part of the world etc. However, I don't think it is only about being able to speak Thai, you also need to have a willingness to be part of the conversation in the first place. If I wanted to I could be quite dismissive of the whole thing and think, it's nothing to do with me.

Going back to frustrations, a very frustrating thing here is the use of assets. The brother of the wife will come over and suddenly "Where's my drill?" I want to use it and it's gone and when you do get it back, it's got a huge scratch on it. You do have to set boundaries as people are quite 'relaxed' about things like that and if you do raise any complaint, you get "oh don't worry, I'll get it fixed" but then they don't.

Talking of which, another frustrating thing is people telling you what they think you want to hear. So, in my company, my staff will tell me, we're going live next month when I know perfectly well, we're not going live next month.

Why do you think that is?

It's a face thing – they do not want to disappoint you. We spend a lot of time in our company dealing with that cultural issue. Trying to tell them to speak up as I won't be angry but I will be in six months' time if they could have told me before.

In places where people do not know you, maybe in your case, in Bangkok, how do you find Thai people react to you? Do they have a look of panic – "oh no, I have to speak English" or do you get in there first and speak Thai?

I actually find it more difficult going to six-star resorts in Phuket and them wanting to speak English with me all the time. Speaking Thai opens up a different door and you get treated differently, for sure – one thousand per cent.

And especially if you talk to them in a way that is respectful about who they are and where they come from.

Any other scary, funny, embarrassing or dangerous anecdotes in Thailand?

I don't feel scared here – I would feel more scared in a dark area of London than a dark area of Bangkok. The more scammy things tend to happen around the tourist areas, not so much in more suburban areas.

Embarrassing mistakes – yes, many but Thai people are very accepting of that so as long as you don't stick your foot on a woman's head or do something very disrespectful, they are very understanding. They will go out of their way to make sure you know where you need to be and do the right thing etc.

What do you think of other expats in Thailand? Do you consciously try to hang out with other expats or do you try to avoid them?

Other expats that I do have a lot in common with, I do hang out with, yeah. Guys that have longevity here, have set up businesses here because we have common issues. A lot of expats are my customers so I don't really try to avoid them – I want to know about their life.

One important point, as someone who hasn't yet reached retirement age, it is a lot easier having friends in Bangkok than Chiang Mai because there are a lot more retirees in Chiang Mai. Bangkok has more people of working age whereas people often move to Chiang Mai to slow down and retire.

Do you agree that there are apart from the main groups of expats such as retirees and English teachers, the only other significant group is of people who have set up their own businesses because it is not that easy to find good employment here in Thailand?

Unless you're coming into a foreign company or any Thai company looking to modernise. In terms of country background, the Japanese population here is huge and the Chinese population is becoming even larger.

What are your plans for the future? Are you fully invested into Thailand or will you and your wife move back to Australia at some point?

I am staying here – life is more interesting here. It's hard to say where I think of as home now – Australia or here. The longer you are here, the harder it is here to think of Australia as home.

Can you summarise in a few sentences your business – the benefits of Dollarsmart, the future etc.

The business was originally set up between myself and a South African guy who had financial systems experience at Morgan Stanley and a Thai university professor. The reason we started the business is typically expats will complain about two things the most – visas and the cost of moving money. We thought we can't fix the first problem but we can do something about the second. We piloted Australia to Thailand about three years ago now and we are now about 20% of the market. The reason for that is that we are fast and we are cheap. It's all completely online and very easy to use so cuts out a lot of the inefficiencies. Also, unlike many others, we support local language support in every market, whether it is in the Philippines or wherever.

Our aim is to be the premier money movement transfer company to and from and in between ASEAN and Asia and the 'between' is the interesting bit – no one else is doing that because the regulatory issues make it quite difficult.

If you were advising other expats, is it better to get a job first from back home or come over here and look for one?

It's better to try and get a job back home unless you are going to be here for a long time and you are prepared to work the network. You need to join the business chambers as things just do not appear on Monster.com or whatever. You have to be out there networking and find out where the opportunities are.

What are cultural differences and challenges of having Thai staff?

Lack of international exposure is the biggest one – a lot of my staff are university kids and we train them up but they will never have the cultural background to think about things like a foreign expat. So, for example, an Australian person may have a girlfriend in Thailand who he is sending money to or a French guy in Hong Kong wants to pay for his villa in France – culturally, these staff have no idea of these people's lifestyle, who they are. I have experience but that is limited to my own life – I don't know about a Taiwanese person's life for example, what they are interested in etc. So, leading an international company with a full Thai team can be the biggest limiting thing – their lack of international exposure.

In terms of other differences with Western office environments, one obvious one is they are very regimented – they will all go out to lunch together. The whole office will disappear to lunch.

243

Another thing we are very sympathetic to is that they are brought to the company in a stable environment so, for example, we built a nursery in the office – so many of the staff have young kids and during the holiday period, it can be very stressful on the family.

In terms of positive aspects of hiring Thai staff, the obvious one is cost base. Also, Thai people are generally very service-oriented and want to please and do the right thing by the customers. It needs to be sharpened and focused but it is there and does not need to be forced. Also, they have a great willingness to learn but they really want to learn in a formal setting. So, whereas I've always thought that 80% of what you learn is through conversations and experiences, they expect the 80% to be in a classroom.

One other big thing that we have gone through in my company is teaching them that they can stand up to me. I can be one of these people who is doing five million things at the same time and I could cause chaos by expecting everyone to work to my speed so people do sometimes need to push back and over time, the message is getting through.

Interview 9: The Filipino

Arnulfo 'Arnie' Aniel is a Filipino who has lived in Thailand for over twenty years, working in education as well as providing consultancy to Thai businesses, public speaking and other topics. Arnie gave us one of the most interesting, opinionated and funny interviews so we hope you like it.

Tell us a bit about your background and why you came to Thailand.

I'm from Manila (in the Philippines) and I've been living in Bangkok for 22 years and 8 months. I came here out of frustration from not getting an immigrant visa for Canada. Fortunately, I had a friend who was working here and I came as a tourist and stayed with him and his colleague in their apartment. I checked things around for about two weeks and decided to find a job after that.

I am a registered nurse and midwife with some teaching experience as a clinical instructor. I was 24, single and had no idea about Thailand except for the fact that they don't speak English, which my friend told me after I decided to come. The only thing I knew about the country was their candidate in the 1994 Miss Universe contest as it was held in the Philippines, the same year when I came here.

My first work was in a small international kindergarten as an Assistant Teacher and now work as an HR Consultant.

I have always lived in Bangkok but I have been able to visit some beautiful places in Thailand both for work and vacation.

Had you visited Thailand before and if so, how many times?

I had never visited Thailand before I came here and didn't know anything except that they spoke a different language which I knew only weeks before I arrived in the country.

What were your first impressions when you moved here?

At first, I thought I won't stay here for a long time because of the language barrier. At the same time, I wanted to work at the hospital or in line with my profession as a nurse and midwife. They found it a bit strange for a male to be a nurse or midwife more than 20 years ago.

Most of my first impressions were influenced by my Filipino friend and his colleagues (also Filipinos). They told me about their experiences here – It is difficult to communicate because Thai people don't speak English and even with some who could, it is difficult to understand because of the accent, they like foreigners with white skin, Filipinos and other Asians are not considered foreigners, traffic is bad.

What were the main challenges and what were the main pleasant surprises of living here?

I was very lucky to have a Filipino friend when I came here. He gave some useful information about Thais and their way of living. Moreover, Bangkok isn't that different from Manila (except for the fact that it's cleaner and safer here), so it wasn't a big adjustment for me.

The biggest challenge was the language. Thai language is a difficult language for me and before, less people could speak English so it wasn't easy to get around (shopping, ordering food in restaurants, asking for directions). From the very beginning it was also a challenge to teach English for me as someone who is from the Philippines – most of them don't like our accent and discrimination was everywhere.

Surprises don't end while living in Thailand. Even though I've been living (and working) here for a long time, every now and then, surprises come my way. In my first job, I had a Thai colleague and she said, Thais are not so fond of Filipinos because they can't accept the fact that we can speak English though we look like them (Thai people). When I became a Head Teacher for a language centre, I was really surprised how Thai people really adore Native English speakers especially from England. They like the British accent and they want to speak English with a British accent.

It is a lot easier to settle now than before since there are more Thai people who can speak English. Moreover, there are more expats now who you can talk to and get information.

What have you learnt about Thailand life that you did not know in the first few months, if anything? What has changed over the years in terms of your development as a resident of Thailand?

I've been here for more than 20 years and living here has changed a lot. In the first few years of living here, I wasn't really interested in knowing more about Thai culture because I didn't have the intention of working here this long. My plan was to move to another country where I could work in a hospital. Moreover, I worked with Filipinos and only a few Thais in my first two jobs, so I wasn't exposed to the culture 100%. But when I got the opportunity to work with more Thai colleagues, that was the first time I learned more about Thai culture, especially how to work with them.

More opportunities came my way when I started learning how to speak & understand the Thai language and Thai people are more at ease talking to me in their own language. Though there are more Thai people who can speak English now than before, they are still more comfortable speaking in Thai than in English. They also find it "cute" to hear me (and other foreigners especially Caucasians) speak some Thai.

My life is a lot better now especially after I changed career from teaching to the corporate world. But I had to invest in making myself more qualified to be competitive in the market. It is important in Thailand to have degrees especially if you graduate from famous universities in the country or overseas. Fortunately, I was able to earn a degree from Thammasat University and now I'm a candidate for a doctoral degree at Mahidol University.

I am more at ease now living in the country and I can relate better with Thai people. One of the keys is the language and my relationship with them. I was able to have some really trustworthy Thai friends who I can definitely depend on anytime.

What are your top tips for settling here successfully? Conversely, what are your top tips on what to not do?

It is not very difficult for some Asians especially Filipinos to settle in Thailand particularly Bangkok. Here are my tips for those who plan settling in this country:

1. Be aware of all the changes in the laws regarding visa and work permit (they change almost every year as far as my experience is concerned).
2. Educate yourself about Thai culture so they won't consider you rude or impolite.
3. Learn some common Thai words, phrases and expressions.
4. When they say "kha" or "krup", it doesn't mean they understand most of the time. Clarify to make sure they really understand (don't just ask "Do you understand?").
5. Be patient especially when you talk to them in English (and worse if you have a strong accent that they are not familiar with) specifically when you talk to those who are not really proficient in English.
6. If you don't eat spicy food you should specify the number of chilies you want to put in your food (a bit spicy for them is still very spicy for most foreigners who don't eat spicy food).
7. Be careful when you go for a massage because of lot of masseuse and masseur offer "Happy Ending" and some of them are really pushy and directly ask for extra tip to give extra service.
8. Be careful in entering relationships. I've heard about some not so good ones that ended up bad.
9. Thai people have preferences on looks and character but it's not difficult to get along with them if you learn how to relate with them.
10. Always keep in mind that Thailand is their country and embrace their culture.

To what extent have you integrated into Thai society?

I strongly believe that I am accepted here and I have been able to establish relationships of different levels – both personal and professional. I can talk to Thai people about similar topics I usually talk with my friends/family back home but there are some things like jokes and stories that they can't relate to (but Filipinos and other foreigners can). In parties or social gatherings, it is not really difficult to relate with them if you can speak the language, drink or sing.

There are many similarities between Thai and Filipino cultures like extended family, respect to elders, the use of 'kha'/'krup' in speaking which is 'po'/'opo' in Tagalog, giving/sending money to parents/family to support financially among others. So, it wasn't really difficult for me to adjust here.

Tell us of any interesting anecdotes, any funny incidents, any scary or dangerous occurrences, any embarrassing mistakes or any other memorable experiences of Thailand.

On my first few weeks, I was told that Thai pronounce the letter 's' with an 'a' (swim becomes sawim etc.) most of the time. I went to a donut shop and ordered sprite and pronounced it "saprite" to make sure the staff would understand me. Surprisingly, he didn't understand me and corrected my pronunciation of "sprite" and I laughed, which baffled him.

– Some of Thai names and nicknames are Tagalog words with different spellings and meanings so I (and other Filipinos especially those who are new here or during their first few months) laugh or smile when we hear those names and nicknames. Some of them have meanings of a sexual context.

- Most people usually expect me to sing every time they know I'm from the Philippines.
- It's always a struggle for me to order "egg" or "chicken" because they sound very similar in Thai. I usually have to use body language to make sure they understand I want an egg, not a chicken.
- One time I caught a taxi and the driver thought I was a Thai TV personality (whom I happen to know). All the way from my apartment to my office, he insisted that I was that person and the more I rejected the idea, the more he was convinced I was that celebrity. He asked for a selfie before I got out of his taxi.

What do you think of other expats who move to Thailand? Do you consciously try to hang out with other expats or try to avoid them?

I think there are different expats who move to Thailand and I will group them as follows:

1. Those who were sent by their companies and those who invest in the country.
2. Those who came to work because they earn better money here.
3. Those who have Thai wives/husbands, girlfriends/boyfriends.
4. Those who just want to experience living in the country for a short period of time

I know some expats from work, some from my affiliation (toastmasters) and others from the church. I think a lot of them enjoy the climate here and the advantage of having the ability of English language. I hang out with my Filipino friends but rarely with other expats from other countries. I guess I have different interests particularly with Caucasians. I had some close friends before who are not Filipinos but most of them went back home for good.

What's interesting in meeting other expats is the sharing of our experiences living in Thailand. It's amazing to know what they think of the country, its people and the culture.

What are your plans for the future? Are you fully invested into Thailand or will you go back home at some point?

I don't have plans to go back to the Philippines and I'm thinking of applying for a resident visa. I am happy with my life here and it's not far from the Philippines, so I can always go back for a holiday. I still have contacts with my friends back home but most of my professional experience is here, so I'm more familiar with working here.

If you have a decent career with a decent package, you can enjoy both personal and professional lives in Thailand. The cost of living is not as high as in Manila or other countries that I know of. It is safer and it's not difficult to work with Thai people.

At the same, I have registered my own business (consulting business: Arnie Consultant) here, which I believe has a better chance of success here than in the Philippines. The exposure here is a lot better since there are more expats here that I can work with and make business with. Not to mention that it is easier to travel from here than from my own country.

Interview 10: The Banker

Tamara van den Ban is a Dutch banking executive who used to work for Thai Military Bank. Tamara was probably one of the few senior female Western bankers here so provides a unique perspective. Her interview was easily the most insightful and best explained perspective of Thai work culture.

Tell us a bit about your background and why you came to Thailand.

I have always worked for ING and my last role before I moved to Thailand was looking on behalf of ING as to where they could start new businesses with a new model. We looked at Eastern Europe and Asia and we bought a stake in Thai Military Bank. And so, they asked me, since you have done all the work and have the experience, do you want to go to Thailand and help us to transform the bank there? And I said sure, why not!!

I was sent there as an expat and they arranged the visas, a housing allowance and a real estate agent who we could liaise with to find accommodation. So, the agent made the trip with us. I also had culture training to prepare us for the move.

The culture training was very, very interesting and I found it really helpful. I have lived in many countries and I have always found that the countries where I did not do the culture training – no matter how close or far the country was – I always regretted it. You can easily make obvious mistakes just because of some things that you need to know that you do not know. It was a 2-day course understanding your own culture and the culture you are going to i.e. Thai, and where there are big differences and clashes, trying to understand the viewpoint of the other side and learning how to cope with that.

They started with what they called the onion model – you know, peel back layers. A lot of people who go abroad for the first time or even a few times, they have certain ways of thinking and behaving and some of it is really yours, embedded in you from a cultural point – your norms and values that you can't change. But there are a lot of other things are things that you do because everyone does it, your mum used to do it, it's just the way it is but you don't really have an attachment to it or a logic or a why.

When you are in your own country, you don't really challenge those things. But then when you go to another country and they do things differently, it's kind of easy to understand why they do it differently and actually, why do I do it the way I do it, which I think is the most important aspect. You peel off these layers and get to the core and then build it up back again with layers that match you and it is a combination between your own culture and your new culture and maybe, every culture you go to, you build up your mixed, blended personality. So you start to become a sort of 'world citizen'.

There were some nice examples of cultural differences in this training I had. For example, picking your phone up in a meeting. What do you do in a meeting if your phone rings? For Dutch people and a lot of Europeans too, you would not pick up the phone, they would put it on silent or not take the call or even send a text to say they are in a meeting and will call back. It's important for them to be in the meeting and focus on that and it is rude to pick up the phone. You don't do that.

But they said, in Thailand, it is actually the opposite – their logic is, when they are in a meeting, it is rude not to pick up because the person who is calling you doesn't know you are in a meeting but everyone else in the meeting knows you are in a meeting so it's fine to take a couple of minutes to just pick up. This is because you never know why they are calling and it may be something urgent or important. It is better to pick up the phone and ask if it is anything urgent and if not, I will call you back. At least then the other person knows. When I learnt that, I thought, actually, that also makes sense and it depends whether you are considering the people in the room or the person on the phone. So, when I got to Thailand and people were picking up the phone, I didn't get annoyed because I knew why they were doing that.

Another example of the training was…let's say I knew that you had a position open in your department and a friend of mine says 'Well, I have someone who I know would be good for position, can you refer that person'. A Dutch person would almost never do that because they would not know whether the person being referred is suitable, good enough, trustworthy and so on – ultimately, it's my reputation on the line. I would only recommend someone who is over-qualified if I was going to do it at all. But the trainer said, a Thai person would always make the referral. Because it's his friend and he asked you to do that and that relationship is more important than your own concerns about your reputation. The fact that your friend asked you to do that, of course you would do it because he's your friend and you are part of this group, this community and it is important. The relationship between him and you would be affected if you did not make the referral.

In the training, they also explained how important the group and the community are in Thailand. I come from Northern Europe, which is a very individualistic culture. Whereas, here, everything and everything you do is about community and group – you are always part of that group. It is very difficult to understand before you have been in it for a while and have seen it happening. I remember when I came here to work, I would see lots of my staff wearing these big, fluffy, animal style sandals – like a lion or Hello Kitty or whatever. And I thought why are they wearing that at work, as these sandals or slippers rustled by my office.

And then I saw that they would come to work in their high heels, change into these childish slipper things and then change back to their heels to go home! And all their desks are full of Hello Kitty toys and family stuff, like one big girl's room almost and when I asked why they have all that stuff, they said, well, this is where I spend most of my time so I want to feel at home. This is my family, this is my home. So, even though the first time I saw all this, I thought 'Oh my God, what is wrong with you?!', I understood later that, yes, this is like their home because they spend 8 or 9 hours here every weekday.

You notice they all go to lunch at exactly the same time – 12pm – and nobody ever eats alone. Again, this is because you always do everything as a group and have that sense of belonging. So, for example, there would be questionnaires with the question – 'Do you have a best friend at work?' – and that is because, again, there is a feeling of this is my place, my community. It is really important and they act as a team. Moreover, it means there is no professional and personal, it is all blended together because it is all one relationship amongst people.

So, you have put a positive spin on it, which is good but was there also a negative aspect to it? So, for example, is it difficult for people to take ownership, as compared to the West?

It's interesting you say that because I wouldn't say individual accountability is that common in Europe either! In Dutch companies, yes, there is a strong sense of individual accountability but when I worked in a British company for a year, ownership was much more distributed!

But coming back to Thailand, I have to admit, I learned a lot along the way over seven years so, yes, in the beginning, I had the same feelings as your question. Thai people can be very childish and irresponsible but there are reasons for this. Most people do not live together before they are married, they stay with their parents for a long time, they marry quite late, when they marry, they often live close to their parents who still take care of them etc. The effect of all this is that they often marry after 30, they live at their parents' home, they earn a salary but they do not have many responsibilities of their own – no mortgage of their own to pay, no bills – so the money they earn is theirs to spend fully and they have no real financial responsibilities. So that maturity that we get when we are younger, they get a lot later in life.

From our perspective, they behave like teenagers because we have already moved on to the next phase of our lives. They do that much, much later. So, a lot of times, even if they just don't like you or they don't like their colleague, they just quit their job! They just quit. They have no financial responsibilities so they can just quit and just say, 'I'll just find another job'. Many people in banking are from families who are reasonably well-off with parents that may be in Bangkok. Even if this is not the case, if they feel offended, that is reason enough to just quit. The unemployment rate is not high at all in Thailand so they will find another job quite quickly.

So how did you deal with this over the years?

I learned – I picked a lot of people in my own team. I was very mindful of how important the culture and the feeling of belonging to the group was, so I spent a lot of time building the team as a team and did a lot of team events to bring up that culture. In terms of childish nature, I just ignored it. As far as delivery, I did not find that as much of a challenge. For me, I could be quite firm with them about delivery on time and so on, as long as it was one to one.

What I found really challenging from a work perspective was what I love about Thailand most in my personal life. So, as Thailand is very strong in Buddhist culture and probably one of the places where people live the most in the now, in the moment. And that is what is makes your personal life so enjoyable because people are fully present, they live in the moment, they don't worry about yesterday, tomorrow is tomorrow, let's enjoy today and make the most out of it. Nothing is really planned and structure is a very spontaneous thing so it is like 'hey, this is happening, let's go over there' with this group and you have fun out of nothing. They make something out of nothing because everything is so of the moment. That feeling of spontaneity, having fun, being relaxed, not that stressed, no planning and so on makes life very comfortable and interesting.

As an example, I remember I was in Bangkok at the time of the floods and I had people in my team who had three or four metres of water in their house and everything gone but they didn't complain, they didn't mention it once apart from maybe asking for a loan or something. They just said, it happened and yesterday was yesterday and maybe it was talked about for two weeks and that was it. If that had in Europe, it would have been talked about for years and years, people would complain and remember. That is a very admirable mindset of being able to live with what is there at that moment and just go forward.

But in work, people have forgotten yesterday so learning from mistakes – forget it! People will make the same mistakes over and over again. Tomorrow – well, people do not plan so a deadline is not really a deadline but a guideline. As such, you can't hold people accountable because everything is a guideline. Since you can't properly plan big deliveries or big projects, it is very difficult to timescale-manage that because they just can't. They really can't. But due to my background I am really good at it so I just took that on me and did the planning.

As they really cannot plan, they have to be really creative to find solutions to be able to deliver things. I found that they are extremely creative, sometimes super committed when they suddenly need to deliver, they almost make it like a party and everyone stays in the office till late, they order some food, some drinks and so on. In Europe, people would say I need to go home but here, since nobody planned anything anyway, so, ok, tonight we have to work until late but we'll do that and come up with a solution and all of a sudden, it is done the day after! I started to see that and learned to trust that things will get delivered somehow. I would trust in their creativity but blend that with planning from me, where I would break down deliveries into smaller pieces that I knew they could do with their creativity. So it was kind of East meets West to deliver.

However, this is a bit of generalisation and there are quite a lot of Thais that have been educated or brought up overseas who are now working in Thailand and they do have that capability to take a piece of work from inception, plan it out and work out how to deliver it by themselves. These kinds of employees might cost more because they command a higher salary but they usually deliver as well so you get value for money. As such you need to get balance between local talent and local creativity and international skills.

As I say, that lack of planning and spontaneity is the best thing about Thai people in non-work situations. It is also why Thai people are so good in roles like marketing, arts, performance because of their spontaneity and creativity. I wouldn't say it is easy to work here – it is one of the most difficult markets to work in, culture wise and getting things done – but once you get to appreciate and understand what they can do really, really well, you get the right balance by having people who can do the planning and the 'boring things', the outcomes can be really great.

You mentioned about personal life and work life blending together here. To what extent was that a challenge or to what extent was that actually a good thing in terms of office dynamics?

I would say there were pros and cons. A big pro was people look after each other and they are generally interested in their colleagues and they take care and know each other well. So, they want to support each other because the relationships are based on a stronger bond than just a working relationship. However, it was also very difficult because there were a lot of emotions to deal with and it was almost like kindergarten sometimes or maybe high school where it was like 'he said, she said'. I'm not sure if it was better or worse than Western office culture but it was different and you have to understand and appreciate that.

What were your first impressions of Thailand and how were they similar or different to what you were expecting, bearing in mind you had the cultural training before you came?

Well, the first couple of months were like a honeymoon and everything was positive and wonderful until you start to adjust and understand a bit better and then everything is bad and then you end up somewhere in between at a normalised level. Everyone goes through that cycle, faster or slower and sometimes there are multiple cycles. I was well-prepared and it still wasn't what I expected. When I look back at myself, how much I changed – you know, how it is to live there, how to adjust, how to let go of some of the planning. Then there were the smells and the sounds of Bangkok and the traffic. When you first live there, it hits you but after a while, it is chaos but more like organised chaos and once you understand how it is organised, you can find your way around. And it is actually pretty easy to live in.

I lived three years on Sukhumvit and four years in Sathorn. In Sukhumvit, I wanted to live in the most hectic area so chose to live on Soi 41, which is near to Phrom Pong and Thong Lor and it was very nice. But after three years I was kind of fed up as every time I stepped outside I was in the middle of the chaos and I wanted to have some more peace and quiet so we moved to Sathorn, which is a bit more of an office area.

To what extent do you think that you integrated into Thai society?

I was more with other English-speaking expats in Bangkok. I mean I travelled a lot in Thailand and for work, I sometimes had to go to more remote places but for my personal life, less. It's not that I didn't have any Thai friends and I still have – Thai friends that came to visit me in Germany – but they were mostly friends who I had met at work and had studied abroad. I found it really difficult or perhaps impossible to have a friendship with 'Thai Thais'. I tried to speak the language at first and I can speak what people call 'taxi Thai' and I can understand a fair bit. A lot of the meetings were in Thai and I would answer in English because I could understand. When I knew the context, I could understand half and guess the other half if it was in Thai whereas, if it was about sport or politics, it was much more difficult. Most of my friendships were with Thai people who could speak English and who had lived abroad.

Also, the lifestyle is so different between the West and Thai people who have lived here their whole life. Everything is about family and community; a big part of life revolves around eating, sleeping, relaxing and shopping. One thing has stuck with me about being Thai – the most important thing is food! In the morning, they speak about breakfast, during the day, it is always about the next meal and it is always about food everywhere. And apart from that, lifestyle is about relaxing and shopping and hanging out, which is not really what I find important.

Also, because you are away from your own family, you tend to form friendships with other expats a lot faster and more intensely than you would do back home because this is now your family. I really enjoyed that. But even that is not really the same as Thais and their family and I could try to understand it but you never really understand it. Also, I am a really sporty person, I am super active and I like outdoor sports and I travel a lot. So, when I would come in with my field hockey outfit, they were always laughing at me at work. I didn't have any interests that aligned with Thai people and I could not really adapt to what they found important or how they wanted to spend their days.

But also, let me reflect that back because if you were to come to the Netherlands, it is really, really hard to make Dutch friends. Because, just like Thais, they have their own rituals and their own routines and so on. They already have their own friends and families and their own communities, clubs and sports and they are really not that interested in making new friends. Even with colleagues at work, well, that's work and then they go back to their own lives and you are not really part of it.

What wisdom, beyond everything you have said already, have you or did you pick up about living in Thailand to make it a success and want to stay there long term?

I learned a lot about losing face and what it means for me and what it means in Thai culture. I still can't really understand it but I understand it, you know. What I consider losing face is not what Thai people consider losing face and what Thai people consider losing face, I do not. For example, if I would be in a meeting, in a big group and I would say something wrong, factually wrong, they would not want to correct me in that meeting because they would say I would be losing face. They would tell me after the meeting, maybe, if I was lucky, or one to one later. And I would be like…well, why did you tell me because now we have to do the whole meeting all over again. Now I am losing face because I have to do it all over again and you could have just told me in the meeting – I don't mind if you correct me. In the end, I managed to get a compromise out of them where they would send me a message or a signal to give me a sign I was wrong.

But then, on the other hand, there are situations where I definitely felt like I was losing face where they thought it was perfectly normal. In my first week, I was in a conference with 500 people and they said that they always do karaoke and we always ask the new people to sing a song! So they were like "You have to sing a song in front of these 500 people". And I told them I really can't sing but they just said it doesn't matter. Now I would consider that loss of face because I don't know all this and I can't sing. But for them, they did not see it like that and you are just showing you are willing to build the relationship and be part of the group and just, you know, have fun. But I have to say, I went through so many personal barriers because of things like this – I had to do so many things like this that I would never have done before that seem to me to be childish or whatever. By the end, I really did not care anymore and I really opened up and I started to understand the fun of it and let go of the shame and just enjoyed it. I realised how important that spirit and heart and soul is in the things you do when you work together.

What is your overall impression of Thailand as you look back now? Would you say it is a good place to live?

I would view it positively but you definitely do need to be open and willing to adjust but that is for every country you go to actually. I always say to people that you are a guest, like when you are a guest in someone's house and you have to adjust the place where you are and when you are willing to do that, you can have fun and have a good time. Don't expect it to be your home, meaning, don't expect things to be as they are at home. You cannot demand your own rules and what you are used to. If you are willing to be open and understand why and what is different…and also really question yourself why you think or do certain things. If you can challenge yourself and think whether how you do things is right or wrong, you can have a great time in Thailand.

It is a really affordable place, it is an easy place to get around, people live in the moment, there's so many things to enjoy, the weather is great, there's lots of things to do – there are a lot of positives. But there are a lot of difficulties and you need to adjust yourself if you want to be happy here.

What I have seen of my colleagues who fail both in work life and personal life, is that unwillingness to adjust. They come here with a mindset of 'I've come here to fix things because it's such a mess in this country, it's disorganised and it is chaos and they don't know what they are doing and they are childish and have no responsibility. I'll come and I'll fix things and I'll do things my way'. It doesn't work!

Like I would say if it was a Dutch colleague, 'You're not in the Netherlands. You have to take your skills and work out how can that augment or help impact the culture to improve or change things. Don't think you will change things overnight. You need to be a part of that in order to change it. You can't make it like your own culture.' You cannot expect the same conditions and way of life as you are used to in your own country and if you want that, go back to your own country! What are you doing there? You should be here because of the differences in culture and how that can change you and what you can learn by being open and willing to adjust. If you are not willing to do that, you will not last more than two years because you will be totally frustrated.

Richard McCully & Stephen Saad

Interview 11: The Expat Who Did Not Stay

Bob Guntz is an American expat who decided not to stay here, after a few visits. His thoughts provide an interestingly different perspective to the other interviewees'.

Tell us a bit about your background and why you came to Thailand.

I lived in Thailand for about five months in 2013. I had a job in the education industry and was considering moving to Thailand full time, probably Bangkok. I had been living in China for several years and was just interested in a change of scene.

Had you visited Thailand before you came to live here?

I had visited Thailand a couple times before on vacation, both Chiang Mai and Bangkok. I had met and talked with foreigners who had lived in Thailand for long periods of time. The reviews were mixed, so I wanted to find out for myself.

What were your first impressions when you moved here?

When I lived in Bangkok I interacted more with people than I while I was on vacation, both foreigners and Thais. It seemed there were a lot of foreigners who got dragged down by the cheap alcohol (and perhaps drugs) and, in the case of men, women who perhaps did not have the capacity for love.

I did not like the fact that the government made the visa process more difficult than it needed to be, even for long-term foreigners with jobs who were married with children.

I also want to say that I found Thais to be generally friendly and, in some cases, really very helpful. I also met foreigners who I thought were perfectly reasonable and nice people. It might have been that after spending more time in Thailand I would have found a nice community to be a part of. However, my early experiences and knowledge indicated that living there might have been depressing. After a few months I decided not to stay.

What were the main challenges of living here?

Having relationships with Thai women was a challenge. I briefly dated a Thai girl who had divorced an American man after some time in the USA and moved back to Thailand. Her sister explicitly told me after our second or third date: "She causes problems." I also overheard a conversation in a coffee house between an American man and a Thai woman in which he was clearly emotionally distraught that she had not taken their relationship of several months more seriously. It seemed that their cultural backgrounds created different expectations for a relationship, and perhaps she was opportunistic, it was

261

hard to tell. I had heard of relationships ending like this from other foreigners before. I knew two people, one Thai and one European, who each had a foreign male friend who committed suicide, one after a bad relationship with a Thai woman, and one for unclear reasons.

One European woman I knew who had become fluent in Thai after living in Chiang Rai and Bangkok for several years felt that the Thai women she had worked with and helped open a restaurant did not show reciprocity in their relationship with her when she needed help. She also worked in Bangkok for a medical company in a customer service position. She felt that generally both the Thais and the foreigners who lived in Bangkok were not very ethical. She gave one example of a phone call in which she was explaining to a foreign man the preparations he had to take before a surgery, one of them being not to smoke for a certain period of time and her supervisors told her not to inform him of this pre-op requirement.

What are your top tips for settling here successfully?

Don't jump into relationships. Be judicious about who you befriend, whether foreign or Thai. Avoid too much partying.

Tell us of any interesting anecdotes or any other memorable experiences of Thailand.

I was not able to open a bank account on my tourist visa so a Thai woman I knew for only a short time opened one in her name so that my company would have some place to deposit my salary. There was absolutely no other way to get paid. The sums were not huge, but not insignificant. Long story short, I wound up with only half the money my company deposited, which wasn't too unexpected given human nature. On the other hand, this woman was kind of a pillar of her community and she owned and operated a restaurant where she could have offered me credit to compensate for the loss. We were never on bad terms. Indeed, she had been helpful to me previously and we had no romantic relationship.

What are your plans for the future?

I might return if I could be reasonably confident of plugging into a healthy community without too much difficulty. There are a lot of expats who are in a cycle of drinking and meeting women which is unhealthy in my opinion.

Interview 12 – The Sportsman

Colin Devonshire is a British expat who has spent most of his time playing and coaching football and cricket (yes, cricket!) in Thailand, alongside various jobs in print and advertising. Having had a stroke, his sporting days are over and he now spends his time writing books by the sea in Hua Hin.

Richard McCully & Stephen Saad

Tell us a bit about your background and why you came to Thailand.

I came here first in 1980 and at that time I worked on newspapers, earned a good salary and enjoyed lots of vacation time! The first holiday was a two-centre package – the usual Bangkok/Pattaya combination. My second Thailand visit was to Hua Hin, I loved it here and so, I kept coming back. Eventually I moved here full time, that was over 30 years ago. I wasn't sure what I was going to do for work and my savings would not last forever so I decided to start a magazine, The Hua Hin/Cha Am Observer. I'm still here but sadly the magazine isn't.

What were your first impressions when you moved here?

Living here and holidaying here is very different. In those days there were very few Thais who could speak English and there were also very few expats, so learning the language was important to make friends and learn about the place.

Thirty years ago, all foreigners were considered wealthy, but now Thais know better. Getting started with a home and starting to work was easy. Nobody worried about work permits, forming a company or any of that stuff. As long as we were respectful we were allowed to do anything we liked more or less.

Why did you choose to live in Hua Hin?

I had always dreamed of living by the sea. Life here is much more relaxed than city living. The palm trees and the cocktails are here as you can imagine. Not everyone can live on the beach, it is far too expensive, but at least it's only a short walk away from most condos and houses. Problems seem to float away when you take a stroll along the beach.

Hua Hin is like a mini city these days, so most things you need are at hand. However, our airport is a bit limited, and you have to go to Bangkok for the Embassy. I would not swap Hua Hin for Bangkok ever!

What were the main challenges and what were the main pleasant surprises of living here?

Local people were always offering help. They knew a quick way to do something or they knew someone who could solve a problem.

It takes a while to accept that if you ask directions somewhere, the three people you ask, are all pointing in different directions. They would rather not say they don't know.

One example of a challenge would be, employing a tradesman to complete a job. When he uses a screwdriver instead of a chisel, you may ask if he is qualified to take on such a task, and he replies, "of course I'm qualified, I watched my mate." Get used to it! The fact that he has ruined your tool should not worry you!

What have you learnt about life in Thailand?

It is very important to accept that Thailand and Thai people are not the same as 'back home'. The thinking of Thai people is not the same as Western folk. We always try to plan ahead, Thais don't worry, and let things happen. Often, but not always, it all works out fine.

You must never ever lose your temper. Where in the West sometimes showing your feelings can help, here it doesn't. I no longer expect things to happen quickly but sometimes I get a nice surprise.

What are your top tips for settling here successfully?

Make as many friends as you can from every level of society from the guy who picks rubbish to the company boss. They all have something to say. Listen to them. Never lose your cool, it may not be easy, but it is very important, I can't stress that enough.

To what extent have you integrated into Thai society?

I've always been a keen sportsman so that makes it easy to make friends. In my early days here, I joined a football team and straight away I had a dozen or so mates. The other day I saw one of them at my children's school and it was great to catch up with him.

Through those men, I met their families and joined in with social gatherings etc. At home, you tend to mix only with people of the same level, but here you are welcomed at every stratum.

I joined the Rotary, it was a bit too much of a 'meetings about meetings' kind of club, but I was accepted and welcomed from day one. Here at a function the person who is deemed the most senior picks up the bill. He or she accepts that, as do all the guests, so there is no embarrassment.

You worked as a sports coach in Thailand?

I am a qualified FA Coach and spent some time coaching both here and in

265

England trying to pass on some skills. Language is no problem, as you have to show, rather than talk.

I was very proud to play for Thailand – at cricket. Yes, Thailand do have cricket here! As, an emerging nation, Thailand were allowed to play foreigners who had lived here for 5 or more years.

Golf I only took up when I lived here. It was too cold and wet in the UK! There are wonderful courses in this country.

Unfortunately, all my sports playing stopped when I suffered a stroke. But I started writing!

Tell us of any interesting anecdotes or any other memorable experiences of Thailand.

Once a senior male was extremely drunk. I removed his vehicle keys and hid them. He was not happy. He explained that he was safe to drive. "Buddha is above me." Eventually, I had to return the keys. The following day he really believed that his faith saved him from harm, "You see, nothing happened, Buddha looked after me."

Another example of drink driving involved a mate with a well-known sur-name who had a serious accident, hurting a pedestrian. The attending police officer looked at my friend's license, noticed his name and instead of arresting him, he offered to help him home. It has to be said, that the next day, my friend did everything he could to settle the hospital bill for the injured man. That would not happen everywhere.

You can also read my book 'Not Far Enough From Worries' for more examples.

What do you think of other expats who move to Thailand?

I hate meeting the expat who keeps saying their home country is better. Far too many people say: "At home we would do it like this or do that". God save me from people like that!

Are you fully invested into Thailand or will you go back to the West at some point?

I can't see the family ever moving back to England. It's great living in Thailand, particularly Hua Hin.

Interview 13: The Filmmaker

John Danylkiw is a Canadian film producer with a company in Thailand. He spends time in Thailand for his various projects and returns to Canada and is, therefore, one of the many short-term staying and frequently returning expats.

Richard McCully & Stephen Saad

Tell us a bit about your background and why you came to Thailand.

I'm a Canadian Film and Television Producer who has been coming to Thailand for almost 9 years and am planning on establishing myself in Thailand going forward. I love the country.

9 years ago, I was introduced to an Australian film producer who was established in Bangkok and was looking for help in producing movies in Thailand. Long story short – He was a fraud.

As it turned out, I was able to obtain a development deal from some local Bangkok entrepreneurs which allowed me to move my project forward. I moved away from this chap and I ended up creating my own operation in Thailand. Following that, I was able to meet one of the richest ladies in the country who was very interested in assisting my operation to open a fully-fledged production and entertainment facility in Thailand.

Ultimately, I was able to set up a working relationship with this lady in Bangkok. This lasted for approximately a year and a half until I had to leave to go back to Canada. We have stayed in touch since then and I hope to get back in contact with her to move the project forward.

What were your first impressions when you arrived here?

I first arrived in Thailand, in 2009, just after the blow up between the red shirts and the government. My first impression was driving down a road and seeing three burned out houses. It was rather a bizarre feeling.

What were the main challenges and what were the main pleasant surprises of living here?

Obviously, the main challenges in Thailand are language and customs. Getting used to the customs takes a little bit of time but with people who I've made friends with in Bangkok, that was a little less problematic.

Language, on the other hand, is a continual challenge. I have managed to pick up some general terminology but I have to start looking at understanding the written word along with the spoken word in order to master the language better. In so far as that is concerned, I have had wonderful help from my local friends who have given me instructions in speaking the language. I'm still working on the written word.

What have you learnt about Thailand life that you did not know in the first few months, if anything?

As I have been staying in Thailand on again off again for the last eight or nine years, I have enjoyed learning the customs, eating the food and learning the language. When I first arrived the politics was problematic, now it's a little more solidified. I am still not a permanent resident of Thailand and still have the ability to find new things around every corner. It's a lovely country, the people are terrific and I look forward to being involved in the country and its life in my future.

What are your top tips for settling here successfully? Conversely, what are your top tips on what to not do?

First and foremost, do not judge Thai people as third world people. Thailand has the technology and the interest of its younger generation to move the country forward in a more modern vein. The biggest mistake anybody could make is to think that Thai people are not with it. One of the tips I should give is when a Thai person smiles to some comments that you might make, that smile does not mean 'yes', it just means that they have heard you, nothing more.

As a man, you have to be very careful to not get involved with other peoples' women as that could seriously impair the rest of your life. Be very courteous. Thai people understand courtesy and want to help foreigners as much as they possibly can but there's always a lookout for something that will benefit them.

Try to learn and understand the Thai language as it will ultimately help you in the long run.

To what extent have you integrated into Thai society?

At present, I believe that I am still integrating into Thai society. It will be probably a lifelong experience and challenge. I get along with Thai people and I love the culture. I've been to various temples in Thailand and I find them to be extremely calming. I very much enjoy Thai massages not the rub and tugs and happy endings as they are called, but the actual, proper Thai massages.

With regards to Thai girlfriends and wives, I have to say I have not had any experience in that respect. Presently, if things in my life change as they may, that might be something I would look into. With regards to my Thai friends, most of them being male, they're very, very accommodating, very helpful and are very interested in my well-being.

What do you think of other expats who move to Thailand? Do you consciously try to hang out with other expats or try to avoid them?

269

It depends upon what you think and consider expats to be. I have come to know one expat who has been in country for over 31 years. He came to be part of the Peace Corps Service in the countryside and ended up learning the language and has become embraced by the country because of his willingness to understand the customs and the traditions. He speaks perfect Thai, writes Thai and actually acts on Thai TV on Thai lakhorns (soap operas). He has become a good friend and business partner with me in an ongoing business that we are going to be doing in the future. Unfortunately, I cannot say the same for some other people who have come to Thailand who have been escaping their own 'conditione humane' in their own countries. The individual I originally came to Thailand to work with ended up being in Thailand because he was escaping his own issues back in Australia. He came to Thailand and married a Thai lady – funny story there in that they both thought the other was richer than themselves – go figure.

I have had occasion to go to certain Thai Bars and I'm rather shocked and alarmed at the tourists that come to Thailand thinking that bargirls are their private property. That kind of disgusted me and probably the perfect reason why I don't spend very much time with expats. The other reason that I don't spend really anytime with expats is probably because my business keeps me running around little bit more than it does with foreigners. There are some good expats and there are some bad ones like everywhere else in the world.

What are your plans for the future? Are you fully invested into Thailand or will you and your wife go back to the West at some point?

As I have suggested in some of my previous answers I am extremely interested in becoming part of Thailand and Thailand's culture. Staying in Thailand would be because I love the country, it has been great to me.

Staying in Thailand
(Some Final Thoughts)

Richard McCully & Stephen Saad

RICHARD

Something I have really enjoyed about writing this book is getting the chance to meet a lot of different expats living here from many walks of life. Whilst I haven't always agreed with their opinions it has been interesting to see the different ways people live here. I will also say that most of these people have achieved some form of success in Thailand and it shows what is possible. It's helped me a lot and I hope you get something from their advice too.

Most people interviewed for this book have talked about falling in love with Thailand from the first moment they arrived. That's not the case for me. My first experiences here were pretty negative. I was travelling around Asia with a friend and we planned to use Thailand as a hub for easy and cheap flights to other destinations. In the three days we spent in Thailand I stayed in a hotel which was infested with cockroaches, got sick from street food and was genuinely shocked at some of the things I saw foreigners doing. That was around 10 years ago.

When I returned five years later I planned to stay just a few months to complete a teaching course before seeing where life would take me. I soon realized I needed to get some experience and money before I could move on to greener pastures so I decided to teach in Thailand for the rest of the school year.

I actually lasted 3 months in the sticks before getting a better job in a fancy school in Bangkok who offered a bonus at the end of a one-year contract. As things do my plans changed due to relationships and career development. Who knows if I will be here forever. I enjoy living here but I'm not someone who sees themselves as turning "Thai" or becoming immersed in the culture.

I don't have many Thai friends. I doubt I'll ever get beyond being a pre-intermediate speaker of Thai. I don't really enjoy visiting temples. Cultural issues can create conflicts between people and I have had a few real lows here.

Despite some of these thoughts the main thing I love about Thailand is the freedom. This is THE reason to be in Thailand in my opinion.

I am free to live my life without a lot of the stresses and pressures of the UK. I have a job that pays more than the average UK salary and I could have a low cost of living if I wanted. Along with disposable income I also have a lot of free time. My work-life balance is great. In general, I love life here and have few problems.

I can be on a beautiful beach in a couple of hours. I can see elephants and tigers in the jungle. I can eat out in restaurant for every meal. In reality, within reason, I can do what I want and I don't really get bothered by people.

Some say that learning the language is a must and whilst I would say it is essential to learn the basics, I feel there is a major benefit to not learning much more than beginner Thai. I can't tell you how great it is to live somewhere and not have to be involved in small talk, not understand what the newspapers are saying or all the negative stories you get on the TV.

If you want to live here successfully, you need to learn to stop caring about certain things and definitely don't compare Thailand to your home country. For example, the paperwork to legally work and live here is ridiculous but it is what it is. It's like a lot of things here, there's no point questioning it, just do it because it won't change no matter how logical you feel your arguments are.

You'll quickly realize that Bangkok is a great place to find a good paying job but it lacks the charm of most other parts of the country. My favourite Thai song is actually called "Allergic to Bangkok" and it sums up how a lot of Thai people aren't fans of the big city. If you aren't working in Thailand then I'd certainly recommend living in a different region. However, if you want to make good money then there is no doubt Bangkok is your best option.

Something I do think is vital is that you come here for the right reasons and have a long-term plan.

It's sad to hear stories of people who are just here to meet women. I understand the thought process but living in "holiday mode", hitting the bars every night just to have fun isn't sustainable. It will get boring. It is different living here compared to being a tourist.

Money is important and, in my view, you shouldn't try to live on a shoe-string here. As a teacher I am hit with looks of pity from many as they imagine someone stuck making 30-40,000 THB a month and just getting by. If you're on a gap year or just taking a short career break then do this but if you plan on being here for the medium to long term then you need to be targeting at least 50,000 THB (if not a lot more!) a month to live and have a decent future. Suffice to say that if I hadn't made the progress to where I am today I would be somewhere else right now.

So finally, whilst life isn't always rosy here there are many benefits to being in Thailand. If you put effort in you will be rewarded. If you are positive then good things will happen. If you have a plan you can succeed. Thailand isn't just a place for sex tourists and backpackers, it's a place where you can progress, live a free life and set up your future.

PHIL

I have lived in Thailand for over 25 years and it's been a roller-coaster ride to say the least. I have had many great times but there have also been some very dark times. Most of it has been linked to money! For over a decade, I scraped by on an English teacher's salary. You don't want to be someone who lives in Thailand and scrapes by because life can get very tough indeed. Thailand can be very unforgiving. It doesn't carry passengers or people who think they have some sort of right to live here. Thailand doesn't owe anyone a living!

When I hit my late thirties, I got out of teaching and started to make a decent income. I can't begin to tell you how much more pleasurable life is in Thailand when you have more money around you. I suppose the same goes for anywhere really.

I very rarely get homesick and I don't seek out the company of other expats. I never feel as if mixing with expats is something I need or something I'm missing out on. Yes, I enjoy the occasional lunch with one of my very few close expat friends but by and large I am happy in my own company. I've always been something of a loner.

I got married to the most wonderful woman in Thailand inasmuch as she is the perfect partner for me. She speaks fluent English, has a great job at a multinational company and has an incredibly Western attitude but still maintains her 'Thai-ness'. She also loves animals and loathes children. As a soul mate, she ticks every box. Finding the right partner is essential. I certainly got lucky. I hope you do too.

Why do I enjoy living in Bangkok? It always feels so safe. You can walk home along a dark street at midnight and never feel in any danger. The Thais themselves are generally always helpful and kind. No one's looking for any trouble. Everyone is focused on just keeping the peace.

Thailand's 'lawlessness' does get me down at times but it can also work to your advantage. I get many e-mails from teachers looking to make the move to Thailand and especially Americans seem to want black and white answers to everything. Thailand doesn't work that way. Everything is fifty shades of grey. Seriously, if you are one of those folks who wants processes and systems to run as they would back in your own country, Thailand might not be the right choice for you. You could be opening yourself up to a whole world of hurt and frustration.

I totally disagree with Richard about learning the Thai language and the advantage of staying at the beginner level. I have studied Thai seriously for the past three years after two decades of doing nothing and letting my Thai language skills stagnate. Having a decent intermediate-level conversation with a Thai person is for me, now one of the great joys of living here.

A word about travel. Thailand is a big country and there are some amazing places to see. Don't limit yourself to the Pattayas and the Hua Hins. Get on a plane and go to see some of the wonderful cities and regions in the north and south of the country. I'm angry with myself because it's only in the last five years that I have taken travel in Thailand seriously. I just didn't realize that parts of this country were so magical and unspoiled.

STEVE

To successfully settle in Thailand, you need to ask yourself why you are in Thailand in the first place, as Richard has pointed out several times in this book. If you are a backpacker, young person using teaching as a way to spend a couple of years in Thailand or so on, you will have succeeded if you leave feeling it was an amazing experience and you have lots of stories of Thailand that you could never have got when you came here for 2 weeks on holiday.

The same can be said for those who come here to meet girls and generally 'have fun'. This book does not seek to judge anybody's purpose for being here; indeed, it can be intoxicating being a Western single man in Asia, at least for a while.

The chances are, the people who are in Thailand in the above scenarios, are not very much invested into Thailand, unlikely to speak the language much at all and not all that interested in understanding social and cultural differences. Which is fine – again, we do not want to preach!

Retirees and late 20s-up professionals who are in Thailand for longer will generally be quite different in their attitude to Thailand. Their success factors are whether they have a fulfilling job in Thailand, have enough money to have a lifestyle whereby they do not feel like a loser, when compared to other foreigners, in social situations or when comparing to what they could earn back home and finally, a stable relationship. Career, money and love – the universal determinants of success and happiness; they apply just as much in Thailand as anywhere else. Indeed, you could argue they apply even more here because you are in a foreign country, away from familiar things, hearing a foreign language every day and out of your comfort zone in pretty much every way. You need at least two, if not all three of those elements to make your stay in Thailand successful.

There are differences within this group of people though. Older retirees will rarely learn the language to any credible level as a foreign language is quite difficult to learn at a later stage of your life. Adapting yourself to a new culture is also quite tricky because you are quite set in your ways by that age (something which Thai girlfriends or spouses actually respect and desire by the way – a Western man who is confident in himself, mature and knows what he likes and no desire to be like Thai men!).

Conversely, younger professionals usually will either have a very good appreciation of Thai culture and social interaction norms because they need to learn this in order to function properly in their work life amongst Thai people. Many will not, however, be good at speaking Thai or have any desire to be so. Generally speaking, these are the executives, high-earning teachers in international schools with non-Thai partners or the expats with a large network of friends from the same country or social background. Some, however, will be focused on learning Thai from the start because they are in a mainly Thai environment at work and/or have a Thai partner and are young enough themselves to have the energy required to learn a new language that is not easy!

What I enjoyed so much about doing this book was that, through the interviews, I was able to see these different classifications of expat in Thailand for real – the responses to the questions we posed to the interviewees painted such an accurate landscape of expats in Thailand. Richard and I have been able to bring a little bit of expat Thailand to you, the reader, by telling you our opinions and experiences and also a fairly broad cross-section of other expats' here.

But what was even more amazing, or perhaps bemusing, to me was that I found myself nodding along to virtually every single interviewee even though, if you have read the 13 interviews intently, they are all quite different and many say the opposite of each other. Several interviewees gave opinions that seemed to contradict with someone else in the 13 or had quite different experiences of Thailand and yet, I found myself agreeing and identifying with pretty much all the opinions. This is even to the extent where some interviewees (and Richard) did not learn Thai very much and have little interest in doing so while others like Max and Dwight (and Phil) thought the exact opposite and I can see both points of view. Thailand can be a place where it is hard to have firm opinions about anything and everything is 'go-with-the-flow'.

Ultimately, of course there are negative aspects to living in Thailand as a foreigner. Ways of life, standards of public safety, hygiene and a hundred other things will not be the same as back home. And then you have the added pressure of a new culture. Moving here is, for 99% of people, not one long chill-out on a white sand beach while bashing out a blog or two at your leisure and beautiful Thai girls all over you every day. And it is not like your holiday here either. There are situations almost every day where there is potential for frustration and misunderstanding. And, at some point, if you have been here long enough, you will wonder what on earth you are doing here and feel quite lonely in a foreign country far away from where you still call home i.e. a Lost in Translation moment.

To mitigate all of the above, if you are clear about whether you are here for 'fun' / extended sightseeing, or work, or love, you will be able to deal with any annoyances and cultural barriers just fine. You will see Thailand is an absolutely amazing country and has something to offer every type of expat. If you have been transferred here for a couple of years for work, you can live in fantastic condos, have all the luxuries you want and shield yourself from the more challenging aspects of real life in Thailand.

If you are here to live a more 'normal' life, the real beauty of Thailand keeps on increasing for you the more you invest into Thailand. The more you understand the culture, the more you speak Thai, the more you mix with Thai people and the more you see of the country, the more those annoyances and inconveniences melt away and the less you feel you need to go back to your own country.

Tamara, Dave, Arnie and some of the other interviewees gave some tremendous insight into how to succeed in Thailand. I hope their words, along with Richard's and mine have helped you in your decision on whether to move here or not. If you will, we hope you will be happy here and fully appreciate Thailand for the wonderful country that it is, no matter how brief or long your stay is. I find myself rooting for Thailand whenever I hear of, or see, new developments – roads, trains, buildings, trade deals – emerging because I want to see Thailand succeed. I guess that means I love Thailand.

Some Useful Resources

Although there is a huge amount of information and advice in this book we wanted to share some extra resources to help you. If you do have any questions about anything in the book then feel free to email me: richard@ lifeinanewcountry.com

RESOURCE LIST

Below you will find a list of useful online resources to supplement the information in this book.

General Life in Thailand
lifeinanewcountry.com
thailandstarterkit.com
thethailandlife.com
expatlifeinthailand.com
whatsonsukhumvit.com
tielandtothailand.com

Babies and Children in Thailand
Babyblueinbangkok.blogspot.com
bkkkids.com

Online Shopping
lazada.co.th
aliexpress.com
central.co.th

Property Rental / Purchase
ddproperty.com/en
hipflat.com

Thai News
bangkokpost.com
nationmultimedia.com

Nightlife in Thailand
bangkok.com
stickboybkk.com

Finding a Job in Thailand
jobsdb.com
monster.co.th
linkedin.com

Visas
mfa.go.th
immigration.go.th

Banks
scb.co.th
bangkokbank.com
ktb.co.th

Forums
thaivisa.com/forum
internations.org/thailand-expats
expatforum.com

Teaching in Thailand
ajarn.com

Learning Thai
learnthaiwithmod.com
thai-language.com

There are hundreds, maybe thousands of sites on learning Thai, as there are for several of the categories above. If you are keen on learning Thai, whether just to a beginner level or beyond, check out Steve's books at any Asia Books store in Thailand or on Amazon.

Some Twitter Suggestions

@RichardBarrow – British expat who is a reliable source of up to date information.
@Bangkokpostnews – Account for Bangkok Post, popular Thai newspaper.
@stickboybangkok – Expat who looks at the naughtier side of Bangkok's nightlife.
@ajarncom – Number one teaching site in Thailand, daily life tweets too.
@iamkohchang – Life on Koh Chang

About the Authors

Stephen Saad is a British expat in Thailand, having lived in the country for over four years. Three of these years were back in the early 2000s when Steve was based in Saraburi, working for a financial software company. Having had a 15 year plus career in investment banking and banking systems, Steve returned to Thailand in 2017 to continue writing Thailand related books, something which he had started in the previous year while planning his exit from his banking career.

Steve has written '100 Thai words that make you sound Thai' – an intermediate level book aimed at helping people speak everyday Thai fluently and naturally – and '100 Thai words to start speaking Thai' – a beginner level pocketbook that offers more than a phrasebook. Having expanded into distributing books, Steve now spends his time developing his book publishing and distribution business – Arun Press – further. You can contact Steve at stephen.saad@arunpress.com.

Richard McCully is the founder of expat website lifeinanewcountry.com which looks at the practicalities and cultural aspects of living in Thailand. Richard has been in Thailand for over five years and has worked as a writer, teacher and business consultant. Richard's writing has been published on many popular expat websites in Thailand and he has a vast experience of teaching in Thailand having worked at all levels of schools over the last five years.

Before moving to Thailand in his mid-20s, Richard worked in the travel industry in London for three years and developed a passion for visiting new countries which led him to Thailand. Outside of work Richard is normally either on the golf course, scuba diving or scouting out new restaurants to try.

You are welcome to contact Richard with any questions or inquiries at richard@lifeinanewcountry.com.

Printed in Great Britain
by Amazon

77023672R00168